Downing Street Blues

Downing Street Blues

*A History of Depression and
Other Mental Afflictions in
British Prime Ministers*

JONATHAN DAVIDSON, M.D.

McFarland & Company, Inc., Publishers
Jefferson, North Carolina, and London

LIBRARY OF CONGRESS CATALOGUING-IN-PUBLICATION DATA

Davidson, Jonathan R. T., 1943–
  Downing Street blues : a history of depression and other mental afflictions in British prime ministers / Jonathan Davidson, M.D.
      p.   cm.
  Includes bibliographical references and index.

  ISBN: 978-0-7864-4846-3
  softcover : 50# alkaline paper ∞

  1. Prime ministers — Mental health — Great Britain — History. I. Title.
  DA433.A1D39. 2011
  941.009'9 — dc22   20010045014

British Library cataloguing data are available

© 2011 Jonathan Davidson. All rights reserved

No part of this book may be reproduced or transmitted in any form or by any means, electronic or mechanical, including photocopying or recording, or by any information storage and retrieval system, without permission in writing from the publisher.

Front cover image © 2011 Shutterstock

Manufactured in the United States of America

McFarland & Company, Inc., Publishers
  Box 611, Jefferson, North Carolina 28640
    www.mcfarlandpub.com

To Meg, who brought this book to life — without her encouragement it might have remained unrealized.

Table of Contents

Acknowledgments — xi
Preface — 1
Introduction — 5

THE PRIME MINISTERS

Sir Robert Walpole (1676–1745) *(1721–1745)* — 15
Earl of Wilmington (1674–1743) *(1742–1743)* — 15
Henry Pelham (1694–1754) *(1743–1754)* — 16
Thomas Pelham-Holles, Duke of Newcastle (1693–1768) *(1754–1756; 1757–1762)* — 16
William Cavendish, 4th Duke of Devonshire (1720–1764) *(1756–1757)* — 17
John Stuart, 3rd Earl of Bute (1713–1792) *(1762–1763)* — 18
George Grenville (1712–1770) *(1763–1765)* — 20
Charles Wentworth, Marquess of Rockingham (1730–1782) *(1765–1766; 1782)* — 21
William Pitt the Elder, Earl of Chatham (1708–1778) *(1766–1768)* — 23
Augustus Henry Fitzroy, 3rd Duke of Grafton (1735–1811) *(1768–1770)* — 27
Lord North (1732–1792) *(1770–1782)* — 27
William Petty, 2nd Earl of Shelburne (1737–1805) *(1782–1783)* — 33

William Cavendish Cavendish-Bentinck,
 3rd Duke of Portland (1738–1809) *(1783; 1807–1809)* 34
William Pitt the Younger (1759–1806) *(1783–1801; 1804–1806)* 34
Henry Addington, 1st Viscount Sidmouth (1757–1844) *(1801–1804)* 40
William Wyndham Grenville, Baron Grenville (1759–1834)
 (1806–1807) 42
Spencer Perceval (1762–1812) *(1809–1812)* 42
Robert Banks Jenkinson, 2nd Earl of Liverpool (1770–1828)
 (1812–1827) 44
George Canning (1770–1827) *(1827)* 47
Frederick Robinson, Viscount Goderich,
 Earl of Ripon (1782–1859) *(1827–1828)* 47
Arthur Wellesley, 1st Duke of Wellington (1769–1852)
 (1828–1830; 1834) 49
Charles Grey, 2nd Earl Grey (1764–1825) *(1830–1834)* 55
William Lamb, 2nd Viscount Melbourne (1779–1848)
 (1834; 1835–1841) 59
Sir Robert Peel (1788–1850) *(1834–1835; 1841–1846)* 66
Lord John Russell (1792–1878) *(1846–1852; 1865–1866)* 68
Edward Stanley, 14th Earl of Derby (1799–1869)
 (1852; 1858–1859; 1866–1868) 69
George Gordon, 4th Earl of Aberdeen (1784–1860) *(1852–1855)* 73
Henry John Temple, Viscount Palmerston (1784–1865)
 (1855–1858; 1859–1865) 75
Benjamin Disraeli, 1st Earl of Beaconsfield (1804–1881)
 (1868; 1874–1880) 76
William Ewart Gladstone (1809–1898) *(1868–1874; 1880–1885; 1886; 1892–1894)* 79
Robert Gascoyne-Cecil, 3rd Marquess of Salisbury (1830–1903)
 (1885–1886; 1886–1892; 1895–1902) 93
Archibald Philip Primrose, 5th Earl of Rosebery (1847–1929)
 (1894–1895) 96
Arthur Balfour, 1st Earl of Balfour (1848–1930) *(1902–1905)* 103
Sir Henry Campbell-Bannerman (1836–1908) *(1905–1908)* 105
Herbert Henry Asquith, 1st Earl of
 Oxford and Asquith (1852–1928) *(1908–1916)* 107

David Lloyd George, 1st Earl of Dwyfor (1863–1945) *(1916–1922)*	112
Andrew Bonar Law (1858–1923) *(1922–1923)*	117
Stanley Baldwin, 3rd Earl Baldwin of Bewdley (1867–1947) *(1923–1924; 1924–1929; 1935–1937)*	121
James Ramsay MacDonald (1866–1937) *(1924; 1929–1935)*	127
Neville Chamberlain (1869–1940) *(1937–1940)*	131
Sir Winston Churchill (1875–1965) *(1940–1945; 1951–1955)*	135
Clement Attlee, 1st Earl of Prestwood (1883–1967) *(1945–1951)*	141
Sir Anthony Eden, 1st Earl of Avon (1897–1977) *(1955–1957)*	142
Harold Macmillan, 1st Earl of Stockton (1894–1986) *(1957–1963)*	147
Sir Alec Douglas-Home, Lord Home of the Hirsel (1903–1995) *(1963–1967)*	154
Harold Wilson, Lord Wilson of Rievaulx (1916–1995) *(1964–1970; 1974–1976)*	155
Sir Edward Heath (1916–2005) *(1970–1974)*	158
James Callaghan, Lord Callaghan of Cardiff (1912–2005) *(1976–1979)*	160
Margaret Thatcher, Baroness Thatcher of Kesteven (1925–) *(1979–1990)*	161
Sir John Major (1943–) *(1990–1997)*	161
Anthony (Tony) Blair (1953–) *(1997–2007)*	162
Conclusion	163
Appendix: Tables of Psychiatric Issues, by Prime Minister	181
Notes	187
Bibliography	203
Index	213

Acknowledgments

I am indebted to the contributions of several friends and colleagues who have most generously given their time and thoughtful comments. Their input has been of great help in many ways, including the review of chapters, direction to useful reference sources, and responding to specific questions. My thanks go to the following individuals: Marjorie Bloy, Reed Browning, Richard Cutler, Travis Crosby, Naomi Davidson, Ann Edmundson, Peter Garrard, Robert Gilbert, Irving Gottesman, Gregory Guenthner, David Hay-Edie, Kenneth Jobson, Arnold Ludwig, Lord David Owen, Jon van Heerden, Richard Weisler, Stephen Wentworth and Andrew Zimmerman.

Special thanks are owed to Ann Tamariz for her patient and skillful preparation of the manuscript.

Preface

Downing Street Blues presents an account of mental illness in prime ministers of the United Kingdom from the first generally acclaimed occupant of the position, Sir Robert Walpole, all the way through to Tony Blair, the 51st prime minister. This spans a period of almost 300 years, and, since biographical material is available on every holder of the office, it ensures that findings are based on the entire sample and are thus fully representative.

The physical health of political leaders, monarchs or elected heads of government has deservedly been studied in considerable detail. The consequences of poorly managed illness in leaders, or concealment of health problems, may be harmful to society or even the world. Impaired mental health has not received as much attention, and there is perhaps the temptation to assume that only the most resilient reach the "top of the greasy pole," to use Disraeli's phrase, and that psychiatric disorders must be rare among such people. A quite different picture emerged when, along with two colleagues at Duke University, I conducted a survey of mental illness in all U.S. presidents from George Washington to Richard Nixon.[1] We found that nearly 50 percent of the sample likely experienced psychiatric disorders during their lives, that a significant number met criteria while they were in office, and that sometimes it had a clearly detrimental effect on leadership. Thus, having established its frequency in U.S. presidents, it was logical to apply a similar method of enquiry to another series of political leaders, and assess the consequences of psychiatric disorders, for better or worse.

This topic has been one of considerable personal interest since, as a psychiatrist, I have become well aware of the individual impact of mental illness on daily function and quality of life in countless numbers of people. On a societal level, mental illness imposes an enormous burden on the economy due to lowered productivity or time lost from work. Stigma continues to be a major problem, which deprives people of access to treatment or proper acknowledgment of their suffering. Psychiatric disorders are equal opportunity disorders, sparing no one on the basis of class, color, gender, intelligence or education. When they affect leaders of government a unique set of difficulties arise. Secrecy means they may go unrecognized, misdiagnosed or improperly treated. Mismanagement can result in impaired decision-making by the sick leader. With some disorders, like dementia or severe depression, the impairment can be so great that transfer of power may be required. So for these and other reasons, mental illness in leaders is a topic of high importance.

The approach followed here is similar to that used in our previous report on U.S. presidents, but is based on more extensive biographical material. An attempt is made to assess each prime minister for psychopathology (i.e., abnormal psychiatric symptoms or behaviors) using the conventional diagnostic labels in the Diagnostic and Statistical Manual of Mental Disorders, Fourth Edition Text Revision (DSM-IV-TR) of the American Psychiatric Association (APA).[2] As described in more detail in the Introduction, it must be stated that diagnosis is a process normally based on direct contact between doctor and patient, along with supplementary information such as laboratory tests and an interview with relatives. Therefore, when the term "diagnosis" is used in this book, it is more in the way of shorthand communication to say that the reported symptoms, behaviors and third-party reports broadly correspond to the features upon which a diagnosis would be based if they had been evident in an interview.

Source material for the book was drawn from biographies of each prime minister, internet sources (such as the *Oxford Dictionary of National Biography*), press articles or web-postings (e.g., information relative to bipolar disorder and Churchill). Several scholarly books on mental illness in political leaders were consulted (e.g., Lord David Owen and Arnold Ludwig), as were authoritative summaries of prime ministers by political historians (e.g., Eccleshall and Walker; Englefield, Seaton and White); these and other sources are referenced throughout the book.

The book begins with an introduction laying out the terrain, setting context, and explaining principles of diagnosis, the pathographic approach, and methods used to assess subjects and assignment of confidence levels in diagnosis. The introduction also discusses the significance of mental disorders in political leaders. Individual assessments then follow for each of 51 prime ministers, and the conclusion attempts to integrate the findings. In the appendix, tables illustrate key details about particular prime ministers, relative to a variety of illnesses and disorders.

While several authors have taken up the task of examining mental illness in prime ministers, including Bert Park, David Owen and Hugh L'Étang, I am unaware of any who focus exclusively and comprehensively on the complete roll call of prime ministers from 1720 to present times. There is only limited work of this type written by a psychiatrist. Hopefully *Downing Street Blues* brings a perspective which can enrich the relevant health-related information given in the many outstanding biographies which were consulted for this work. It is my modest hope that such a perspective will offer a well-informed clinical interpretation which holds up psychiatrically and extends our understanding of many prime ministers. While being keenly interested in biographies and history, I profess no expertise in these fields or in matters of politics. If it appears at any point that I have strayed beyond my area of competency, then it has been unintentional. This book is directed at specialists and general readers. As a result, while the use of some technical language ("jargon") is inevitable, all efforts have been made to explain such terms in plain language and to enliven the text with anecdotes or sometimes peripheral details on the prime ministers.

For those interested in the links which have existed between Great Britain and the United States, it is worth drawing attention to a little-appreciated historical curiosity about Number 10 Downing Street, the home of all British prime ministers since around 1730, and where many of the dramas described in the book have taken place. It may be thought that there could be nothing more "British" than this address, yet the person after whom it was named, Sir George Downing, was one of nine students in the first class to graduate from Harvard College in 1642, a time when North America was a distant and sparsely-populated outpost of Great Britain. Who would have thought that a 17th century Harvard alumnus would give his name to the Prime Minister's home all those years ago? Downing subsequently became Harvard College's first tutor before returning to his country of origin. It was to be almost 300 years until any of the occupants of Number 10, or their chief representatives, paid a visit to the former North American colonies.

Winston Churchill reputedly described the United States and Great Britain as two countries divided by a common language. Certainly the same word may have a different meaning, or may be spelled in a different way. Thus it has been necessary at times to use different spellings, wherein the British form is used when quoting from original sources but the American form in all other situations. It should also be kept in mind that the use of a word might change over time. Another issue of terminology concerns the changing use of diagnostic labels as medicine adopted different terms for psychiatric disorders. For example, "gout in the head" during the 18th century is probably the same as "neurasthenia" in the 19th century or "depression" today. Throughout the book, the original terms were used if they appeared in the biographical sources, and an attempt was made to "translate" outmoded medical terminology into current language. Where it seemed called for, technical medical terms (e.g., iatrogenic) were also explained in plain language, and it is hoped that this is not seen as insulting to the reader.

Introduction

Politicians depend as much as anyone else on the services of psychiatrists, and it has been said that "a frighteningly large part can be played in British politics by various types of mental illness and psychiatric abnormality. Some aspirants to the Highest Office have had some very peculiar psychiatric quirks and oddities...." This is no flight of fancy, for such an opinion comes from William Sargant, a distinguished consultant psychiatrist at St. Thomas' Hospital, London, during the 1940s to 1970s, whose patients included a number of prominent politicians. Dr. Sargant went on to suggest that it could be instructive for history if case details were to be made available to teach posterity.[1] While privacy rights make this unlikely, much can be gleaned from the study of biographical and publicly accessible medical information. The abundant biographical material on British prime ministers varies in quantity and quality, some being quite effusive about personal health, whereas others say little. Only rarely has medical history been written about in-depth by a prime minister's personal physician, as, for example, Lord Moran, Winston Churchill's physician. Another example exists in the essay of Dr. Kidd, who was Disraeli's personal homeopathic doctor towards the end of the prime minister's life. While his writing reveals perceptive insights on Disraeli's competitive character, it says little about his psychological health, since these were not issues at that time.

While political leaders are often set apart from others by their uncommon talents, they do not differ in their liability to illness. There have been many instances where a head of state became impaired due to sickness, without adequate disclosure to the public. L'Étang cites Prime Ministers Ikeda of Japan and Nehru of India, General Franco of Spain, Presidents Wilson of the United States and Charles de Gaulle of France as all having undergone major illness which was kept concealed or for which the full consequences were not made known.

The list, of course, is much longer, but these individuals serve as good examples.[2] The impact of strokes on U.S. presidents has been described by Jones and Jones,[3] who found that 11 of 43 presidents suffered a stroke, four during office, with variable restriction on their decision-making and ability to provide leadership. In Britain, Churchill is a recent example of post-stroke mental impairment too. The consequences of stroke, of course, include physical and mental deterioration. It was partly on account of these events that mechanisms were introduced in the U.S. Constitution to arrange for transfer of power and/or to disclose necessary medical information when a president has become impaired.

The question of mental illness in heads of state has long been of interest, and I, along with two colleagues at Duke University, evaluated all U.S. presidents up to Richard Nixon for possible psychiatric disorders and their effects. We found a high rate and several presidents whose disorders clearly compromised them in office. The considerable number of British prime ministers since 1720 offers an excellent opportunity to carry out a similar study. The main questions include: How many had psychiatric difficulties? How were they affected? What were the disorders? Did they occur during office? Did mental illness impair job performance? Conversely, did mental illness in some way have a strengthening effect? These questions will be examined here in the full cohort of prime ministers.

As summarized by Sartorius,[4] effective leadership is based on (i) good communication skills, (ii) the ability to identify others who share the leader's vision and recruit their committed participation, (iii) an ability to sense the "right time" to act, and (iv) behavior shaped by past experiences, physical and mental stamina and the ability to handle stress. It is obvious, therefore, that mental illness and poor stress-coping abilities could potentially influence leadership not only in the extent to which they fall directly under the fourth category, but also by interfering with the other three categories as well.

The Individual and the Group: Can the Democratic System Compensate for Deficiencies in the Leader?

It could be argued that democracy offers few examples where mental illness in a leader resulted in catastrophe; the system has generally outlasted any damage which may have resulted from an individual leader. While a good support team can theoretically pick up the slack when the leader is ill and thereby avert disaster, we should keep in mind that between the extremes of no effect and complete disaster there is much room for mental illness to leave its stamp on a leader's performance. It would be a mistake to underestimate the impact an individual can have for good or bad, and Lloyd George[5] observed that "a gifted and resolute person has often postponed for centuries a catastrophe which appeared imminent and which but for him would have befallen. On the other hand, a weak or hesitant person has invited or expedited calamity which but for him might never have happened or which at least could have been deferred." Lord Salisbury was considered by some to be a great prime minister, and "the incalculables of his greatness are the disasters he averted from Britain and the whole human race by wise statesmanship. Disasters have come in plenty after his guiding hand had been removed."[6] During the 1920s and 1930s, by a remarkable accident of history, when central Europe was in the grip of brutal dictators, British government was successively lead for 15 years by three prime ministers who were significantly troubled by irresolution, exhaustion, fear, poor decision-making ability, low morale and, in one case, dementia. Long periods of rest and psychotropic medications were prescribed for Baldwin; while Chamberlain, who had depressive tendencies, nearly had a "complete nervous breakdown" after his meetings with Hitler. MacDonald was manifestly unable to discharge the responsibilities of leadership as he became progressively more demented. Small wonder that the Continent bumbled its way into war. This unfortunate record evokes the lines of William Butler Yeats,[7] who in 1921 had foreseen the rise of a new and destructive world order in "The Second Coming":

> Mere anarchy is loosed upon the world,
> The blood-dimmed tide is loosed, and everywhere
> The ceremony of innocence is drowned;
> The best lack all conviction, while the worst
> Are full of passionate intensity.

Passionate intensity ... not much in evidence among the tired British prime ministers of the 1930s, as they allowed themselves to be outmaneuvered in a worsening world crisis. With hindsight of history we know that the fourth prime minister, Winston Churchill, was fortunately full of the same passionate intensity as his dictator counterparts, proving to be more than their match. It is hard to understand MacDonald, Baldwin and Chamberlain without taking into account their psychiatric conditions: the muddle-headedness of MacDonald from 1930 ("my brain is going"), to his being "no longer in a mental ... condition to be capable of ... high office" in 1933, and "inane and gaga" in 1936; the fearful apprehension of Baldwin; and the combination of hubris and a near-nervous breakdown in Chamberlain. A large part of Baldwin's and Hoare's capitulation to Mussolini over Abyssinia has been put down to Baldwin's anxiety and depression.[8] We may legitimately ask if they would have stood up more firmly had they been in better mental health. Churchill, on the other hand, provides an instructive contrast in that his previous encounters with depression produced new strength and more effective ways of coping with challenges.

Diagnosis at a Distance: Steering the Middle Course

A medical diagnosis is made after a doctor has taken a history from and examined his or her patient. Other information is often brought to bear (e.g., laboratory tests, meeting with a relative or friend), and on the basis of all this information the doctor forms an opinion as to the likely diagnosis.

Prevailing ethics discourage a doctor from giving a diagnosis in the absence of direct patient contact. With psychiatric conditions, there are additional issues related in part to the negative emotional responses that often accompany some psychiatric labels, like paranoia, megalomania, and alcoholism, and there is also the stigmatizing effect which may lead to public perception of personal weakness or unsuitability for leadership. Partisan feelings can also intrude, thereby depriving the subject of a "fair hearing." There have been some celebrated instances where psychiatrists offered a "diagnosis at a distance," including the U.S. presidential candidate Senator Barry Goldwater in 1964, who in a magazine survey of psychiatrists was seen by many as too unstable for the presidency. Such remarks were quickly condemned by the American Medical and Psychiatric Associations, and the so-called "Goldwater Rule" was formulated which stated that it was unethical to offer a professional opinion about a public figure unless based on an examination and appropriate authorization to make such a statement.[9]

So it goes without saying that opinions arrived at via biographic study are made in the absence of any direct contact with the subject. As long as this limitation is recognized, and if one stays with the facts, there is no reason why such analysis should raise ethical concerns; indeed, recent initiatives have been taken by the Board of Trustees of the American Psychiatric Association to revise its ethical guidelines over assessing public figures. The draft states that academic scholarship can legitimately make provisional diagnostic assessments of historically important figures in accordance with relevant standards of scholarship.[10] Good quality biographies offer perceptive accounts of health and mental well-being from which a clinically trained person can often draw conclusions on the medical significance of reported material in a way which the biographer is unable to do. On the other hand, biographers and "diagnosticians" without proper qualification cannot allow themselves to be drawn out too far in expressing their own political or historical opinions. Making value judgments or appraising the success of a politician is difficult. According to how one looks at things, for example, Churchill could be seen as a heroic success in his first administration, or well below par during his second term. Longevity in office may seem one criterion of success, but that is not always the case.[11] Such judgments are best avoided in pathography, the main objective of which is to apply biographic data to a better medical understanding of the person, or, as is the case here, to a psychiatric understanding of every individual who achieved office as prime minister.

Another temptation best avoided is to move beyond the facts into a world of psychological speculation. For example, a statesman may have lost both parents in childhood and may have later been subject to depression or taken ridiculous risks. It can be tempting to allow one's pet theory to explain why the person did this or that — to compensate for deprivation or personal inferiority, to prove some sort of loyalty to the deceased parents, to expiate their ghosts, to respond to a punitive super-ego (a tyrannical father may be said to create rivalry in his son), and so forth. All of this is unprovable, albeit interesting to some.

Principles of Diagnostic Assessment Used in This Analysis

In order to relate yesterday's disorders to current terminology, it is desirable to attempt some correspondence between the reported symptoms and the conditions as they are presently described in official diagnostic systems like Diagnostic and Statistical Manual of Mental Disorders 4th Edition (DSM-IV) of the American Psychiatric Association (APA) and the World Health Organization's International Classification of Diseases 10th Edition (ICD-10).[12] Accepting the limitations already mentioned, this task is attempted as far as possible. In some cases the correspondence is virtually beyond argument (e.g., Stanley Baldwin); in others it is suggestive but far less obvious (e.g., Pitt's "gout in the brain," Macmillan's "neurasthenia" and veiled suicide attempt). Some level of confidence in the assessment is therefore assigned. A rating of 1 would mean low confidence but some evidence; 2 would mean moderate confidence; a 3 would represent high confidence.

Entering into clinical assessment are the following considerations: (i) details of the reported pathology and whether it (ii) persisted or recurred, (iii) produced distress or (iv) impairment, (v) lead to medical treatment or (vi) was viewed by others as clearly abnormal, or (vii) whether contemporary medical opinion favored mental illness as an explanation. It seemed reasonable to assign the levels of confidence to three categories: level 1 would correspond to the presence of 1 or 2 of the 7 criteria; level 2 would equate with 3 or 4 criteria; and level 3 with 5–7 of the above criteria. At least this provides for a clinically-informed judgment as to the strength of evidence gleaned from biographical and other source material, and is similar to our previous assessments of U.S. presidents.

The spectrum of ill-defined physical complaints which lack any clearly discernable medical explanation has always been a thorn in the side of disease classification. Today they are referred to as the somatoform disorders and include various pain states, hypochondriasis and what was once called "hysteria" (i.e., a profusion of physical symptoms from many different body systems: gastrointestinal, genitourinary, cardiovascular, neurological, etc). Fibromyalgia, chronic fatigue and myalgic encephalitis partly overlap with this spectrum, although they differ in some important ways too. But in cases where vague somatic problems like "neuritis" and "clergyman's throat" affected a person, and were acknowledged to be a form of stress, it seems reasonable to take the position that they belonged to the somatoform group of disorders. However, sometimes these mild symptom eruptions in a person with a known history of depression or anxiety are best understood as relapses of the prior condition rather than a new problem. As in the case of Lloyd George, it is not always easy to decide which is most appropriate.

Possible Consequences of Mental Illness in Leaders

Why is mental illness a concern in heads of state? Common conditions like depression and anxiety can seriously undermine self-confidence: self doubt increases, uncertainty creeps in, and the ability to make decisions is affected (e.g., Baldwin, MacDonald, Rosebery). Energy is sapped, sleep is lost or becomes excessive, isolation builds, and it can become hard to meet the challenges of leadership, especially to occupying a desk where "the buck stops here." Wise or unwise decisions are taken which affect the lives and safety of millions of people, determine the identity of nations, affect the outcome of war, and impact economic and many other critical day to day problems. To succeed one needs good resilience, good advice, respect from ones friends and foes, good judgment and high energy.

Dementia is another important example, especially in older leaders. Neuronal degeneration in the brain can leave an individual progressively unable to remember recent events, learn new information, recognize other people, find their way about, perform complex mental tasks, work under pressure or express oneself in speech. Early signs include deterioration in language function, highlighted by difficulty naming persons or objects, vague and empty speech, use of imprecise words like "thing" and long circumlocutory speech. These changes in language and speech may have been the first sign of the dementia which is believed to have caused Harold Wilson's resignation. His otherwise hard-to-understand increased fear of Parliamentary Question Time may have been driven by awareness of declining mental capacities, including concentration, attention and the ability to think on his feet.

The Culture of Alcohol

A special word should be said about the culture of alcohol which has long prevailed in Parliamentary life, as reflected by one former Member of Parliament (MP).[13] It is peculiar to politics that inebriacy has been long tolerated while conducting important business affecting the nation. Perhaps the proximity of Annie's Bar, along with the practice of late night (10 P.M.) voting, had something to do with it. This has now changed, but a number of prime ministers were known to indulge in pathological drinking in ways which would not have been tolerated in other forms of business; and it could certainly happen again in the future. Even though problem drinking may be on the decline in British politics, it does surface from time to time, as in the recent case of Charles Kennedy, then leader of the Social Democrat Party, who stepped down in 2006 on account of his drinking problem. Appearing drunk in Parliament is no different from a surgeon showing up in the operating theater under the influence, a priest hearing confession while smashed, or a judge hearing cases in court after imbibing heavily. Yet Nicholas Soames, a former Conservative MP, is reported to have said, "A glass of champagne braces the spirits and lifts the soul. My grandfather [Churchill] was right — you can't make good speeches on water."[14] Another MP concluded that "drinking [in Parliament] was good but drunk was not."

Over a 200 year period, Pitt, Asquith, Wilson, Churchill, Eden, Derby and Rosebery were all prone to excessive consumption of alcohol or drugs, and Gladstone also took drugs before speaking in Parliament. Under the influence of alcohol there is always the possibility of making rash decisions, and the wearing-off effects of alcohol can produce insomnia, agitation, nervousness and dysphoria (literally "feeling bad"). Even if there is no obvious short-term impairment, the cumulative effect of heavy alcohol consumption on the central nervous system can be significant, acting as a risk factor for dementia, depression, anxiety and poor resilience under stress. Such may have been the case for Winston Churchill.

In the eighteenth century and thereafter it was not uncommon for a doctor to recommend alcohol, occasionally with disastrous results, as with William Pitt the Younger. Even Pitt the Elder was prescribed alcohol for his "gout." Attitudes and social convention towards alcohol have changed greatly over the past three centuries. In the 1700s and 1800s alcohol may have been safer to drink than water, which was a disease-carrying vector for cholera; and in those days a doctor would generously define moderate drinking as up to a quart of wine a day.[15]

Drug-taking falls under the same umbrella, except for two principal differences: (i) drugs are more often prescribed by doctors than alcohol (which, of course, is a drug), and (ii) alcohol is legally available in stores, bars, restaurants etc., whereas most drugs of abuse are not. (Some over-the-counter drugs like decongestants and diet pills possess weak abuse potential.) But those differences aside, the predispositions and consequences of drug taking and alcohol share so much in common that, for the purposes of this account, they will be considered together. Abuse of drugs can occur either from illicit acquisition or by misuse of drugs which have been lawfully prescribed. Sometimes misuse occurs without the doctor's knowledge, and at other times the doctor is regrettably a willing partner: both scenarios have occurred among prime ministers, although the latter seems to have been more common. Drugs which can be misused include hypnotics (i.e., sleep enhancing medications, such as barbiturates and benzodiazepines), stimulants (e.g., cocaine, amphetamines) and pain-relievers (e.g., opiate drugs like morphine). Today the group of drugs which enhance cognition may also be candidates for abuse (e.g., modafinil).

Possible Benefits of Mental Illness

The effects of mental illness are not invariably negative. It has been said that Abraham Lincoln and Winston Churchill drew strength from prior episodes of depression.[16] The same might be said of two nineteenth-century prime ministers, Disraeli and Gladstone, who perhaps became better at their craft after depression seemed to give them greater resilience in the face of adversity, and maybe the "passionate intensity" to cope with setbacks.

We are accustomed to thinking of mental illness as bringing more pain than gain, and by and large this is true. Yet there is the interesting finding that bipolar (or "manic-depressive") men attribute lasting benefit from their episodes in making them more sociable, more creative, more alert and more psychologically sensitive people. Unipolar depressives (i.e., depression without mania or hypomania) felt they became more sensitive too.[17] Without doubt, leaders could turn some of these gains to good effect.

Grief was often described in the biographies, along with phrases like "never being the same man again," "he was broken by it," "never recovered," "profound." That some leaders failed to regain their former health and were impaired by grief has been noted by Davidson and Connor in the cases of Presidents Pierce and Coolidge.[18] At a time when life expectancy was short and death during childhood and childbirth quite common, bereavement was to be expected. Society has always put in place mourning rituals to help the grief process run its course, and in the Victorian era these were elaborate, prolonged and perhaps quite ostentatious. So the task is to determine whether grief was "normal" in this sense or if it left unfortunate scars which might have influenced competence in everyday work. Grief has also spurred much creativity,[19] and in work, grief may somehow be resolved, or guide and inspire focus. While sometimes this occurred (e.g., Eden), in other prime ministers it left an overall deficit rather than gain (e.g., Asquith, Andrew Bonar Law). In others, the loss seemed not to have overtly affected health or performance (e.g., Lloyd George).

The Different Disorders

Of the many possible disorders described in DSM-IV, only a few are suspected of having affected British prime ministers. These are as follows: mood disorders — unipolar depression (referred to throughout as "depression"), bipolar disorder or manic depression (where episodes may be of mania [elation, anger, overactivity, risk-taking], depression or both together), seasonal affective disorder ("winter depression"); anxiety disorders (generalized anxiety, social anxiety disorder); alcohol abuse and dependency, drug abuse and dependency; sleep disorders (narcolepsy, sleep apnea); sexual deviation (paraphilia); developmental disorders (Asperger's disorder, a form of autism where communication skills and social development are affected); tic/impulse disorders (Tourette's disorder, tic disorder not otherwise specified); somatoform disorder (i.e., physical symptoms with no credible physical cause but presumed to be of psychological origin); dementia (global deterioration of mental and intellectual function — for example, after stroke or from Alzheimer's disorder); mental disorder due to a medical condition (hypothyroidism); and two disorders which are still viewed as somewhat provisional in DSM-IV, bereavement and relational problems. These disorders are not described here in detail in order to avoid tedious listings of the numerous symptoms, but fuller descriptions are provided as appropriate for the individual prime ministers. For exhaustive descriptions, the best source would be DSM-IV.

When considering whether symptoms are pathological rather than simply a normal manifestation of life (e.g., prolonged sadness versus transient unhappiness; persistent or recurrent worry versus brief stress reaction), it is helpful to gauge whether there was (i) substantial distress, (ii) impairment/incapacity, or (iii) treatment was prescribed by a doctor.

The Prime Ministers

SIR ROBERT WALPOLE (1676–1745) *(1721–1745)*

Robert Walpole, first Earl of Oxford, is widely regarded as the first prime minister, although the term had been used previously and was not to become official until the time of Campbell-Bannerman almost 200 years later. As well as being the first, he remains the longest serving prime minister in British history. He dominated public consciousness and the political scene in a way which has been matched by very few; Bagehot described him as "coarse and barbarous."[1] Walpole's longevity is believed in part to be the result of the monarch's distrust of opposition politicians at the time, Walpole's decision to remain in the House of Commons, and his skill in forging a partnership between Commons and King. Walpole was also able to engage the fledgling press on his behalf.[2]

Although his health was poor, he did not suffer any form of mental illness as far as is known.[3] It is of some interest, though, that his daughter Katherine most likely died from anorexia nervosa at the age of 19.[4]

EARL OF WILMINGTON (1674–1743) *(1742–1743)*

Spencer Compton, Earl of Wilmington, was prime minister for one year. During his brief administration he was concerned with maintaining British participation in the War of the Austrian Succession. On the domestic front, his administration passed a bill to limit public drunkenness by increasing liquor taxes. At the time of his appointment he was in poor health from kidney stones and died 16 months later. Wilmington never married, although he fathered several children; one of his daughters married James Glen, for whom

Wilmington procured the governorship of South Carolina.[5] Wilmington also gave his name to two cities in the states of Delaware and North Carolina.

Wilmington was described by a contemporary as a "plodding, heavy fellow, with great application, but no talent," and he rarely spoke in the House of Lords. There is no indication of any mental disorder.[6]

HENRY PELHAM (1694–1754) *(1743–1754)*

Henry Pelham was the younger brother of the Duke of Newcastle, who succeeded him as prime minister. Pelham served in office for 10 years between 1743 and 1754. Among the major events of his administration was Bonnie Prince Charlie's 1745 Jacobite rebellion, which Pelham successfully put down, and the establishment of peace with France and Spain upon conclusion of the War of Austrian Succession. Pelham appears to have been the first prime minister with a record of combat experience, which occurred during his military service in the first Jacobite Rebellion of 1715.[7] He was well-regarded, and his stable government inspired new confidence in the country after a period of uncertainty.[8]

After 1748 his health deteriorated, and in 1751 he tried to resign on the grounds of ill-health, which the King refused to accept. He died in office. There is no record of mental illness.

THOMAS PELHAM-HOLLES, DUKE OF NEWCASTLE (1693–1768) *(1754–1756; 1757–1762)*

Thomas Pelham-Holles was born Thomas Pelham but later took the name Holles on acquiring an inheritance. He was the older brother of Henry Pelham, who had preceded him in office. Serving as prime minister between 1754 and 1756, and again between 1757 and 1762, his administration was preoccupied by the onset of the Seven Years War, which saw hostilities against France in North America. Defeat at Monongahela and the loss of Minorca lead to his resignation, but he returned to office the next year. After King George III ascended the throne, Newcastle lost influence, became embroiled in Parliamentary disputes over financing of the war in Europe and resigned again in 1762. His two terms are currently viewed as no better than mediocre, and have even been termed "disastrous."[9] Newcastle was considered to be a "hypochondriac of the first order,"[10] who worried constantly about his health and hired his own personal apothecary (pharmacist).[11] However, there is some inconsistency over Newcastle's hypochondriasis, and it is possible that Newcastle's wife was the hypochondriac,[12] although the Duke was himself troubled with constipation. In any event, whatever the extent of his suffering, it did not impair his ability as a politician, and "like most hypochondriacs, he was in fact quite healthy."[13] There is thus some doubt as to Newcastle's level of hypochondriasis.

Newcastle has been described as one of the strangest men in 18th century politics, "a strange, unbelievable person" with "a pathetic demand for affection," "a bit neurotic," and given to restlessness, jealousy, peevishness and fearfulness. In social conduct he came across as clownish and given to inappropriate expressions of intimacy and touching. His constant profligacy was termed "irrational" in its recklessness.[14] He wept easily, which would suggest an emotional liability often associated with anxiety disorders. He refused to sleep in "unaired" beds, abhorred drafts and feared sea travel. His need for approval was viewed as excessive.

Despite holding great affection for his younger brother Henry, Newcastle developed suspicion towards him when the latter was prime minister, "falling prey to his streak of jealousy and paranoia, in his letters accusing Pelham of imagined slights."[15] At times the brothers stopped speaking to each other. It appears that Newcastle was largely responsible for these contretemps and that Pelham showed the greater maturity in dealing with the situation. A common friend, Lord Hardwicke, the Lord Chancellor, used his considerable diplomatic skills to keep the two brothers in business. Newcastle spent recklessly, and lavish entertainment lead to the "evisceration" of his estate, heavy debt and considerable hardship for his wife and relatives.[16]

Newcastle suffered a stroke in 1767, which left him impaired in memory, speech and energy, yet he soldiered on in politics until his death the next year.

On the matter of psychopathology, biographical material is insufficient and at times conflicting, but few would disagree with the assessment of Newcastle as being a strange individual who displayed abnormal psychopathology. His constant overspending does not fit the picture of mania, yet it was called "irrational" and harmed his family. There were streaks of paranoia and an unusually high need for approval; his habits suggest some anxiety and possible hypochondriasis, but it is hard to put this together into a coherent diagnosis. Some of his temperamental qualities most probably hindered his effectiveness as prime minister, but much remains unclear in this regard.

WILLIAM CAVENDISH, 4TH DUKE OF DEVONSHIRE (1720–1764) *(1756–1757)*

William Cavendish was prime minister for a brief seven-month period in 1756–1757 between the two Duke of Newcastle administrations. He displayed "solid if not outstanding abilities ... devotion to friends and duty, patriotism, and unswerving integrity," and was "a political broker rather than a leader."[17]

He died at the age of 44 from a stroke.[18] There is nothing to suggest any psychological disorder.

JOHN STUART, 3RD EARL OF BUTE (1713–1792) *(1762–1763)*

The Earl of Bute became prime minister largely due to his position as "finishing tutor" to the future King George III. Unfortunately for Bute, his personal relationship with the king created many enemies and produced considerable resentment on the part of his rivals. He was also the first Scotsman to be prime minister at a time when the Stuart rebellions were still fresh in the memories of many Englishmen, which would hardly endear him to the population. So Bute carried two significant disadvantages from the start. Being the chief agent of King George's efforts to increase executive power of the monarchy set him in an adversarial position with respect to the political establishment. Bute's ambition for political advancement was accompanied by much ambivalence, and he remained uncomfortable holding the reins of power. His term as prime minister was short and unpopular. When he resigned in 1763, ill health (mostly stress) was troubling him, and shortly after leaving office he retired to Harrogate spa for recuperation.[19]

While Bute was once seen as an abomination, historians now view his political career in a more positive light. Among his achievements was the treaty ending the Seven Years War on quite favorable terms for Britain. As he withdrew (or was forced out) from his advisory functions to the royal court, Bute increasingly devoted his energy and talents to encouraging growth of the arts and sciences. He became an important patron of the Scottish enlightenment, establishing chairs of rhetoric, botany and materia medica at Edinburgh University, setting up the Royal Botanical Gardens in the same city, and supporting Glasgow University in like manner. Largely on his account, Aberdeen became a center of astronomy and medical training. Besides the above, Bute generously supported the work of eminent writers, artists and architects, such as Samuel Johnson, Tobias Smollett, John Home and Robert Adam. He wrote a number of books on botany, developed and expanded the Royal Botanical Gardens at Kew, and supported the work of others in fields of anatomy and mineralogy. Bute died at the age of 78 from long-term complications of a fall on the cliffs near his home while collecting plants.

Bute's Mental Health

From the psychiatric view, Bute showed symptoms which affected his activity as politician, although it did not trouble him in his work as patron of the arts and sciences. Schweizer states:

> As with Pitt, his political woes can be ascribed in part to his personality. Although an affectionate friend and devoted family man, in public he appeared invariably cold, distant, and haughty, probably more from shyness than arrogance. Happiest in scholarly seclusion, Bute was ill at ease and insecure on the political stage. His entire ministerial career is the tragic story of a man called into politics in middle age to assume a position he initially feared and eventually came to detest. His limitations, ultimately, were not ones of achievement as of personality and will — an inability to kindle enthusiasm among his colleagues and the public at large, and failure to convince others that he was an effective minister.[20]

Given the suggestion that abnormal personality factors may have interjected themselves into Bute's life as a politician and in his dealings with people, a closer look at his psychological health seems warranted. Hibbert reports a contemporary who said that Bute "never looked at those he spoke to or who spoke to him."[21] He was reputed to have shaky self-confidence, to be deeply insecure, aloof and incapable of mixing comfortably in society.[22] Under stress he was prone to insomnia and gastrointestinal symptoms, which likely corresponded to what was then referred to as "bilious fevers." Such observations strongly suggest a high degree of social anxiety as it is defined in the DSM-IV: avoiding eye contact, shyness, unease in company, social deficits, and fear in high-profile or high-pressure situations where a person is the center of attention.

There are allusions to other difficulties with depression, and at the time of his resignation he was "allegedly on the verge of a nervous breakdown."[23] Within a year he was in a "deep depression" as his relationship with the king continued to unravel.[24]

According to Sher,[25] Bute's friend John Home, a celebrated poet and playwright of the day, was privy to "the private regions of his psyche, where he works to ward off the bouts of depression to which the Earl seems to have been prone." These were particularly bad during his term as prime minister. By March 1763, less than a year after assuming office, Bute strongly desired to retire from political entanglements; he had "sorely underestimated the amount of resentment that his promotion would generate.... Quite simply, office was too much for him. He bore all the symptoms of a man facing physical exhaustion and nervous breakdown."[26] Bute described his condition in the following terms:

> My health is every day impairing; a great relaxation of my bowels of many years standing is increasing on me continually; the eternal, unpleasant labor of the mind and the impossibility of finding hours for exercise, and proper

medicine, the little time I get for sleep, the little I ever enjoy, even when abed ... my health therefore dictates retirement from the greatest weight, that ever lay on any man in this country.

For his problems, Bute was taking "enough of Hemlock every day to kill a horse if given him at once without perceiving any good effect of it."[27] This highly toxic poison used to be given as a sedative and as an antispasmodic for symptoms which today would fit the picture of irritable bowel disease or severe anxiety.

Bute held others responsible for his plight, including the king, to whom he angrily wrote in 1766 that "I have for ever done with this bad public, my heart in half broke and my health ruined, with the unmerited, barbarous treatment I have received."[28] We do not know how long this episode of depression lasted, nor in what other ways it affected him, but the parsimonious view would regard his multiple symptoms of depression, lack of sleep and "bilious fever" as part of the same condition, which either recurred or was chronic. His health improved somewhat as he settled into more scholarly pursuits and greater solitude ("melancholy grandeur," as described by Schweizer). However, two subsequent periods of illness coincided with Bute's actual or potential return to the political stage; in 1768 he was re-elected to parliament as a Scottish representative peer, then spent much of the next three years traveling in Italy because of ill health.[29] Again in 1778, when attempts were made to return Bute to the political mainstream, the ensuing public outcry caused a recurrence of his illness.[30] The political fray and his immense unpopularity, it seems, greatly disturbed Bute's mental well-being.

Bute was spurred by considerable vanity and a drive for power, but he was otherwise poorly equipped to handle the rough and tumble of politics; his thin-skinned nature, proneness to excessive social anxiety, depression and autonomic instability (diarrhea) were all aggravated by high office. He was ill suited to be prime minister, being more comfortable pursuing a life of scholarship, and promoting the arts and natural sciences. He had the misfortune to be forever branded as the king's favorite and all the baggage that entailed. It brought him intense and lifelong public castigation.

GEORGE GRENVILLE (1712–1770) *(1763–1765)*

George Grenville came from a prominent political family. His father had been an MP between 1715 and 1727; a younger brother was First Lord of the Admiralty; and three other brothers were MPs. His sister Hester married William Pitt (Lord Chatham), and his fourth son, William, became prime minister in 1806.

Grenville succeeded Lord Bute and served for two years between 1763 and 1765. While he made more enemies than friends, he was widely respected, being dubbed both "the most disagreeable man to do business with" and "nevertheless, the fittest person to be at the head of this country."

Among the main events of his administration was the passage of the controversial North American Stamp Act, which provoked wide protest in the colonies. Grenville did not get on well with King George III, who found him insolent and disliked the fact that Grenville tried to curtail Lord Bute's continuing influence on the monarch. Grenville was removed from office in July 1765, to be succeeded by the Marquess of Rockingham.[31]

CHARLES WENTWORTH, MARQUESS OF ROCKINGHAM (1730–1782) *(1765–1766; 1782)*

Charles Wentworth, Marquess of Rockingham, was born on May 13, 1730, and died July 1, 1782. He was twice prime minister, first between 1765 and 1766, and again, sixteen years later, in 1782.

In Rockingham's first term, which lasted a mere three months, he repealed the unpopular Stamp Act following protests in the North American colonies. Cabinet conflict resulted in his resignation and replacement by William Pitt the Elder, later to become Lord Chatham. During his second administration, Rockingham opened peace negotiations with the American colonists and championed political reform in Ireland. These initiatives were affected by his sudden death from influenza one year after taking office, and the brevity of his administration makes appraisal of his contributions difficult.

Evidence for Mental Health Problems

Although Rockingham's political career was not undermined by mental illness, he did show signs of social anxiety and hypochondriasis. Thus, in Walpole's memoirs,[32] Rockingham is described as being "of unpromising disposition...so weak a frame of person and nerves, that no exigency could surmount his timidity of speaking in public."[33] Rockingham was prone to anxiety if he considered that he failed to measure up to proper standards. He also had "an intense relish for private life...and lacked a taste for politics as a professional game." The writing of political letters sapped his energy, and "any sort of bustle ravaged him," as he had "neither ambition nor appetite for employing power."[34]

Christie[35] notes Rockingham suffered from "a crazy constitution" and was "several times disabled by illness." Highly-strung nerves left him tongue-tied in Parliament. In 1769, at the age of 39, Rockingham reported to the Duke of Portland as follows: "I was from beginning to end, in a most violent agitation and was obliged to speak notwithstanding, three times. I got a good draught of Madeira before I went to the House, and had a comfortable breathing of a vein, by Mr. Adair's lancet afterwards."[36] His anticipatory fear of speaking in Parliament was so severe that he fortified himself with alcohol and then, as was the custom of the time, underwent a bleeding session with his surgeon. While he eventually overcame some of his performance anxiety, Rockingham kept public speaking to a minimum. In the words of Horace Walpole, "Mere necessity alone made him at all a speaker in Parliament, where, though he spoke good sense, neither flattery nor partiality could admire or applaud."[37]

Other Health Problems

Beyond that, Walpole noted him to be "indolent" and "dilatory of execution." Hoffman[38] remarked on chronic chest and side pain, which Rockingham attempted to treat himself. Reference to this complaint ([my] "old complaint") recurred throughout his correspondence, and it is quite possible that this "old complaint" was from a sexually transmitted disease contracted in his youth, which allegedly left him with erectile dysfunction. A friend, Sir George Saville, wrote that "9 or 10" of his friends had observed his "unalterable and continued recourse to medicine with hardly any reason," which Saville referred to as a "game of quacking." Some years later the Duke of Richmond reproved Rockingham for being "so often ill without being dangerously so, and ... so often doctoring yourself" that when he became truly ill, it was either due to the effects of all the medicines he self-administered, or to not leaving the illness to manifest itself. Iatrogenic illness is always a possibility.

Summary

With these qualities, one may wonder how Rockingham could have found himself in such a prominent position, and how he could have achieved any success. Compensating for his tendencies to anxiety, self-doubt and hypochondriasis, all of which suggest a man prone to worry, Rockingham was driven by *noblesse oblige*, a sense of duty borne from his Whig inheritance. His moral resolution, personal charm, decency, integrity and good intentions and talent for attracting dependents have been noted.[39] Somewhat surprisingly, he enjoyed combat, having enlisted at age 15 as colonel in a regiment of volunteers to fight the Young Pretender. He was ambitious and well-liked, which perhaps accounted for his success as a conciliator.[40]

One assessment holds Rockingham and his party as the *enfant perdu* of British politics[41] on account of a reluctance to confront the responsibilities of government: to be in opposition was more congenial. It is not a far reach to believe that, in part, this was a result of Rockingham's constitution and proneness to anxiety. It has been said that "Rockingham was palpably unfitted for the career of a politician."[42]

WILLIAM PITT THE ELDER, EARL OF CHATHAM (1708–1778) *(1766–1768)*

The Pitt Inheritance: Destined for Mental Illness?

William Pitt (the Elder) was born November 15, 1708, and died May 11, 1778. He was the youngest son of Robert Pitt, MP, "a mean and cantankerous" man, and of Lady Harriet Villiers, who came from a "notoriously unstable" family. His inheritance was referred to as being "explosive,"[43] and this seems well to have been the case. Pitt's grandfather, Thomas, was a very successful "buccaneer and interloper" who became governor of Madras. Thomas was described as acting erratic towards his family, sometimes solicitous and at other times "choleric" and contemptuous. Pitt's father, Robert, was known for extravagant spending as a young man, which drained his and his wife's fortunes. Robert Pitt grew into a milder clone of his father — stormy, quarrelsome, complaining and critical. Of William Pitt the Elder's siblings, his sister Ann showed signs of the same illness that affected William, becoming "wild." In 1779 she required restraint and died 2 years later in a mental hospital. William's brother Thomas was regularly in debt and fled England to escape his creditors. Thomas was a "bad man," in the words of Horace Walpole,[44] and "never was ill-nature so dull as his, never dullness so vain." Thomas lived abroad, ruined and "more than a little mad," of sharp temper and unbridled violence.[45] A visitor to Thomas Pitt commented, "It was no scandal to say that there was a degree of madness in the family." As though that was not enough, Pitt's sister Elizabeth possessed her "own draught of the family madness, laced with a dose of nymphomania."[46] She was something of a "loose cannon," and at one stage handed to an opposition newspaper some letters from her brother (incorrectly) purporting to show that William had robbed her of her allowance.

Multigenerational impulsivity, recklessness, overspending, intractable debts, hypersexuality, madness, violence, psychiatric hospitalization, buccaneering, notorious instability — all of these would suggest a genetic predisposition to bipolar disorder in the Pitt family.

Pitt's Health Problems

William Pitt was considered to be truculent and passionate. His intemperate ways, impulsivity, rapid energy, imperious will and "eager nature fit for a great crisis" were regarded by Bagehot as desirable during times of war but a disservice in conducting everyday domestic affairs.[47] Pitt's reputation had been built through his spectacular successes in the Seven Years War with France. In this vein, it is interesting that Black writes of Pitt that "when the heroic aura of war was absent by the end of 1766," and "while the entanglements of office ... were pressing home on him," he simply was unable to make his administration work effectively: his ministers were poorly chosen and Pitt's indifference to others in the party from whom he could have received support drove many of them into opposition.[48] Pitt was frequently in debt and displayed "grandiose extravagance," with disastrous financial consequences. His wife spent much of her own fortune in rescuing him.

There is strong evidence of depression. For over two years, between 1751 and 1754, Pitt was laid low by illness beyond the gout which also afflicted him, and he withdrew from public life. His friends were puzzled by its nature and thought of it as just being "out of sorts," or a "sullen illness," to quote Horace Walpole.[49] By mid–1753, Pitt was much better, but he suffered a relapse in March 1754 and was "much sunk by extreme dejection," according to his friend Gilbert West.[50]

It is interesting that Pitt's doctors prescribed opiates for insomnia, about which Pitt correctly said, "Though they may procure a temporary ease, yet often after recoil upon the spirits." West went on to express the opinion that Pitt's physicians had missed the boat somewhat in their preoccupation with his gastrointestinal symptoms, "not sufficiently regarding the distemperature of his spirits, a disease much more to be apprehended than the other." Among the symptoms which Pitt experienced were prolonged insomnia, severe anorexia, disorder of his bowels, "extreme dejection" of spirits and withdrawal, all of which would be consistent with Pitt experiencing major depression between 1751 and 1754. Initial recovery in 1753 was followed by a relapse the next year, perhaps precipitated by the lengthy absence and deteriorating health of his sister Ann.

Between 1765 and 1768, Pitt's health was poor, and when he assumed office in July 1766, he could barely function. Already, by 1765, Pitt had suffered from what was called "gout in the head that led to bouts of insanity."[51]

It is beyond doubt that Pitt suffered from major mental illness between 1766 and 1768, and the details suggest this to have been depression, but with manic elements. In 1766 he was uncharacteristically defeatist and pessimistic about his own power to influence the administration.[52] Things were going badly for Pitt: gout had flared up, he was in pain, his government was in disarray, there was trouble in the American colonies and his own standing in the public eye as "the Great Commoner" had suffered following his elevation to the peerage. By January 1767 he was close to resigning, but somehow pressed on as he became more deeply mired in melancholia. His appetite again deserted him, he was barely able to concentrate, and his physical condition was poor, with "fever" and weakness.[53] His wife, Hester, often served as front and correspondent in his name. Pitt's government was "leaderless" and "in tatters."[54] It fell to King George to intervene through his representative, the Duke of Grafton, who was shocked at Pitt's appearance and could barely get Pitt to understand that a political crisis even existed. Grafton did succeed in winning permission from Pitt to proceed appropriately. As to the King's entreaties, Pitt refused his suggestion to consult with the King's doctor, professing full confidence in his own physician, Dr. Anthony Addington. Pitt's condition deteriorated throughout 1767, and he sat in silence — brooding, weeping, distanced from his children and servants. Among his symptoms were palpitations, light-headedness, shaking, refusal of food, and insistence on a darkened room. In the midst of all these developments, Pitt would engage in unrealistically grandiose plans to enlarge his country home by 34 bedrooms and buy up neighboring properties to protect his privacy, even when it was abundantly obvious that he lacked the means to do this. By August of 1767 his wife assumed power of attorney. All the while, Pitt remained in name the prime minister (or, more precisely, Lord Privy Seal) of Great Britain. Serving as *de facto* prime minister was the ill-prepared Duke of Grafton, who seemed unable to control increasing discontent in the American colonies. The Townshend Duties Act of 1767 was unpopular in North America and lead to riots. Grafton could not remedy this growing problem, and relations between the colonies and Britain deteriorated to an almost irreparable extent. It is clear that Pitt was seriously disabled by mental illness and totally unable to provide any direction. By the summer of 1768 he had recovered from depression,[55] reappearing in Parliament to criticize his own ministers before submitting his resignation in October of that year. He remained critical of Grafton and his ministers through much of the next administration.

Another 10 years of life remained, but Pitt's health took a turn for the worse in 1776, with many other problems besides gout and mental illness, including arthritis, hernia, kidney and possibly heart disease. But amidst all these disorders, Dr. Addington remained of the opinion that some of Pitt's symptoms were due to his "hypochondriasis."[56]

Black notes that Pitt's health deteriorated in 1767, with exacerbation of gout ascribed to stress and depression. Even as he was supposed to be leading the government, Pitt took to his house, unwilling to see more than a few people and refusing to conduct any business away from home. In June 1767 he excused himself from an audience with King George because of "extreme weakness of the nerves."[57] The Duke of Grafton commented that Pitt could only with great effort discuss politics, and that "his nerves and spirits were affected to a dreadful degree...his great mind bowed down, and thus weakened by disorder." He was "disabled by dejection of spirits almost approaching to insane melancholy." This state of affairs lasted throughout 1767 and far into 1768. Although King George had initially refused to accept Pitt's resignation, by October of 1768 the "weak and broken state" of his health had convinced him of the necessity to resign in favor of Lord Grafton. But, as noted by Black,[58] the government had for a long time been run by others, and was in no meaningful way a Chatham ministry. Considering the powerful influence he had wielded over politics for such a long period, his two-year term as first minister was anticlimactic, and his reduced health had much to do with this.

While it is easy to see in Pitt the indicators of major depression, we need to further consider the evidence for bipolar (or "manic-depressive") disorder. A feature of bipolar disorder, or of the bipolar temperament, is extravagance with money. Even as an undergraduate, Pitt wrote to his father not to think harshly of his son's overspending, so this trait may have been present at an early age. What is more obvious, however, is that financial irresponsibility landed him in a perilous position. He over-reached himself in purchasing and improving country estates, and had to borrow excessively from his friends, as well as depend upon his wife's fortune. Although the landed gentry commonly overspent and incurred large debt, the parsimonious explanation in Pitt's case is that it was due to bipolar disorder. In support of this are the other indicators of bipolarity, such as his hot temper, impetuosity, and heavy drinking. It is possible that some of Pitt's pathology could be accounted for by the hubris syndrome,[59] a proposed but unvalidated condition, which overlaps with mania. For example, during the Seven Years War, Pitt "alone was not tired of the war. He never considered its carnage or the ruin facing a bankrupt country. He had tended to concentrate the whole conduct of government into his own hands and worked with furious energy. His haughty manner, which alienated many, and his high-handed treatment of affairs had earned him ... little friendship."[60] His remark "I know that I can save this country, and that I alone can,"[61] which was made while he was secretary of state during the Seven Years' War, bespoke of arrogance, if not outright hubris; while an "egoistic obstinacy and honorable single-mindedness" and "megalomaniacal demands" made him hard to work with.[62] Almost surely Pitt suffered from incapacitating depression and episodic bouts of mania or hypomania that would qualify for a diagnosis of bipolar disorder. Some of his "furious energy" and "megalomaniacal demands" may have been manic, hubristic, or adaptive to the demands of the situation, or a mixture of all three (there is room for debate). But as to the presence of depression, which impaired his competence to lead government, few would disagree.

AUGUSTUS HENRY FITZROY, 3RD DUKE OF GRAFTON (1735–1811) *(1768–1770)*

The Duke of Grafton's short term as prime minister between 1768 and 1770 was preoccupied internationally with ongoing problems in the American colonies, and domestically with the attempts of John Wilkes, who had been convicted of seditious libel, to take his seat in Parliament. Grafton was also intermittently embroiled in conflict with Chatham at a time when the latter's health brought uncertainty to the matter of government. Grafton was, in fact, a reluctant replacement to Chatham as prime minister.

Grafton's Personality

Grafton has been referred to as "having little interest in aspiring to political supremacy" and a "political lightweight."[63] He was by nature a conciliator and disliked stirring up trouble; while advocating a consensus approach to policy, he was "all too often unable either to achieve a collective view or to quell dissent."[64]

Descriptions of Grafton's personality refer to a "moody and capricious temper ... disgusting coldness ... mutability, sullen[ness], [and a] profliga[cy] without gaiety" by those who were unfavorably disposed to him. More complementary aspects of his character were offered by those of greater sympathy, such as being "kind to his domestics, hospitable to strangers, [and of] honorable character."[65] As with a surprising number of other prime ministers, Grafton was "shy and disliked ceremonial."[66]

There is nothing to suggest that any of these personality traits or temperamental qualities reached a level of pathology or put him at risk of depression, anxiety or other mental illness, but they made him poorly suited for leadership.

LORD NORTH (1732–1792) *(1770–1782)*

Lord North was born April 13, 1732, and died August 5, 1792. He was appointed prime minister in January 1770 and remained in office for twelve years before resigning in March 1782, making him one of the longest serving 18th century prime ministers. North is best known as the man who lost the North American colonies, which was seen at the time as a monumental calamity in Britain. Barbara Tuchman sees North as a key example of the folly which characterized British policy towards North America.[67] However, this folly should not detract from the fact that he is now seen in many ways as "a successful politician, managing king and Parliament with consummate skill ... and as a prime minister whose policy initiatives were in many respects innovative and successful."[68] He excelled at finance[69] and left a positive legacy with regard to Treasury administration. His management of the Falkland Island crisis averted likely war with Spain, and he showed an enlightened view towards the French Canadian settlers which went some way towards creating a solid foundation for Canada as a new nation (in contrast to his handling of the other American colonies). However, despite his successes, there is abundant evidence to suggest that North's career as prime minister was at times impaired by depression and anxiety, leading to periods of indecision and inactivity.

Lord North: A Doubting Thomas

King George III saw Lord North as the natural choice for prime minister, and Walpole considered him to be "more able, more assiduous, more resolute and more fitted to deal with mankind," in comparison to his predecessor.[70] Yet North harbored many doubts as to his adequacy for the job, clearly in excess of the self-deprecating language which was customary at the time. In December 1759, two months before taking office, he wrote to his father as follows: This day has been so charming, that I envied you at Waldershare. Indeed, my situation is such, that I envy everybody; I always hated my part, but this aversion increases daily. It is very hard, that when a man has no favor to ask but his own dismission, he is not able to attain it in two years. I can not bear to live this life any longer.[71]

North annually threatened to submit his resignation to King George, yet was seen by contemporaries as having done a commendable job, and his personal misgivings were not always well-founded. Ambivalence about leadership is revealed by North's own description of "being tied to the stake," as he referred to his reluctant continuation in office.

For the first few years of North's administration, the situation in North America was relatively calm, but passage of the Tea Act in 1773 produced strong reaction in Massachusetts, since it essentially gave a monopoly for tea importation to the East India Company, for which the colonists were forced to pay import taxes. This ill-judged measure culminated in the Boston Tea

Party. Further repressive measures were enacted by North, which ultimately lead to war. In 1775, North offered to resign, but this was rejected by the king. Again, in 1781, after the defeat at Yorktown, North offered to resign, and once more the king rejected it. His resignation was tendered again on March 20, 1782, and this time was accepted. However, he remained a presence in Parliament for years to come, acting as home secretary under Fox for a brief period in 1783. The final years of his life were dogged by blindness, and he died at the age of 60 in 1792.

Lord North: Anxiety and Depression

During 1779 Lord North almost certainly suffered from clinical depression. Butterfield[72] has characterized the prime minister as behaving like "a prisoner seeking release," and, in describing a revealing correspondence between John Robinson and Charles Jenkinson during 1779, provides strong evidence that North was markedly depressed.

Jenkinson, the First Lord Liverpool, was a confidante of the king, and Robinson was senior secretary of the treasury and mentor to North. By late 1779, because of North's "incapacitation,"[73] Jenkinson had become in effect the king's adviser, a role traditionally taken by the prime minister. The picture emerging from their letters is of a man who considered himself unfit for office and who suffered misery and anguish to the point of paralysis. Problems in Ireland were almost as serious as those in North America, and issues of control in India, along with domestic problems, overwhelmed North. In December 1779, Ireland was in such turmoil that it seemed likely to go the way of the American colonies. A report had been submitted by the lord lieutenant of Ireland in July, which he felt demanded urgent attention. Nothing happened, and he again expressed further concern in December after there had been practically no correspondence from North's minister for Ireland. In between these dates, on August 11, we find that Robinson is writing, "Nothing done, or attempting to be done, no Attention to the necessary arrangements at Home, none to Ireland, nothing to India ... a Cabinet totally disjointed.... Lord North, indeed, is the most altered Man I ever saw in my Life. He has not spirits to set to anything." North wrote to Robinson, saying that "nothing can be more miserable than I am."[74] Five days later North pleaded that he had no time, that no-one would do anything—and then "he fell into one of his distressing Fits."[75]

On September 30, Robinson tried unsuccessfully to persuade North to read the abstract of the Irish report, failing to convince him that a crisis loomed or that there was a real possibility of the government falling unless some action was taken. He stressed that time had almost run out.[76]

Neglect of the Irish situation lead to the resignation of Lord Gower, president of the Council. This brought to a head North's failure to complete ministerial reassignments. It also may have triggered an attempt to replace North, but this was ultimately thwarted by others in the government allied to the King.

Butterfield is of the opinion that North's increasing depression and its "attendant creeping paralysis" corresponded to the escalation of North's ministerial crisis. In November, North acknowledged that everyone was deserting him, although he failed to comprehend the reasons. He felt himself to be incapable of anything, unable to make decisions or to pay attention to business matters, and to suffer from indescribable "torments of mind." As North expressed all this to Robinson, he became so upset that Robinson himself became tearful,[77] an observation which resonates with the medical maxim that if a doctor can empathize with the depressed patient (i.e., share the feeling) it is a helpful clue as to the presence of a depressive disorder. There was also an element of self-pity, as illustrated in North's view that he had gone through "torture and anguish" on the King's behalf and did not deserve the cold shoulder from His Majesty.[78] North also bewailed the fact that so many of his ministerial colleagues had deserted him. Overall, the evidence of mental disorder was so stark that even Jenkinson, in December of 1779, opined that North's condition was "a Disease of the Mind which comes and goes."[79]

We can presume that some of North's depression was related to the mounting problems of the time, which left him overwhelmed. But so often in these situations, it can be difficult to distinguish chicken and egg. While stress is known to produce depression, the symptoms of the illness lead to further stress. Indecisiveness, poor concentration, withdrawal and fatigue are not conducive to effective leadership, and the more things are neglected, the worse the problems become. The more a person withdraws, the less likely it is for colleagues to remain engaged; they go their own way and by default make decisions in times of crisis. It is conceivable that in 1779, when the issue of North's resignation was again on the table, his ambivalence brought about further gloom. In sum, around 1779, Lord North spent a minimum of one year in a state of deep depression which paralyzed him and could not be remedied by compensatory initiatives from his associates, try as they might. Many colleagues deserted him, and the de facto acting prime minister was ill-equipped for the task. In accounting for the things that did or did not happen during Lord North's administration during 1779, some part of this can be laid at the feet of the prime minister's depression.

Whiteley[80] quotes North as saying that prime ministerial burdens were more than he could undertake. He feels that two sets of factors contributed to North's increasingly frequent attacks of illness and "certainly to his periods of depression and inertia in the face of difficult decisions." He pinpoints long hours of overwork, although these were limited to particular months of the year, and a proclivity to become bogged down in detail at the expense of the overall picture. North would consult with many people of different opinion on an issue without reaching a firm decision. Thomas Hutchinson, the governor of Massachusetts, wrote in 1774 of "[North's] delays which attend business of all sorts, [his] consulting so many persons, who of different opinions; and from this difference he remains undecided himself for some time, [and] is apt to change." Such indecision in the face of pressure suggests either the worry of high anxiety or presence of depression.

Lack of confidence is illustrated in a letter written by North to his father in May 1772, just after preparing the budget, in which North stated his wish to be released from his position, as it was too large for his abilities. He went on to express fear that he would lose whatever respect he had earned, and he was worried lest his incompetence cause public damage.[81] To most people, North was doing his job well; he was still comparatively young and in good health. The five years preceding the troubles with North America were North's "high noon," which was tainted by underlying anxiety. North's sentiments about his performance were at variance with the views of others, such as Chatham, who effusively praised North's service.[82]

In September 1776, Lord North sustained a serious riding injury when he was thrown from his horse and fractured his right arm. While he recovered from the immediate physical injury, his general health began an irreversible decline. North, who was so corpulent that he was unable to stand for very long, lost weight to the extent of being able to feel his ribs for the first time in years.

In August 1777, when things were going badly for the British campaign in North America, and in the run-up to one of the most humiliating defeats in British history (at Saratoga), North wrote to his father indicating severe worry and depression. He claimed that over the previous three months he had been more "hurried and vexed" than usual, being worn out with continual fretting. He thought it possible that his uneasiness arose from his own failings, but "the fact is that so long a continuance in a situation which I dislike, and for which I am neither adapted by temper or capacity, has sunk my spirits, weakene'd my understanding, impaired my memory, and fill'd my heart with a kind of uneasiness from which nothing can deliver me but an honorable retreat. I am sorry to say that I do not foresee the moment when that happiness will fall to my lot."[83] These changes in Lord North even prompted King George, who was destined to experience his own mental torments, to express concern for his prime minister's mental state.

Here North indicates that his cognitive faculties are impaired by diminished thinking, concentration, attention and memory, that he feels trapped, that he is self-blameful and gloomy in outlook, and in low mood. His use of the words "hurried," "vexed," and "fretting" suggest very high levels of anxiety, as in generalized anxiety disorder.

Later, in 1787, when he was in his mid–50s and going blind, North was in "extreme depression of spirits" and was read to at night by his wife until he went to sleep, suggesting a delay in falling asleep, as is often seen in depression.

Possible Sleep Apnea

Many references to Lord North's "corpulency" appear, which was felt by some of his contemporaries to be a health problem that reduced his expected life span. Such marked obesity, coupled with his frequent tendency to fall asleep in Parliament, made him the butt of jokes. It also raises the possibility that Lord North could have suffered from sleep apnea, a condition associated with daytime fatigue, involuntarily falling asleep during the day, memory disturbance, poor concentration, disinterest and reduced performance. Sleep apnea used to be known as the "Pickwick syndrome," named after the Charles Dickens character Mr. Pickwick. As set out in the DSM-IV,[84] excessive sleepiness is the most common presenting complaint among patients with sleep apnea (or "breathing-related sleep disorder," to use its current name). The individual's failure to control sleepiness is often noticed when they are at rest or in meetings, as they may fall asleep during conversation.

It is therefore relevant to the argument that in Parliament North fell asleep involuntarily during important debates.[85] The first known reference to North's soporific habit appears in a 1770 quote from Edmund Burke's brother, William, who said, "I wish the noble Lord opposite had some one at his elbow, to pull him every now and then by the ear, and give him a gentle tap on the shoulder." His sleep was accompanied by obvious snoring, a habit which was occasionally mimicked by his parliamentary colleague George Selwyn — to the great amusement of all in the House. Edmund Burke remarked, "Brother Lazarus is not dead, but sleepeth."[86] North's "constitutional somnolency" has been put down to overwork and attendant lack of the opportunity for sleep, as well as to a willful inattention to certain things in Parliament and even to his short-sightedness. While these may have been factors, the possibility of a breathing-related sleep disorder seems more likely.

Summary

In brief, Lord North was one of the most self-doubting of all British prime ministers, and he expressed his perceived inadequacies in many letters to his father and to King George. He "fretted" and worried excessively, which caused him considerable distress. One of his biographers has used the term "debilitating" in this context. Superimposed on his anxiety were numerous periods of paralyzing depression, the severity of which were indicated by the extent to which he neglected affairs of state. If sleep apnea supervened as his weight increased, this would have been an additional hindrance to his health and political effectiveness.

North had many talents, and if not for the North American debacle he might have received a more favorable judgment by history. His survival as prime minister for 12 years — unusual for 18th century British politics — was due, in part, to his ability to obtain and keep the support from a disparate group of colleagues, and not simply through party loyalty. Given the short terms of many 18th century prime ministers, North's longevity was quite an achievement. (Discounting the 50 years covered by North, Walpole and Pitt, there were 15 different prime ministers in the 30 remaining years of the 18th century.) North was affable, diligent, principled and well-liked. He successfully handled some international crises and was a staunch defender of the constitution. But he was uncomfortable with conflict and prone to indecision, a well-recognized effect of anxiety and depression. While perhaps a good peacetime leader, he was a poor war leader; and it was in the context of the American war that this chronically anxious man eventually submitted his resignation, probably not without a feeling of relief.

WILLIAM PETTY, 2ND EARL OF SHELBURNE (1737–1805) *(1782–1783)*

The Earl of Shelburne was one of the first prime ministers who entered office with a distinguished military record, which in this case was acquired from service during the Seven Years War at the battles of Minden in 1759 and Kloster Kampen in 1760. For his actions he was promoted to the rank of Colonel and appointed aide-de-camp to the King.[87] He is also one of the few prime ministers to have fought a duel, which occurred after some sharp remarks in a parliamentary debate with the Scottish MP Lieutenant-Colonel Fullerton in 1780. The duel left Shelburne with a wound in the groin but also brought him a degree of brief heroism for this action.

Shelburne headed the government for only 8 months between July 1782 and March 1783, resigning after his proposed peace agreement to end the war with America was narrowly defeated in the House of Commons. For five of these 8 months, parliament was in recess, so his active term as leader was an ephemeral three months.

From the medical perspective, his physical and mental health remained good, and illness did not significantly interfere with his career.

WILLIAM CAVENDISH CAVENDISH-BENTINCK, 3RD DUKE OF PORTLAND (1738–1809) *(1783; 1807–1809)*

The Duke of Portland was twice prime minister, between April and December 1783 and again between March 1807 and October 1809. Portland's first administration came to an abrupt end when the King dismissed him; his second term ended when he died after a stroke.

Portland is widely seen as a failure in his two administrations, but he served politics as a whole with distinction over a period of almost 50 years.[88] His health was good until old age, although in his final administration he was barely able to function. His fear of public speaking was longstanding: "[He] was even more averse to public speaking than Rockingham," and "[he]contributed nothing more than mute votes to the party's profile in the House of Lords."[89]

He inherited from his father traits of shyness and aversion to public speaking, and also found it hard to make decisions, attributes which would hardly be desirable in a leader yet were strangely common in eighteenth-century prime ministers (e.g. Portland, Rockingham, Newcastle, North, Grafton and Addington). Perhaps in part this reflected the pathology of the King, who had much influence in the choice of ministers. Portland did at least function, but gout, stones, shyness and a stroke made a poor recipe for leadership, of which he offered none. He was "totally unfit for the task," delegated extensively and made little effort to coordinate policy among the departments of government.[90] Portland must go down in history as one of several prime ministers whose poor health resulted in serious impairment of leadership, especially in his old age. While in his case, the proximate conditions were physical, a secondary role was played by his anxiety and retiring personality which today would be suggestive of possible social anxiety disorder, performance type.

WILLIAM PITT THE YOUNGER (1759–1806)
(1783–1801; 1804–1806)

William Pitt the Younger remains the youngest to take office as prime minister — at age 24 — and also served as prime minister for a total of 19 years before dying at the age of 46. Despite his precociousness, selfless dedication to his country, and distinguished record, Pitt suffered for most of his adult life from increasingly serious alcohol problems and, quite possibly, phobic anxiety.

Pitt came from politically successful families on both his paternal and maternal sides. His father was prime minister between 1766 and 1768, and his maternal uncle, George Grenville, was prime minister between 1763 and 1765.

Early Years

Due to frail health in childhood, Pitt was educated at home, taking readily to books and learning, while neglecting the fashionable athletic activities of his day. He entered Cambridge University at the remarkably young age of 14, when fewer than one in five freshmen was below 18 years of age.[91] The Master of Pitt's college hailed his "extraordinary genius." While he was an undergraduate, Pitt made important connections to the world of politics, most notably Lord Camden, as well as finding time to attend debates in Parliament. It was during one of these debates that Pitt's father collapsed and died shortly afterwards. Although Pitt the Elder left a financial legacy for his son, it did not prevent him from quickly falling into debt, a problem which shadowed him throughout his life.

By 1780 Pitt had completed his law studies and was called to the Bar during that year. Not long afterwards he was elected to the House of Commons as member for Appleby. His maiden speech was given with neither warning nor preparation, yet was impressive in its "cool, incisive ... and reasoned argument."[92] Pitt also took an opposing position towards the American war and the power of the Crown over Parliament. By 1783, at the age of 23, Pitt was appointed Chancellor of the Exchequer after having declined the offer of a relatively minor cabinet post under Lord Rockingham.

Record as Prime Minister

Pitt became prime minister in December 1783 and was successfully re-elected as Member of Parliament for Cambridge University in 1784. At the time of his appointment, a popular verse[93] commented on his youthfulness for such an important job:

> A sight to make all nations stand and stare:
> A kingdom trusted to a schoolboy's care.

For the first six years of his premiership, England was at peace, and Pitt was able to restore his country to fiscal security after the costly American War of Independence. His competency in overseeing the country's finances contrasts markedly with the irresponsible neglect of his own finances. Pitt ran further into debt when he purchased his country residence in 1785, and seemed to neglect his affairs to such an extent that he was robbed by his servants.

Among the causes which Pitt championed were parliamentary reform to reduce royal influence, union with Ireland, centralizing rule in India, reduction of the national debt, Catholic emancipation and promotion of free trade. Major crises which Pitt had to face included King George's mental illness and the determination of whether sovereignty should pass to the King's oldest son, a move which was ultimately rendered unnecessary by the king's recovery.

In 1801, Pitt resigned following defeat over his efforts to grant the vote to Catholics. Three years later, after Addington's ineffective administration, the King asked Pitt again to form a government as the rise of Napoleon posed a renewed threat to Britain. Eventually war broke out, for which Pitt was blamed by his opponents. While Britain enjoyed some notable successes, such as Nelson's victory at Trafalgar, Napoleon's defeat of Russia and Austria in 1805 was a major setback for Pitt, who died a few months later. His last words were, "Oh my country! How I Love my country."[94]

Pitt's Health

Within a few weeks of arrival at Cambridge, Pitt fell ill and had to return home for a prolonged period, where he was cared for by his father's physician, Dr. Anthony Addington, who gave advice that may have had dreadful consequences for Pitt. While some of Addington's recommendations were doubtless good, such as to take up daily exercise by riding, to cultivate regular sleep and a healthy diet, his advice that Pitt should drink port wine every day very likely set him on a troublesome path which ultimately lead to alcoholism. The specific details of Addington's advice have generally been interpreted as endorsing liberal quantities of alcohol. Medical recommendation to drink was not unusual in those times, and Pitt responded well to Addington's ministrations in the short term, shaking off his history of chronic ill health. But even in the 18th century, just as today, recommending the daily consumption of liberal amounts of alcohol to a 15 year old would be considered perilous advice. To someone prone to alcohol problems, this is truly playing with fire, no matter how well-intended.

Alcohol Problems

What is the evidence that Pitt suffered from serious abuse of, or dependence on, alcohol? Pitt remained in good health until his mid-thirties, by which time he had been prime minister for about 10 years. His alcohol consumption had become a problem, coinciding with increasing work pressure and a diminishing social life. It has been estimated that by the 1780s Pitt was drinking about one and two-third bottles of strong wine daily, and in this alcoholic haze Pitt would plan his Parliamentary speeches. On one occasion Pitt and his boon companions, Dundas and Jenkinson, had been drinking and then allegedly rode through an open toll gate, where they were fired at by the toll booth keeper, an incident which gave rise to the following satirical lines of verse:

> Ah, Think what danger on debauch attends!
> Let Pitt o'er wine preach temperance to his friends,
> How, as he wandered darkly o'er the plain,
> His reason drowned in Jenkinson's Champagne,
> Rustic's hand, but righteous fate withstood,
> Had shed a premier's for a robber's blood.[95]

It is perhaps surprising that Pitt's alcohol consumption failed to interfere greatly with his mental acuity or performance. There was one occasion, in 1788, when Pitt was unable to give a speech in Parliament after being attacked by Charles James Fox over legislation about India. The previous night Pitt and friends had been drinking, and, according to Hague, this was one of the rare times that alcohol had impaired Pitt's competence in Parliament.[96] In 1793, Pitt and Henry ("Hal") Dundas appeared in Parliament inebriated, which gave cause for the following lines in the press:

> I cannot see the Speaker, Hal, can you?
> What! Cannot see the Speaker, I see two![97]

During 1793 Pitt was under heavy pressure after France declared war against Britain on February 1, setting off twenty-two years of hostilities. His excessive drinking started to concern others, particularly at the time of the British retreat at Dunkirk in September of 1793. One of Pitt's closest colleagues, George Rose, wrote that Pitt's failure to answer letters began to irritate others.[98] Even Pitt expressed concern, confiding to his friend Henry Addington that he feared the newspapers would disclose his problem.[99] George Canning, a future prime minister, observed that Pitt drank "I know not how much Madeira" at a dinner, while another colleague stated that the failed siege of Dunkirk coincided with "the first visible effect of Public Affairs upon his health." Even the *Morning Chronicle* newspaper remarked that Pitt was "observed, in walking to his carriage, to oscillate like his own bills."[100]

There were many other stresses in Pitt's life, including the difficult decision he made in 1794 to dismiss his brother, Thomas, who was First Lord of the Admiralty, a move which Thomas not only disputed but which caused an irreparable breach in their friendship. William Pitt wrote that he had experienced more sleepless nights during that year than at any other time, and an observer commented that he "had no leisure, and lost all relish, except for the company of his intimate friends."[101] By 1795, when his physician Sir Walter Farquhar first saw Pitt, Farquhar found his patient in a state of much debility and resistant to Farquhar's advice for relaxation to regain strength. Farquhar warned that continued neglect of Pitt's health would have a damaging effect.[102] Three years later, in 1798, Pitt fought a duel with George Tierney, an opposition MP. A few days afterwards, Pitt took to his bed and was absent from the House of Commons for weeks. In June 1798 he was noted to be "seriously ill," and either exhaustion or alcohol frequently kept him from rising before 11 A.M.[103] Many times Pitt would take to bed after having managed some major challenge. Despite public comment about his frail health, Pitt remained in denial, telling his mother that he was growing stronger by the day and was as well as ever.[104] Pitt's health, drinking and suggested insanity became the subject of opposition newspapers for a while in 1798.

While some of Pitt's illness was the result of gout and/or gastrointestinal problems, it is surely the case that excessive alcohol consumption was also a significant factor. Addington may have been the only person who could tell Pitt to stop drinking, and in 1800 Pitt spent a period of rest at Addington's home, intent on bringing his drinking under better control. Even then, Pitt pushed his limits: despite being advised by Dr. Farquhar to only drink with lunch but not at supper, he pressed Addington for a nightcap; fortunately for Pitt, Addington held firm in refusal. Pitt's health continued to deteriorate, and his cough and unhealthy complexion was widely apparent, as well as his continued need to rely on alcohol at the end of the day, when he would rapidly take several glasses of port wine.[105]

The Duke of Wellington was probably correct in attributing Pitt's poor health to "long and previous exertions in the House of Commons, and by deluging his stomach with port wine and water, which he drank to excess, in order to give a false and artificial stimulus to his nervous system."[106]

So the question comes up whether Pitt suffered from pathological alcohol use disorder (i.e., either abuse or dependence), or whether he was merely a heavy drinker at a time when it was not unusual to imbibe port wine or ale on a regular basis among his circle. With reference to the current criteria for diagnosing alcohol abuse, it is clear that Pitt's misuse of alcohol caused impairment and distress, and recurrent failure to fulfill major role obligations (resulting in absences from work and most likely problems in relationships). As to the possibility of alcohol dependence, he would have qualified for two of the required three symptoms: he continued to drink despite knowing that it was harmful and aggravating of other health problems, and he missed important occupational activities (i.e., attendance in the House of Commons) in part as a result of drinking. However, it is possible that other medical problems contributed to his behavior.

Social Anxiety Disorder?

When we consider Pitt's personality and social relationships, the possibility is strong that he displayed features of social anxiety disorder (SAD or social phobia). Nobody relishes embarrassment; criticism is often hard to take; and most individuals would admit to some mild fear of certain interactions. In SAD, the threshold for these fears is much lower than in the general population and the level of discomfort substantially greater. The anxiety can be unbearable and lead to marked withdrawal from most social encounters or from selective types of interactions, such as dating relationships, public presentations, speaking, athletic activity, examinations, performing arts, meeting strangers or making new friends. It is not uncommon for people with SAD to drink alcohol to lower their level of anxiety, and secondary alcoholism then develops because of persistent and excessive drinking.

We think of politicians as having a thick skin and being able to deal with rejection. To be exceptionally afraid of scrutiny, criticism or embarrassment may seem unlikely in one who chooses the high-profile life of politics, where being the center of attention is inevitable, but surprisingly it does happen, and other notable examples have been described, such as U.S. presidents Thomas Jefferson, Ulysses Grant and Calvin Coolidge. With Pitt, SAD is a strong possibility.

Pitt had an easy-going, pleasant demeanor and bookish manner. Pitt the Elder wrote of his son's tendency to sequestrate himself at family events, which in his opinion "agrees better with his contemplative constitution than more talk and more romps."[107] As Pitt grew into manhood, he overcame some of these retiring ways and, at Cambridge, was described as lively in company, witty, but never one to cause offence or distress to others. He was perhaps unusually concerned with not disgracing himself in any way, and therefore "avoided every species of irregularity."[108] In other words, he was cautious in his conduct and perhaps less of a risk-taker than many of his peers. William Wilberforce referred to Pitt's "playful facetiousness which gratifies all without wounding any."[109] While none of these characteristics alone is sufficient to claim the presence of SAD, they suggest a person who is more intent to please others than to offend, and who is more concerned than average with avoiding disgrace — both attributes of those with SAD, and almost the polar opposite of Pitt's father. By the time he graduated from Cambridge, Pitt's character was set: "a brilliant and tireless interest in practical questions, a tremendously relaxed and talkative enjoyment of chosen company, and a stern face presented to the outer world."[110] While aloofness can easily be mistaken for arrogance, this is not always so: shyness is often behind such an attitude. Was Pitt shy? Wilberforce regarded Pitt as the shyest man he'd ever known, to the extent of awkwardness that "often produced effects for which pride was falsely charged on him."[111] Pitt himself said, "I am the shyest man alive."[112] Of course, shyness is not "all or none," and under the right circumstances and with sufficient motivation it can be selectively overcome. Thus it could be that Pitt was described as socializing with "relaxed good humor" at a visit to the French court.[113] Taken together, Pitt's social avoidance, failure to establish intimacies with women, exceptional shyness and uncontrollable use of alcohol build a strong case for clinically significant social anxiety beyond mere shyness. However, we should not overlook some other explanations, such as alcohol abuse, which could produce social avoidance due to shame; and his failure to establish close relationships with women could be the result of homosexual preferences; but these seem less likely. That social anxiety failed to prevent Pitt from launching himself to political stardom may perhaps be explainable by many offsetting factors, including ambition, genius, opportunity, family pedigree and expectation.

HENRY ADDINGTON, 1ST VISCOUNT SIDMOUTH (1757–1844) *(1801–1804)*

Henry Addington was born May 30, 1757, and died February 13, 1844. His father, Anthony Addington, was a prominent physician specializing in psychiatry who had opened a private psychiatric hospital near Reading. As previously noted, Dr. Addington's patients included King George III and the Elder and Younger Pitts. He remained a distant figure to his children, who drew greater warmth and affection from their mother, Mary Addington, herself "a shadowy figure who lived her life uneasily in the interstices of her husband's prejudices."[114]

Addington has been referred to as the first middle-class prime minister, a background which proved to be an obstacle, although obviously not an insurmountable one.[115] Because he once proffered medical advice on how the king's madness should be treated, Addington was derisively known as "the Doctor." The advance of his political career was due, in part, to royal patronage arising from his father's ministrations during the king's psychotic episodes. Addington became prime minister in 1801 and was removed in 1804. On either side of his administration were those of William Pitt the Younger. One notable event during Addington's premiership was the negotiation of the Treaty of Amiens, which was seen by many as more favorable to France than to Great Britain. Shortly afterwards, Napoleon was again threatening the peace, and Addington resigned. While relieved to give up the premiership, he remained active in Parliamentary affairs (as Lord Sidmouth) for the next twenty years and survived to a ripe old age, outliving both his wives.

Addington and Mental Illness: Is There a Case?

It has been said that Addington was relieved to give up leadership, in part because he was poorly suited to the demands of being prime minister, especially in time of war.[116] A notoriously poor speaker, Addington sat in

Parliament for two years before giving his first speech, which only happened after strong persuasion by Pitt. As noted by Ziegler, excellence as an orator is not a prerequisite for being a good prime minister, as other qualities, like efficiency, calmness, good judgment and integrity, can compensate. But in times of war, what is needed is one who can inspire, like Churchill or Lloyd George, and in these qualities Addington was sorely lacking.

Is there enough information about Addington to support the presence of psychiatric disorder? Fear of public speaking, lack of confidence, reluctance to thrust oneself forward, and fear of being snubbed or made to look a fool were all characteristic of the man.[117] Added to these were poor confidence in his oratorical skills and a lack of ambition. Ziegler likens Addington to a hedgehog: "shy and reticent ... prickly when trodden on but otherwise inoffensive, lying extremely low and toning in well with his background. And like the hedgehog in the light of day, Addington's inclination when trapped in a glare of publicity was to run away and hide."[118] It's scarcely the stuff of which great prime ministers are made. These qualities "went far to create that lack of confidence which was ultimately to nullify all Addington's efforts and to lead to the classification of his government as a hopeless failure."[119] A contributory factor to this might have been Addington's social anxiety and, possibly, liberal use of alcohol.

When Addington resigned in 1804, although it was a personal relief, there is evidence that he was experiencing considerable depression, or the signs of withdrawal from excessive use of alcohol. "He was close to being a broken man ... his mind had been thrown too much, perhaps, off its bias by the nature of the opposition."[120] He was observed to be carrying a load too heavy for his shoulders: "He wants spirits and courage for his situation and though a temperate man, now drinks perhaps 20 glasses of wine at his dinner before he goes into the House of Commons to invigorate himself."[121] The once affable and complacent Speaker of the House had become a "haggard neurotic, sleeping badly, short-tempered ... doubting his own capacities and pathetically uncertain of his closest friends.... The last few months in office had come close to destroying his spirit."[122] In approaching the question of alcohol consumption, it is true, as noted earlier, that in Addington's time alcohol was less likely to spread disease than water, and society's attitude was more permissive towards alcohol. It is also important to keep in mind that port wine was fortified with brandy and thus somewhat weaker than today's port. Furthermore, the smaller port bottles of the time would correspond to about half a bottle in 2009.[123] But even making these allowances, Addington was drinking very heavily by any standards. Quaffing even 20 small glasses of alcohol immediately before attendance in the House would, in today's world, be the subject of censor.

In looking for a multigenerational pattern of mental illness as supportive evidence, it is relevant that Addington's son, Harry, was abnormally shy and lacking in self-confidence, and made a suicide attempt which ultimately proved fatal. How much of Harry's predisposition came from his father and how much from his mother is difficult to tell, since they both had excessive levels of social anxiety, and were "shy and retiring."[124]

WILLIAM WYNDHAM GRENVILLE, BARON GRENVILLE (1759–1834) *(1806–1807)*

William Wyndham Grenville was the third son of George Grenville and Elizabeth Wyndham. His father was prime minister between 1763 and 1765. The younger Grenville hesitantly took office as prime minister — a reluctance determined partly by the necessity of having to give up a lucrative sinecure. Fearful of its mental and physical burdens, he adapted uneasily to the tasks of leadership.[125]

Although Grenville wanted to create a national government, the manner in which he went about it alienated the king and stirred up party rivalries. After Grenville resigned in 1807, he reportedly said, "The deed is done and I am again a free man, and to you I may express what it would seem like affectation to say to others, the infinite pleasure I derive from emancipation." He achieved relatively little as prime minister, other than the admittedly signal accomplishment of abolishing the slave trade.

Grenville's health was extremely good, apart from chronic insomnia and increasing obesity. In later life it was necessary for him to withdraw from active politics because of a stroke in 1823. Another stroke followed in 1827, and towards the end of his life, according to Grenville's son, he lost his "firmness of mind," suggesting that dementia had set in. However, while late-life cerebrovascular mental pathology may have been present, it had no impact on his political career.

In temperament, Grenville joins the many prime ministers who have been described as publicly aloof, reserved and austere,[126] but was affectionate with his wife, to whom he was close. In summary, there is no evidence of mental illness, but Grenville may perhaps be counted among the ranks of former prime ministers who showed decline of mental functions in old age.

SPENCER PERCEVAL (1762–1812) *(1809–1812)*

It has been said that Spencer Perceval became prime minister as the result of good fortune,[127] but it was a stroke of extremely bad fortune that brought an end to his life — Perceval is the only prime minister to have been assassinated, an event which occurred in the lobby of the House of Commons at the hands of a disgruntled businessman. Throughout his life, Perceval was sustained by devoutly evangelical beliefs, being known as a man of probity and earnestness; in these respects he was very similar to Gladstone. He always dressed in black, although not from any prolonged mourning. Politically, Perceval was in some ways a reformist, opposing slavery and unregulated child labor, but he was in other ways quite conservative in his views. For example, he tried to enforce punishments against adultery and successfully obtained sufficient funds to prolong Wellington's campaign in the Peninsular War against Napoleon. Among the numerous problems with which he had to contend were those relating to the king's re-emergent insanity, the matter of the regency and the conduct of the regent's wife.

Perceval's Health

Although described as "pale" and "sepulchral" in appearance, his health was apparently good. The only hint of any kind of mental disorder is a brief allusion to the fact that "after two years in office, the strain of continual political crises was beginning to tell. He looked frail and anxious."[128] Of these crises, Iremonger wrote that "his ability to keep government functioning in the teeth of strong opposition was a tribute to his resilience."[129] Wilberforce characterized him as one of the most conscientious and generous men he ever knew.[130] Perceval was shy, apologetic and self-effacing, yet succeeded nonetheless in making an impact on others. Aspects of Perceval's character which offset his lack of self-confidence and modesty included religious enthusiasm and aggressiveness.[131] Other character traits included a tendency to gloom, austerity, extreme self-discipline, excessive concern with religion and eschatology: he was sure, for example, that the world would come to an end in 1926, and his study of the book of Revelation lead him to the conviction that Napoleon was "the woman who rode the beast, who is drunk with the blood of saints, the mother of harlots."

Perceval was a clear example of the conflict often found in prime ministers between the necessity to appear genial and sociable and the intense sensitivity, isolation and solitariness of their true natures. Some public men resolve this conflict better than others.[132] Perceval's life illustrates the adage that far from being invariably a community of "handsome, gregarious, strong men of genius, many British prime ministers suffered from the handicaps of an unimpressive face and body, unattractive and even repelling personality, and other crippling disadvantages," often including early bereavement and deprivation of parental love. The forces which drove Perceval and others like him to overcome these handicaps were strong indeed.[133]

On the possibility of mental illness in the context of unceasing stress, it is relevant that Perceval's family life was nearly ruined, he was looking frail, mental strains were telling on him and the crack was imminent — but it never came because of his untimely death on May 11, 1812.

ROBERT BANKS JENKINSON, 2ND EARL OF LIVERPOOL (1770–1828) *(1812–1827)*

The Earl of Liverpool's term as prime minister lasted for almost 15 years between 1812 and 1827.

Background and Political Career

Liverpool was the only child of his father's marriage to Amelia Watts, a woman of partial Indian heritage. He was educated at Charterhouse School in London, then at Oxford University, from whence he graduated with a Master of Arts degree in 1790. In the same year he was elected member of parliament for Rye, and progressed rapidly up the ladder due in considerable part to his father's influence. Early in his political career, after war broke out with France, Liverpool enlisted in the militia and was away from Parliament a considerable amount.

As secretary of state for foreign affairs, Liverpool (or Lord Hawkesbury, as he was then known until his father's death in 1808) negotiated the Treaty of Amiens. Much of his time as secretary was taken up with French and North American issues. In 1806, when Pitt was ill, King George III asked Liverpool to form a government, but he declined. A year later he was named home secretary in the Duke of Portland's government. In 1809 he was appointed war secretary in Spencer Perceval's administration, and after Perceval's assassination in 1812, Lord Liverpool succeeded him as prime minister.

Among the events which took place during Liverpool's long administration were the War of 1812 with the United States and further Napoleonic campaigns, culminating with Napoleon's defeat at Waterloo and the Congress of Vienna, which set the stage for many years of peace. At home, Liverpool had to face serious post-war economic problems, partly arising from massive war debts, economic recession, repeal of the wartime income tax and passage of the Corn Laws, all of which lead to scattered unrest, riots and the Peterloo massacre. In 1820 his administration passed repressive legislation to limit free speech and public assembly. In the aftermath of these unpopular measures, Liverpool was targeted for assassination by the Cato Street conspirators. In the final years of Liverpool's leadership his government adopted more liberal policies and economic prosperity was restored.[134]

Liverpool's Personality and Evidence for Mental Illness

Although successfully retaining office for 15 years, Liverpool did not achieve the stature which might be expected. Evans speculates that this was partly because of his "fussy, nervous and detail-driven" nature,[135] best summed up by Disraeli, in his novel *Coningsby*, as a man whose highest attribute was "meager diligence" and who earned the sobriquet of "Arch Mediocrity."[136] Iremonger describes Liverpool's colorless personality, displayed in his marriage of 25 years, as one of "dullness in private reflected by dullness in public," and "modest entertainment [which] reduced their guests almost to the same state of morbid apathy as that in which they lived." He had no hobbies, no friends and died in isolation without any outpouring of grief for one who had served as leader for so long.[137]

It is important to distinguish features of character or temperament from those present in a psychiatric disorder. Certain personality features may increase the risk of developing such a disorder, or may even be an attenuated form of the disorder. One example of the latter is so-called avoidant personality disorder (APD), which represents a persistent form of severe shyness or social anxiety disorder (SAD) beginning in childhood and persisting into adulthood, thereby creating the impression of being a "personality" type — that's "who the person is." In reality, it is better thought of as SAD, which develops very early in life and pervades one's entire existence. The distinction is important from a therapeutic point of view in that APD responds to the treatments which help SAD. Similarly, the chronic worrier may have an attenuated (mild) generalized anxiety disorder and/or be at greater risk for the development of the full disorder later in life under conditions of stress. With Liverpool, there is reason to suspect that biographical portrayals suggest anxiety *disorders* rather than merely character traits, as in the following descriptions.

Liverpool is described as being "totally without social grace or ease of communication ... never really easy in oratory ... and, in debate as if he had been on the wrack three times and saw the wheel preparing for a fourth." For all this, he was considered to be a "brilliant debater,"[138] and there was discrepancy between actual performance and inner state, as is quite commonly seen with performance anxiety. His gaucherie "verged on the clownish ... above all he was nervous. He suffered from a terrible anxiety at the thought of offending others, and worried constantly simply at what the next day would bring, or at what others thought of him."[139] Such a description could suggest social anxiety, paradoxical as this may sound for one who lead his country for 15 years and made a career of speaking in Parliament. Lending further credence are the comments of a contemporary who referred to Liverpool's "grand fidgets," while the king found him to be conspicuously depressed, which affected his health and temper.[140] Alison believed that Liverpool's "greatest failure was a constitutional nervousness, which made him, as he himself said, never on one day during which he held office break the seals of a heap of letters without a feeling of apprehension."[141] Yet he was seemingly able to turn these peculiarities to good effect, for "his mind was stored with a vast variety of facts on every important question, which he brought out with equal judgment and skill in debate, and he left behind the reputation of being, if not the greatest, certainly the most prudent and fortunate minister that ever conducted the affairs of Great Britain." Attention to detail, conscientiousness, level-headedness, conciliatory skills and mediating abilities all offset his tendencies to anxiety and may have played a big part in explaining Liverpool's longevity as prime minister. These same qualities might explain how he was able to retain an exceptionally talented cabinet for so long: four of his colleagues were eventually destined to become prime minister.[142] Gash noted how, by 1812, time and experience had mellowed Liverpool such that "his nerve had hardened and his judgements ripened."[143]

Liverpool's irritability and depression at times threatened to undermine his health, and actually did so in 1824 when he had to conciliate over disputes in his cabinet.[144]

Gash noted the strain of office which produced in Liverpool periods of worry, fatigue and irritability. He cites an occasion when Robert Peel commented how well Liverpool looked, only for Liverpool to reply that no-one knew what it was like to have been prime minister for 15 years and "never in all that period to have opened his morning letters without a feeling of apprehension."[145] The true cost of anxiety is often underestimated.

In 1820, Liverpool was under considerable stress by King George IV's divorce crisis and the terminal illness of Liverpool's wife Louisa. For a time he thought seriously of resigning. Louisa's death in 1821 was followed by severe grief and some impairment and decline in health. Irritability and "gusts of passion" became evident after Louisa's death, along with episodes of fatigue. Canning commented that "Liverpool's agitation has, in some stages of this business, amounted almost to illness."[146] At times his explosive behavior would be out of all proportion to the inciting cause. There was also evidence of developing circulatory insufficiency in his legs, resulting in peripheral pain and, later, impaired eyesight (such that when reading he would miss a few words in each line). It is possible that Liverpool had suffered mini-strokes prior to the major stroke in 1827 which caused him to resign.

Summary

In sum, Liverpool experienced many symptoms compatible with generalized anxiety disorder throughout his life, often triggered by stress. For a period of time he kept these under check, or at least out of public view, but he nonetheless experienced them on a daily basis. With the death of Louisa and the onset of circulatory disease, his anxiety worsened. It is also possible that he became depressed. His somewhat solitary manner and excessive sensitivity to offending others raises the question of social anxiety, but the picture is too sketchy to arrive at a firm view. Liverpool's anxiety rarely got in the way of effective function until around 1820, when cerebrovascular disease began to complicate things. Although Louisa's death produced deep grief, Liverpool remarried quickly, and there is nothing to suggest the development of chronic, complicated grief, as occurred with some other prime ministers.

GEORGE CANNING (1770–1827) *(1827)*

George Canning's term as prime minister lasted for 118 days, coming to an unexpected close with his death in August of 1827. Unlike many of his predecessors, Canning blended together a mixture of quick temper, sarcasm, contempt, arrogance, fieriness, combativeness, pride and recklessness.[147] Famously, he was challenged to a duel by Lord Castlereagh and received a wound in the thigh from that encounter. While dueling was not unusual, in Canning's case it dealt a major setback to his political ambitions, delaying their fulfillment by many years.[148] Canning's self-confidence amounted to a belief in his infallibility, that he had "godlike powers," and that only he could handle foreign policy, obtain Catholic Emancipation and save his country, an attitude redolent of Pitt the Elder.[149] While this character profile suggests the possibility of bipolar disorder, no further support exists for such a diagnosis. There is no more than scant evidence for any kind of psychiatric disorder, being limited to the fact that he did undergo severe grief upon the death of his 19-year-old son, and for a time questioned the pursuit of politics as a career.

FREDERICK ROBINSON, VISCOUNT GODERICH, EARL OF RIPON (1782–1859) *(1827–1828)*

Frederick Robinson, First Viscount Goderich, was chosen by King George IV as an acquiescent compromise whom the king would be able to control, and in the belief that he was unlikely to take an independent line. Goderich is regarded as one of the least effective prime ministers, and he stayed in office for only 130 days. In his obituary, the *Times* asked, "Who was Lord Ripon? What did he do?" He has also been characterized as being among Britain's most obscure and inglorious prime ministers, one overwhelmed by the duties of office.[150] Goderich took the helm in the face of daunting challenges which would prove difficult for most, among which were the Corn Laws, Catholic emancipation and Parliamentary reform. Goderich was dealt a poor hand, lacked support and contended with a quarrelsome cabinet. Moreover, he lacked powers of leadership and persuasion, handicaps which perhaps proved fatal.

Goderich's Emotional Difficulties

Little has been written about Goderich, but from the standpoint of his mental health, there is good, if limited, evidence that emotional instability was a major reason he was relieved of his duties. The king quickly found that Goderich was unable to cope with the strain of office and accepted his resignation after only 4 months.

Signs of Goderich's emotional fragility include proneness to weeping in public. On one occasion in Parliament, when he rose to defend his actions in the face of a murder charge, he lost control of himself and became so embarrassed that he lived in constant fear of a repetition, and was "scarred for life" by the experience. From that time on "he wept without provocation," and his foes knew him as "the Blubberer." Even conceding that politicians sometimes break down in public, Goderich was worse than most.[151] His personal life was problematic too, as he was enmeshed in his wife's hypochondriacal anxiety, which sapped his confidence and at times interfered with his attention to the demands of politics. Iremonger describes Goderich as "appallingly thin-skinned," a trait which was to grow with the passage of time.

Bereavement left a deep impression on Goderich. As chancellor of the exchequer in Lord Liverpool's cabinet, he lost two children and suffered a major emotional breakdown after the death of his second child. Deep as his wife's grief was, she ended up having to placate her husband, whose recovery took longer than hers.[152] His grief was considered excessive by the standards of the time. At the time of his distress, coupled with the subsequent deterioration in his wife's mental health after the birth of a third child, Goderich pressed his resignation unsuccessfully on Lord Liverpool. After the death of Liverpool, and very shortly before he was to assume the mantle of prime minister, Goderich was in clear emotional distress and "almost driven out of his mind" by Lady Sarah's post-natal depression and hypochondriasis.[153]

When Goderich was appointed prime minister, the omens did not look good. King George essentially bullied him into acceptance so as to gain greater control of the cabinet. Goderich's first act was to postpone the assembly of Parliament, presumably as a means of avoiding the worst. In fact, he never met with Parliament,[154] and Jones has described Goderich as "the most timid and fearful individual to hold office on British affairs."[155] One contemporary observed that he "cut a pathetic figure" and presented a "most pitiful state," with his "spirits ... worn out" and "all power of decision gone" due to the worry over his wife.[156] It did not take Goderich long before he wrote to the king about his inadequacy to serve. He noted his and his wife's health to be poor, and that this kept alive "anxiety to a degree not easily compatible with the due discharge of duties which require the exertion of all the energies of the strongest mind."[157] Whether or not this letter was meant as a submission of resignation, the king took it as such and dissolved the government. It is reputed that the king lent Goderich a handkerchief as he (again) "blubbed" while handing over the seals of office.[158] What can we make of the unfortunate Goderich from a psychiatric perspective? A thin-skinned nature, weepiness, indecision and timidity all suggest an anxiety disorder or, at the very least, marked tendencies to be anxious — "neurotic" in lay language. In Goderich's case, this became quite severe and apparent to others, and interfered with his leadership. He could not cope. Complicated grief may have also supervened, although we have no clear time line as to its course and/or degree of resolution. It is of interest that in his retirement Goderich became happier and gained weight.[159]

ARTHUR WELLESLEY, 1ST DUKE OF WELLINGTON (1769–1852) *(1828–1830; 1834)*

Arthur Wellesley (né Wesley), First Duke of Wellington, is one of Britain's greatest heroes on account of his military triumphs against Napoleon. He was upheld in Victorian times as embodying all the best qualities of his country: loyalty, courage, hard work, simplicity, and sense of duty.[160] He was also unique in that for much of his life he pursued a dual career of political service and active military duty, being remembered primarily for his achievements as a soldier. Given his iconic status, it is perhaps surprising that Wellington may have suffered throughout his life from a variant of autism — Asperger's disorder — categorized in the DSM-IV as a developmental disorder of social and communication skills.[161] In old age it is also possible that he suffered from other psychiatric ailments.

Background and Early Years

Arthur Wellesley was the sixth child of Garrett Wesley, Earl of Mornington, and his wife Anne. At the time of his birth in Dublin, the family name was Wesley, which was later changed somewhat pretentiously by his oldest brother to the more socially impressive name Wellesley, this change being adopted later by Arthur in 1798 when he was aged 28.

Arthur's father was a professor of music at Trinity College in Dublin.[162] Garrett Wesley died when Arthur was 12, leaving him in the care of his mother and oldest brother, Richard, a brilliant person with strong political ambitions of his own. Arthur was held in low regard by his mother, who viewed him as clumsy and stupid, and later expressed the opinion that her "ugly son" was "fit food for powder," sending him off to a military academy in France. Regardless of his mother's motivations, this decision helped turn the tables of history, given the outstanding successes which awaited him on the battlefield. About the only activity at which the boy showed any accomplishment was playing the violin, a talent which he subsequently disowned by burning his instrument amidst the turmoil of an unsuccessful courtship of Kitty Pakenham.

Arthur was a poor student and a socially isolated child. He was sent to Eton College, where he fared poorly and was removed after three years by his mother and oldest brother, who needed the money which was being spent on Arthur's schooling. At Eton, and later at the military academy, Arthur was unsociable, combative, and a poor scholar, but he "had the power of rapid and correct calculation." He was more interested in his pet terrier, Vic.[163] As a teenager, Arthur abhorred organized games, preferring to look on, shy and friendless.[164]

Adulthood and Career

At 18, Wellesley joined the army as an ensign in the 73rd Highland regiment. Nine months later he was made a lieutenant in the 76th, and then received four further commissions over the next 5 years, eventually leading a company in the 18th Light Dragoons. During these early years he served as an aide-de-camp to the lord lieutenant of Ireland, as well as member of the Irish Parliament for the constituency of Trim from 1790 to 1795, drawing accolades for his performance.

Wellington's first active engagement took place in Belgium during 1794. Between 1796 and 1805, Wellington was assigned to military duties in India, where he distinguished himself and earned a knighthood. The presence of his brother Richard as governor-general in India may have helped in the progress of Arthur's career. Besides having command of 50,000 soldiers, his duties extended to civil administration and diplomacy. Upon returning home, Wellesley was elected to Parliament as the member representing Rye. He continued with his dual career and fought successful campaigns in Portugal and

France, culminating in his most celebrated victory over Napoleon at Waterloo in 1815, one year after Wellesley had been given the title of Duke of Wellington. He was thereafter appointed commander-in-chief of the army in occupied France between 1815 and 1818.

On the political front, Wellington had served in the Duke of Portland's cabinet from 1807 to 1809 as chief secretary for Ireland, then again under Lord Liverpool from 1819 to 1827 as master-general of the ordnance. In 1828, Wellington was called to lead the government upon Goderich's resignation. His administration continued until 1830 but was marred by internal dissension, partly due to Wellington's authoritarian style, which, while appropriate in the army, was not welcomed in the world of Parliamentary politics. He was unused to being contradicted, took criticism poorly and expected obedience from his underlings. English notes Wellington's lack of tact, egotistical manner, poor public speaking skills, inability to manage people well [in the world of politics] and indifference to public opinion.[165] One notable event which occurred during Wellington's premiership was the duel between Wellington and Lord Winchilsea in March 1829 for defamatory words which the latter had spoken against the prime minister over the Catholic question. Winchilsea claimed that Wellington had "treacherously plotted the destruction of the Protestant constitution."[166] The duel was intended to be more of a formality, as both parties shot far wide of their targets and no harm was done, but Wellington's breach of the law upset many of his colleagues.

Despite Wellington's conservatism, one remarkable achievement of his first administration was the passage of the Catholic Relief Act, which permitted Catholics to sit in the London Parliament, as well as making it possible for middle-class Catholics to obtain civil service posts. Wellington again served as caretaker prime minister in 1834 for a number of months, then as foreign secretary between 1834 and 1835, and as leader of the opposition in the House of Lords from 1835 to 1841. He remained active in party politics until the resignation of Peel in 1846, although from 1837 he became progressively less involved, perhaps related to numerous epileptic fits which occurred over the next several years, along with other physical and psychological problems (to be described).

Wellington's Marriage and Relationships with Women

Prior to being sent overseas, Wellington had pursued Kitty Pakenham in marriage. Kitty's family was resistant because of Wellington's poor financial prospects, and largely due to opposition from Kitty's brother, no engagement took place. The matter did not die, however, and while he was in India some correspondence took place between Wellington and an intermediary,

Colonel William Beresford. It was enough to keep the flames alive, and when Wellington returned from India he proposed marriage to Kitty. Not having seen Arthur for 11 years, and after another failed romantic relationship, Kitty asked if the two should not at least meet one another. Wellington did not think it necessary and somewhat bizarrely said that he would go through with the marriage anyway because "they asked me to do it and I did not know myself."[167] As Holmes points out, Wellington was 37 years old and would be expected to have taken a more carefully considered approach to such an important question. He thinks it may have been more a matter of pride, in that Wellington was "righting a wrong" — in his mind at least — due to the initial rebuff he had received from Kitty's family over his courtship. Somewhat incredibly, immediately after the wedding, Wellington turned to the minister (his brother) and exclaimed, "She has grown ugly by Jove!"[168] Not surprisingly, the marriage proved to be a disaster.

Wellington had relationships with many other women, some of which were almost certainly sexual, others perhaps more platonic. These were the result of just plain infatuation or pathetic efforts to overcome the loneliness of bereavement in old age, as with the rather strange correspondence of over 390 letters that he wrote to Anna Maria Jenkins during the final 18 years of his life. Anna Maria was a 21-year-old orphan who took a liking to Wellington and initiated a correspondence with him, which he did much to encourage, although they met rarely. At one point Wellington did broach the question of marriage to Anna Maria. The content of his letters has been described as "abject twaddle,"[169] yet there was a bullying tone to Ms. Jenkins' letters, which the Duke thoroughly enjoyed. Many of his relationships with women were characterized by domination. Mrs. Harriet Arbuthnot, to whom Wellington was deeply attached, was referred to as La Tyranna, and Wellington took great pleasure from being bossed by her. Iremonger believes that Wellington's indulgence in bondage and sadomasochism came close to being pathological.[170]

Between 1831 and 1839, Wellington suffered the loss of three women. Kitty died in 1831, and in response to reports that he might marry again, Wellington reportedly said, "No woman ever loved me, never in my whole life."[171] Such was his repudiation of Kitty, who, for all her faults, had been devoted to her husband.

In 1834 his close friend and confidante, Harriet Arbuthnot, died. When Wellington received the letter bearing this news, he dropped it in a "paroxysm of grief" and flung himself on the sofa, but recovered sufficiently well to deal with matters which needed addressing.[172] In bereavement after Harriet Arbuthnot's death, Wellington was described in the following way by Charles Greville, the son of Wellington's lover, Lady Charlotte Greville: "The Duke has no tenderness in his disposition.... His nature is hard, and [he] does not appear to have had any real affection for anybody, man or woman, during the latter years of his life, since the death of Mrs. Arbuthnot, to whom he probably was attached."[173]

Yet another close friend, Lady Salisbury, died in 1839, leaving Wellington devastated by the shock. He experienced a stroke not long afterwards, with temporary loss of speech and vision. Although Iremonger believes it to have been precipitated by the shock of bereavement, we have no way of knowing if this was the case. However, we do know from Lord Rosebery that two years later Wellington lived through a period of "extreme depression," and that he "fell into morbid ways ... retired for a time into a gloomy and silent solitude, denying access to everyone with passionate and almost brutal vehemence."[174]

Wellington and Asperger's Disorder

McElearney and Fitzgerald, both of whom are psychiatrists with expertise in autistic disorders,[175] have argued that the Duke of Wellington met the diagnostic criteria for Asperger's disorder. On a 24-point scale, they assign a score of 18, basing their case on the following findings.

Wellington showed abnormal social interactions in his personal and professional life. The peculiar nature of his marriage is a good example of this. Coldness, neglect, and failure to relate in marriage, to empathize and to share intimacy, are viewed by McElearney and Fitzgerald as features compatible with high-grade autism. On the professional front, while Wellington often showed distress at the carnage from battle and concern for the welfare of surviving family members of the slain, it is also said that he "deliberately alienated any affectionate feeling of all ranks from him, and when the war was over he parted from his soldiers without regret and never troubled himself again about them. He was in fact glad to be quit of them, and made no pretence to the contrary."[176] As a child and teenager he was socially maladroit and isolated. Preference for gadgetry or animals has been noted, and he experienced difficulty integrating with his peers. Indeed, Wellington appeared to lack much need for any emotional connection with others, as observed again towards the end of his life by Lord Rosebery. Wellington's son, Douro, said that his father had never shown him kindness nor ever patted him on the shoulder when he was a boy.

Marked impairment in the use of non-verbal communication is one hallmark of Asperger's disorder. This covers such behaviors as gaze, eye-contact, facial expression and body posture. Wellington's stiff gaze is illustrated by Stanhope in his report of a dinner conversation with the Duke in 1827.[177] On the subject of how to deal with "madmen"— those with psychotic depression, like

Lord Castlereagh, who committed suicide — Wellington said, "The effect of the eye upon insane persons is very singular and very certain. I have tried it many times. I always look them full in the eye, and they cannot stand it." Comment has been made on Wellington's intense, piercing, strange and penetrating stare.[178] What we cannot be clear about, though, is the degree to which Wellington's peculiar gaze resembled the gaze of high-functioning autism, which is typically a gaze *away* from the eyes (e.g., at the mouth, body or other objects).[179]

Speech and language problems were noted by Wellington's mother, who was aware of his slowness of speech and dullness of manner. Direct brevity characterized his written communications. Longford referred to a "flick of his logic" which made Wellington sound harsh while being kind. Acerbic words gave offense when none was meant. Once when a recipient of a letter complained to the Duke about his caustic language, he replied to the complainant by asking that he return the letter with the offending words highlighted. Such a concrete and literal manner of communicating is compatible with Asperger's disorder.

Other features included being bound by rules and routines, which Wellington imposed on others, his indifference to public perception and, early in life, motor clumsiness.

The features of Asperger's disorder which impaired the Duke in his personal life, and to some extent in his political life, may have served him well in the military. For example, his expectation that others should submit to his will and abide by (his) rules, matched with his coolness in the thick of battle, tactical dexterity and strong self-belief, would serve him and his army well. On the other hand, qualities of empathy and flexibility in negotiation would not be so useful. McElearney and Fitzgerald comment that the qualities found in those with Asperger's disorder can be adaptive for military leaders, as they facilitate absolute focus on the battle plan and an ability to cut through the fog of war and identify what could be ignored or postponed. These same qualities would be of less value in peace-time politics and may partly explain why Wellington was more successful as military strategist than prime minister.

McElearney and Fitzgerald's argument deserves serious consideration. However, some caution is in order, since Asperger's disorder itself is not firmly established as differing from other forms of autism, and in the next edition of the DSM (DSM-V) it is expected to be subsumed under a broader diagnosis of autistic spectrum disorder. Moreover, much important diagnostic information on autism comes from direct observation or conversational cues.

Wellington and Depression: Considerations

In the final years of his life Wellington showed changes which suggest possible depression, although assessing the exact nature of these symptoms is not easy, since they occurred in the context of stroke, seizures and progressive deafness. Chronology of these symptoms is such that he experienced acute severe grief in 1834 after the death of Harriet Arbuthnot, and the degree to which he recovered is not clear. It is not without significance that 1834 was the year when Wellington struck up his relationship with the much younger Anna Maria Jenkins, who perhaps helped the Duke cope with his loss. In 1837 he suffered the first of several epileptic seizures. In 1839, Lady Salisbury died. Shortly afterwards he experienced a stroke, from which he recovered. Rosebery noted in 1841 "morbid" changes in his demeanor which are compatible with depression, and which in due course passed. Charles Greville's remarks, however, seem to indicate that Wellington did not fully recover from the loss of Mrs. Arbuthnot, and that he underwent further hardening and coldness towards people for the rest of his life. What makes it doubtful that he sustained a full melancholic depression are the comments of Stanhope in 1840 that, at the age of 71, the Duke had grown old, careworn and pale, had developed a stoop and a tendency to fall asleep even in the morning, and that "the fire of his eagle eye was quenched."[180] Yet, "he walks firmly and well, often 4–5 miles a day at once. He was, in general, gay and in good spirits.... His great mind is certainly as great as ever ... but it is grown somewhat slower, both in the conception and expression of ideas. He seizes upon facts less rapidly, and conveys his thoughts with longer pauses."

A number of possibilities arise. One is that Wellington was indeed depressed but that contemporary accounts fail to give the full picture. Second, he might have simply shown an intensification of Asperger's disorder, such as the emotional hardening and isolation, brought on by cumulative grief and loneliness in old age. Third, he could have experienced depressive-like changes from stroke or epileptic seizures, in which case the Duke would have met conditions for the diagnosis of mood disorder due to CNS disease, either stroke, seizures or cerebrovascular disorder. The origin of his seizures invites speculation, with stroke, autistic disorder or post-battle trauma all being possible candidates. The progression of increasing deafness may have contributed to his isolation and emotional hardening. Based on eyewitness accounts, his mental state fluctuated in that sometimes he was in good spirits and physically active, and at other times less so. An undertow of emotional detachment seemed to remain, however.

CHARLES GREY, 2ND EARL GREY (1764–1825) *(1830–1834)*

Charles Grey is best known for two very different things. Politically, his greatest and most enduring triumph was the passage of the Reform Bill, which established that seats in the House of Commons could no longer be bought or inherited but must represent the people.[181] Passage of this bill ultimately lead to universal suffrage and secret balloting. Grey's other principal legacy, outside of politics, was to popularize a blend of tea flavored with bergamot, known ever after as Earl Grey Tea.

Grey was born in 1764, the second son of General Sir Charles Grey and his wife Elizabeth. Grey's father was one of only a few British military heroes from the American War of Independence, having served with distinction at Valley Forge. He had previously given honorable service at the Battle of Minden. While in America, Grey's aide-de-camp was Major André, best known for his treacherous collusion with Benedict Arnold. For his military service, Sir Charles Grey was rewarded with an Earldom.

Grey himself entered Parliament in 1786 at the age of 22 and soon became one of the Whig party leaders. His talent for public speaking made him an expert debater, and for many years he was diligent in attending Parliament. Throughout his long years of opposition he was committed to Parliamentary reform and other liberal causes. He eventually became prime minister in 1830, at age 66, and two years into his administration succeeded in passing the Reform Act of 1832, a major accomplishment for which he is rightly remembered. Other achievements in his three-and-a-half years of office include the Abolition of Slavery Act, the Factory Act, and the setting up of Parliamentary select committees to prepare framing of legislation. His influence was strongly felt in foreign policy, with his foreign secretary, Lord Palmerston, warding off a number of dangerous crises and creating 80 years of stability with regard to the Belgian problem.[182]

Grey and the Possibility of Mental Illness: Temperament

Grey's personality and temperament are well described by Smith, who painted a picture of Grey as a proud, vain and ambitious young man who saw himself as eventually becoming chancellor of the exchequer.[183] He had a violent temper, indulged excessively in alcohol and had affairs with numerous women (both before and during his marriage). One affair with Georgiana, Duchess of Devonshire, produced an illegitimate child and lead to a potentially difficult situation in regard to the Duchess' marriage. Grey was "hasty and impulsive in action, impatient of contradiction, quarrelsome in face of opposition and too overtly ambitious, he was inclined to alternating extremes of enthusiasm and despondency." His personality was "volatile," and he was prone to moods of self-doubt,[184] "a strange blend of headstrong ambition and of moody despondency."[185] By temperament he was "either in the skies or in the depths," and efforts to rouse enthusiasm or inspire others usually faded as his pessimistic moods inevitably came to the fore, a problem which is believed to have affected his ability to lead the opposition.[186] Contemporaries saw the young Grey as being of "imprudent warmth and eagerness," which gave rise to his being misunderstood and misrepresented by others, and of having "dangers in his character."[187]

These descriptions lead to the reasonable conclusion that Grey showed temperamental features of bipolarity, with volatile swings of mood and perhaps intermittent hypomanic episodes. Is it possible that clinically significant depression was superimposed on this temperament? The evidence will be examined.

Depression

Grey was prone to "recurrent fits of depression."[188] Derry wrote that "the winter of 1802–03 saw Grey more depressed than ever,"[189] as he stayed away from London, using his wife's pregnancy as excuse. He was lethargic and under-sold himself in opposition during the 1820s when his health was poor, apparently in part due to depression. In 1808 he wrote to his wife that in the House of Lords, where he had been lately elevated after his father's death, "it is impossible I should ever do anything there worth thinking of."[190] For many years, this "sensitive and easily depressed man ... easily yielded to the promptings of his natural indolence and to the call of his domestic affections." And so it remained: "In the chill and silence of the hostile House of Lords he heard and felt little of the stir of new forces, until his youth returned to him in the miraculous year of the French barricades."[191]

Smith sees Grey as perhaps experiencing chronic, low-level depression. For example, "The decade after 1792 marked a low point in Grey's career, and his mood was restless and irritable as a result." We are treated to the picture of a grouchy and splenic individual who, when entering his club, would cause conversation to dry up, and "was peevish and wayward ... always desponding, always out of spirits unless he thinks he is riding the winning horse ... and always thinking of himself and his failures in life."[192] It was during this decade of personal misery that he ran into trouble over his affair with the Duchess of Devonshire. Additionally, Grey threw in his lot with an organization called "Friends of the People," which lead to deep division within his party. With this background, we might understand how he could have developed his despondency.

In 1801 yet another event took place which caused great disquiet for Grey. His father successfully lobbied the prime minister for a peerage and duly took his place in the House of Lords. Because peerages were hereditary, it meant that Charles Grey Jr. would, of necessity, be required to move to the Lords upon the death of his father, which, given his age, was expected to occur shortly. The younger Grey had seen the Commons as the place to fulfill his ambition; thus he became resentful and angry towards his father, even complaining that his father had not consulted with him over taking a peerage! Henceforth, Grey withdrew to his country home at Howick, four days' journey from London. His friends were frequently exasperated at his prolonged absences, which Grey explained away unconvincingly as due to his wife's many pregnancies. When he did attend Parliament, it was grudgingly, and his colleagues were irritated by his manner, which "cast gloom over the deliberations." His normal self-assurance was replaced by incapacitating nervous tension and insomnia. It is of interest that this renowned debater was overtaken by such anticipatory anxiety before his speeches that he stayed up at night and, in May 1803, cursed his constant "debating nervousness" in the House of Commons, which he now called "this odious place."[193]

When prime minister, Grey, during a storm of controversy about the Reform Bill, was no longer the "peevish and wayward invalid," and his "low spirits" had faded. He became "serene," and his contemporaries remarked on his cheerful enjoyment of life. "From pessimist he had turned optimist."[194] As his term progressed, and once the Reform Bill had passed, disagreement built up within his administration over appropriations to the Irish church and lead to several resignations, all of which Grey was too tired to deal with. "He was at the end of his tether ... and when it [the Reform Bill] was over the effort had left him an old man with broken health."[195] His correspondence revealed exhaustion, lack of zest and a desire to escape from the burden of office.

Other clues suggest that Grey may have experienced some anxiety. As a child, he was "nervous" and from the age of 6 had a series of illnesses at school which are believed to have been psychological in origin.[196] Iremonger relates a curious incident in Grey's childhood which stayed with him into old age. At age 6 he was taken to witness the hanging of six men found guilty of forgery. The experience of seeing their dying contortions close-up left a lasting impression so that 65 years later, "The statesman who had passed the Reform Bill would wake up sweating from a nightmare vision of this old horror of Hogarth's London."[197]

Summary

Grey was a nervous child who had intermittent breakthroughs of anxiety throughout his life, whether performance anxiety or nightmares of a childhood experience. However, while biographical sources fail to support a clear case for any chronic anxiety disorder, the fact that he would stay up at night due to insomnia prior to giving a speech is good evidence of abnormal social fear. Biographers emphasize to a much greater extent Grey's mercurial, volatile mood swings, impetuousness, and periods of sullen irritable despondency, all of which are compatible with a bipolar spectrum disorder. At these times his friends and colleagues wished to keep their distance from him. In his better moments, others found him attractive, but as he grew older the depressions and withdrawal came to predominate and, at times, may have been disabling. However, during his mid–60s, when he was prime minister, the more optimistic, ambitious and engaged Grey returned to life, at least until passage of the Reform Bill. Thereafter, he once again slid back into lethargy and a lack of zest for the rigors of politics. In retirement he may have become again a somewhat happier person, content in his country estate at Howick, no doubt enjoying the Earl Grey tea for which he is best remembered.

WILLIAM LAMB, 2ND VISCOUNT MELBOURNE (1779–1848) *(1834; 1835–1841)*

William Lamb was born on March 15, 1779, and died November 24, 1848. Upon his older brother's death in 1805, Lamb succeeded to the title of Viscount Melbourne, and after his father died in 1828 he became Lord Melbourne, taking his seat in the House of Lords. Melbourne's family was well established in the Whig aristocracy. Melbourne served briefly as prime minister in 1834 and again between 1835 and 1841. His life was remarkable for a variety of reasons.

Melbourne was the last prime minister to be dismissed by personal decision of the king rather than by loss of Parliamentary majority or at an election. However, with the next monarch, in Melbourne's second term as premier, things got off to a flying start. Melbourne ingratiated himself with the inexperienced teenage Queen Victoria when she ascended the throne. Besides being her prime minister, he set himself up as the queen's private secretary and confidante. Such was their dependency on one another that the relationship went far beyond the call of official duties, and for a time the queen was known colloquially as Mrs. Melbourne.[198] When Victoria became engaged to Prince Albert, and Melbourne found himself marginalized, he developed a depressive reaction.

Lord Melbourne is also remembered for his wife Caroline, whose erratic and bizarre behavior, including a very public affair with Lord Byron, exposed her husband to much humiliation. Indeed, the Melbournes' marriage was miserable, and they eventually separated, yet even after Caroline's death in

1828, Melbourne continued to express sadness over the loss. The couple had one mentally retarded son, Augustus, who died as a young man in 1836. Later, Melbourne was the subject of scandal concerning a reputed affair with Caroline Norton. Caroline's husband George attempted to blackmail Melbourne, and demanded a payment of £1400, but this attempt came to nothing when Mr. Norton was unable to furnish evidence of an affair.

Melbourne left two other legacies. At a time when a growing settlement in the Australian state of Victoria was only a series of huts in 1837, Lord Melbourne gave his own name to the community, which as the city of Melbourne has become one of the world's major enclaves. He is also responsible for the "weekend." During the first part of the nineteenth century, the English work week was typically 6 days. Melbourne and his friends, however, would break from work early on Friday and hold lavish house parties at his home in the country. To ensure sufficient time for these sybaritic affairs, it was agreed that no business would be conducted on Saturdays and Sundays: thus the apparent origin of the "weekend."[199]

Stage Fright

While an undergraduate at Cambridge University, Melbourne was haunted by the thought of making a fool of himself,[200] and performance anxiety was quite a serious problem at the beginning of Melbourne's political career. In this regard, Lord Melbourne can be joined to the ranks of several other prime ministers. One factor to take into consideration in the seventeenth and early eighteenth centuries was the young age at which men would enter politics. It was not uncommon to be elected to Parliament in one's early twenties, an age at which social skills, social polish and self-confidence are still being developed. In Melbourne's case, we know that he had been a member of Parliament for a full year before making his maiden speech. His brother Frederick said, "I think he has lately fallen into a want of confidence in himself,"[201] and he was right, for Melbourne affirmed this himself by admitting that he was in "terror at the prospect."[202] He went on to write, "I was always very nervous, I was too vain to expose myself to what I considered the disgrace of speaking in a hesitating manner, and I had not taken the measures necessary for a more fluent and striking performance." Ziegler notes how Melbourne would repeatedly brace himself to speak, only to be left mute, humiliated and unable to even catch the Speaker's eye.[203] It took seven years for Melbourne to overcome his nervousness about speaking, and even then, for another several years, he had some difficulty in speaking with proficiency: any distraction or interruption would easily derail his train of thought.

It appears the social anxiety ceased to be a significant issue, or if it continued, little is heard about it. More serious, however, was Melbourne's proclivity to depression and other mental illnesses. He has been described as experiencing serial depression, Tourette's disorder and narcolepsy.[204] Close examination of the available material suggests that he did, indeed, experience problems of depression and sleep, as well as showing odd mannerisms.

Evidence for Depression

Ziegler refers to Winthrop Praed's description of Melbourne as "mournful in his heart of hearts" and of Lord Grey's observation how, at dinner, Melbourne would "fall into such a state of thought and abstraction that it was quite painful to witness."[205] Another contemporary, Benjamin Haydon, noted, "There is a bitterness in Lord Melbourne's humour that betrays something melancholy." Ziegler rightly points out that occasional moments of gloom should not be confused with morbid sadness, but he goes on to say that in Melbourne's case these observations should not be dismissed as romantic fantasy. Cecil paints a similar picture of a man overtaken by "fits of depression" who would sit in remote silence, and whose good moods were even penetrated by "streaks of disillusionment."[206] A depressive episode occurred in 1816 from which he recovered.[207] In 1835, Melbourne's health deteriorated as a result of gout in the knee, which rendered him immobile for as much as a week at a time, thereby contributing to his lethargy, insomnia, languor and despondency. When Melbourne complained of his mental distress to Lord Russell, the rather blunt rejoinder came back that it was the price of eating and drinking too much and not enough exercise.[208] Since Melbourne was known to eat and drink to excess, there was probably some truth to this. By 1836 he was starting to feel the strain of office, which, along with irregular work hours, helped transform him into a "fretful invalid."[209]

Any understanding of Melbourne's depression would be incomplete without some knowledge of his relationship to Queen Victoria. At the time of her accession to the throne, Victoria was eighteen and Melbourne fifty-eight. The prime minister quickly took a liking to the young, inexperienced queen, whose own father had died when she was 8 months old, and who had received a very sheltered upbringing. The desolate and childless Melbourne formed a deep affection for the queen, which was returned for a while with equal intensity. Melbourne would either be in the queen's presence or writing to her as much as six hours each day during the first five years of her reign: he found in her the chief satisfaction of his life.[210] In 1839 the queen accepted Prince Albert's marriage proposal, despite Melbourne's efforts to dissuade her. While Melbourne did the best he could in terms of advising them both about the responsibilities of monarchy, he could not escape another depression, being afflicted by early waking, "a sure sign of anxiety of mind"[211] and a classical symptom of depressive illness. Leavesley wrote that when Victoria fell in love with Albert, "the discarded Melbourne became acutely depressed."[212] Her attraction to Albert was a contributory factor, but other pressures bore on Melbourne in 1839, including gout, difficulties over constitutional reform, which saw his majority shrink to five, and his mismanagement of an incident which involved Lady Flora Hastings, a maid of honor in the royal household. Since 1835, Melbourne had experienced financial problems, partly due to his neglect, and which were to preoccupy him for many years.[213] Lord Melbourne again developed insomnia, gastrointestinal symptoms and low spirits, to the point where "Melbourne, who for so long had been the most cheerful member of the Government, was now noticeably the most depressed.... 'I do not know what the deuce is the matter with me!' he sighed to the queen."[214]

The final six years of his life saw periods of marked depression. Cecil wrote that one year after resigning, Melbourne missed Victoria more and more as though he was in grief: "[He] bore within his breast a starved and aching heart."[215] In Cecil's opinion, the withdrawal of Victoria from Melbourne's life was "the most powerful cause of his low spirits"; with the "irradiated ... light of the Queen's presence," it was felt likely that Melbourne could have borne the vicissitudes of old age, tiredness and loss of friends and power, but without it his life was empty. Things were brought to a head when Melbourne was asked by Baron Stockmar, an adviser to Prince Albert, to cease the correspondence which had continued after Melbourne left office, and to desist from offering advice to the queen. In fact, it took several more months and further admonishment from Stockmar before Melbourne finally complied. The rest of 1842 went badly for Melbourne's health. His disturbed mental state "began to make its impression on his enfeebled body. His infirmities rapidly grew worse throughout the year. In November he had a stroke. For a day or two people wondered if he was going to die."[216]

In later years, acquaintances who had known Melbourne were shocked at the way he had changed: stiffness of gait and a dragging leg from his stroke; a grave, stern and silent demeanor; absence of the social vitality that had been his trademark; and an inability to summon the energy to hold conversation. By 1844 he withdrew from the London scene and began to spend more time at his country retreat in Brocket, where he would pass long periods sitting with an unopened book on his knees, gazing at the fire, "sunk in apathetic melancholy."[217] He would be heard mournfully reciting lines from Samson Agonistes:

> So much I feel my genial spirits droop,
> My hopes all flat: Nature within me seems

> In all her functions weary of herself
> My race of glory run, and race of shame.
> And I shall shortly be with them that rest.

While friends would visit and attempt to cheer him up, with some level of success, his mood invariably returned to gloom after their departure. He remained preoccupied with Victoria, and his eyes filled with tears whenever her name was mentioned, even to the extent of provoking "hysterical" outbursts.[218] He would still write letters to her, but mostly on trivia rather than affairs of state, and he rarely received a reply. Their few meetings would be stiff, brief and in the company of others — doubtless not the way Melbourne wanted it.

As his life drew to a close, Melbourne found himself well liked by many but needed by none.[219] His sanguine temperament had been defeated by his questioning, destructive intellect: "At last he was forced to feel, as well as think, that life was a vain and empty dream.... 'The fire is out,' he would mutter to himself gazing into the distance."[220]

Melbourne roused himself from the gloom in 1846 when Peel split his party by opposing the Corn Laws, and there was some possibility that the Whigs could return to power. Melbourne journeyed to London and spoke in Parliament. Peel's government fell, and Melbourne cherished the hope of being given office in the new government. This was not to be, the queen writing to explain that his frail health had much to do with it. His disappointment was great, and friends noticed that he had episodes of nervous agitation. Later in the year, while attending a dinner at Windsor, Melbourne exploded in the queen's presence about Peel's behavior. His loss of control embarrassed the gathering, who sat awkwardly and in silence as the tirade continued.[221]

Further changes in mental state took place. Worried preoccupations about trivial or even imaginary concerns overtook him. He believed his friends had turned against him, and he worried (unwarrantedly) about his reputation. He would ruminate about long-past events and the unrealistic possibility of his being held responsible for them. In the final years, although it seems that by then his life was one of unmitigated misery, Cecil noted flashes of geniality with his friends and that Melbourne was still capable of "racy, whimsical" conversation.[222]

Tourette's Disorder?

Melbourne was a person of unconventional habits.[223] He was full of strange idiosyncrasies: gleeful rubbing together of his hands as though he was amused, odd ejaculations ("eh, eh") before he made a remark, and a curious gesture of passing a finger to the back of his head while he was talking. Queen

Victoria observed his odd, comical grimaces and how he would talk to himself in an unintelligible murmur, which would cause her to look his way, thinking he was talking to her.[224] His habit of talking to himself in company was perplexing. Oftentimes the first impression he made was one of eccentricity, with his tendencies to swear or laugh whenever he pleased, and his habit of "jerking out anything that came into his head," not to mention the explosive "ha-ha's" that emanated from his mouth.[225] These descriptions convey the impression of motor and vocal tics (i.e., sudden rapid non-rhythmic movement or vocalization). It is possible, as Leavesley says, that Melbourne suffered from Tourette's disorder, but some key information is lacking. It is not known, for example, if this problem developed before the age of 18, as would be required for the diagnosis. The extent of the problem is also unknown, how often it occurred and how long it persisted. The tics of Tourette's disorder occur many times a day, in bursts, for periods of at least one year with no more than three months of freedom from symptoms. Tics of lesser frequency or briefer duration would be classified as Transient Tic Disorder (DSM-IV code 307.21).[226] If they did not appear until after age 18, the more appropriate diagnosis would be Tic Disorder Not Otherwise Specified (coded as 307.20 in DSM-IV). Regardless of the exact type, the bottom line appears to be that Melbourne was affected by some form of tic disorder.

Sleep Apnea or Narcolepsy?

Melbourne's gluttony and high consumption of alcohol did not escape comment. In her diary, Queen Victoria wrote, "He has eaten three chops and a grouse for breakfast," and she rebuked him for his preoccupation with eating and drinking.[227] Gluttony was one of Melbourne's best known vices,[228] and he was "large of frame."[229] In 1835, Lady Lyttleton expressed flippantly but perhaps accurately her opinion that nothing could remove him from office "unless he contrives to displace himself by dint of consommés, truffles, pears, ices and anchovies, which he does his best to revolutionize his stomach with every day."[230] His excessive eating suggests that he would have become overweight, but it is not explicitly stated in the main sources. However, a September 1841 *Punch* cartoon shows Melbourne as being corpulent.[231]

Among other distinctive features, Melbourne was prone to daytime naps and snoring at socially inappropriate times — "suddenly going off to sleep in company," as the queen noted.[232]

One authority has proposed that Melbourne's abnormal sleep patterns were due to narcolepsy.[233] For this diagnosis, cataplexy and hallucinations would both be required. Cataplexy refers to brief sudden attacks of muscle paralysis, often in the context of emotional arousal. We have no evidence for this, and if it occurred, it would have not escaped notice. The hallucinations of narcolepsy are associated with either falling asleep or waking, and there is some evidence that this might have occurred. One illustrative account described Melbourne as being in a "trance" and laughing to himself as though he was having an amusing thought.[234] Suddenly he woke and rounded on the observer, Lady Clarendon, asking if she loved her neighbor as herself. Could this have been a hypnopompic (i.e., waking from sleep) hallucination? Against the diagnosis of narcolepsy is the fact that the condition usually starts in adolescence and almost always before age 40; on this matter we have no information here. However, there are exceptions, and, just as cataplexy and hallucinations have been traditionally required for the diagnosis, sleep experts today now recognize subtypes of narcolepsy without cataplexy.[235]

Breathing-related sleep disorder (or sleep apnea) is the other main explanation of Melbourne's abnormal sleep habits. To support this diagnosis, nocturnal attacks of apnea (i.e., suspension of breathing) broken by loud snoring, excessive daytime sleepiness or marked nighttime insomnia are required. There were daytime naps and snoring, but good accounts of his nighttime sleep are lacking. Obesity is a risk factor for sleep apnea, and Melbourne's voracious eating appeared to have caused such a state. Obesity is also linked to narcolepsy.[236] It is possible that Melbourne suffered from a primary sleep disturbance pre-dating his stroke, and that this disturbance could have been narcolepsy, sleep apnea or both. The disorder could have aggravated a pre-existing tendency for depression and is likely to have contributed to his altered mental health. It may, too, have rendered him somewhat less effective in his work.

Stroke

Melbourne's health deteriorated in his final years. The stroke which affected him in 1842 could have triggered another depressive episode, as well as emotional volatility of the type he displayed at a royal dinner in 1846. Depression both contributes to the risk of stroke and is a complication thereof. (We now know that it responds well to treatment with current antidepressants.)[237] For Melbourne, worse was yet to come: In April 1848 he experienced another stroke, and from that point deteriorated mentally and physically, with the development of jaundice and seizures at the end of the year. Death occurred on November 24, 1848.

Summary

Melbourne was in many ways a sad figure. He came from a family known for its flamboyant lifestyle and instability, made a poor choice in marriage and was unable to establish any satisfying family life of his own. Melbourne's marriage was disastrous, and the behavior of his wife exposed him to public humiliation. His only child, Augustus, suffered from probable mental retardation, and for several years after Caroline Lamb's death, Melbourne had sole responsibility for raising Augustus until the boy died at a young age. Although seen as cautious, unable to commit and an aristocratic anachronism left over from the previous century, some commentators now regard him as an underestimated prime minister and note that he was held in high esteem by Gladstone and Disraeli.[238] Another view holds that Melbourne's inertia debilitated his party and let the country "drift rudderless towards disaster."[239]

At the start of his Parliamentary career, Melbourne was handicapped with severe public speaking fear which he slowly overcame, at least to the extent that he no longer avoided speaking in Parliament, although debating never came easily to him. Melbourne later suffered from gloomy moods of a type which his contemporaries considered abnormal, and which gave rise to more severe episodes of clinical depression. The degree to which this caused his "rudderless" leadership is a matter for conjecture, but it can scarcely be maintained that chronic low-grade depression, excessive daytime sleepiness, gluttony and high alcohol intake would produce optimal function. In the final years of his life there is no doubt that Melbourne's mental state seriously interfered with his political abilities, and Queen Victoria explained that it was not possible to offer a cabinet position to him because of his frail health. On the other hand, Melbourne has the reputation of being a cautious, non-innovative prime minister who provided stability at a time of high turmoil in Britain, and his gloomy manner may, in some ways, have served him well in this role.

Many of Melbourne's emotional needs were fulfilled in his relationship with Victoria, which became of great importance to Melbourne in the latter part of his administration and provided a *raison d'être* to continue as prime minister. Upon his resignation in 1841 and the progressive withdrawal of the queen from his life, Melbourne's depression worsened, a process that was hastened by his stroke in 1842. In the final years of his life, Melbourne was a pathetic shell of his old self, suffering from depression and other mental changes, such as volatile emotions, forgetfulness, poor concentration and slowness of thought. His mental health was complicated by excessive daytime sleepiness caused by a primary sleep disorder. Tourette's disorder may also have been present, although this did not appear in any way incapacitating.

SIR ROBERT PEEL (1788–1850) *(1834–1835; 1841–1846)*

Sir Robert Peel was born in 1788, became prime minister at the age of 53, and held the office for 9 months in his first term and for almost five years in his second.

Peel's Shyness and Anxiety

Peel's health was generally good. He was of striking appearance, and possessed great physical strength and stamina, possibly the result of his sporting pursuits.[240] Evidence for any mental illness is sketchy, but it cannot be ruled out entirely, and Post identified Peel as having "marked" psychopathology, without specifying whether it was episodic mental disorder such as periods of depression or anxiety, or if it was a longstanding deviation of personality.[241] There is some support for the latter, since Peel was shy and sensitive, and greatly feared ridicule, traits which have been related to his socially cloistered upbringing. As an adult he was never able to overcome his shy, awkward ways and remained "repelling except in his family circle."[242] Iremonger wrote of Peel as both bold and ultra-sensitive, "a leader of men and a loather of mankind, ambitious for power and nauseated by it."[243] He presented a frigid and haughty exterior, underneath which was a state of high emotionality.

In 1824, Peel wrote to his wife that "I feel quite uneasy in society and last night went up to my room two hours before the rest of the party, and read till I went to bed." Peel, in fact, could only be comfortable when he was in the presence of his wife.[244]

Peel's extreme sensitivity of mind was matched by an equal sensitivity to physical pain, both of which may have cost him his life.[245] After falling from his horse on June 29, 1850, Peel was taken home and laid out on a table. For three days he endured extreme pain but refused to let his doctor examine him, fearful of even more pain — this despite the availability of chloroform anesthesia. On July 2 he died from his injuries. Cecil drew an interesting and somewhat unexpected connection between Peel's shyness and his death when he wrote, "He was a bad horseman, but it appears that he had also a bad horse, against which he might have been warned, if he had been less shy and stiff, by an acquaintance who recognized the animal and perceived the danger Peel would be put in if he rode it."[246]

Peel's shyness receives further anecdotal confirmation from the description of his first meeting with Queen Victoria, where his severe shyness made the queen feel awkward too, while his "nervous mannerisms, his irritating habits of pointing his toes and thrusting out his hands to shake his cuffs reminded the queen of a dancing master."[247]

It is not far-fetched to propose that Peel suffered from excessive social anxiety, possibly even social anxiety disorder — at the very least, and in line with Post's categorization, he displayed pathological levels of shyness and fear of embarrassment, which perhaps even contributed to his fatal injury. However, shyness did not prevent him from attaining the highest public office, and from the twentieth-century perspective, some historians consider Peel to be among the greatest of prime ministers.[248] Gladstone thought highly of Peel for his financial discipline and success in foreign policy.[249] One of Peel's most enduring legacies was the creation of the first police force, popularized by the names given to police officers such as "Bobby" and "Peeler."

LORD JOHN RUSSELL (1792–1878) *(1846–1852; 1865–1866)*

Lord John Russell was born prematurely, and it seemed at first as though he would not survive. Short of stature, physically weak ("delicate") and prone to coughs, colds and fainting spells, he appeared an unpromising candidate to climb all the way up the greasy pole. Russell confounded the odds. Having failed as a poet, dramatist and writer, he made an inauspicious start in politics. Characterized as a pigmy who reached the peak, Russell was of the most unlikely and unsuitable of prime ministers.[250]

Iremonger cited his grotesque appearance, squeaky, high-pitched voice, stammering and uncertain manner, and suddenly deteriorating health, and noted, "Because he had little to say and said it pitifully, badly ... [he] made either no impression or a bad one."[251] Russell may be among the shyest of prime ministers; his nephew put down his uncle's stiff and frigid manner to incurable shyness.[252] As with Peel, Russell was deficient in social skills, largely the result of his upbringing, which limited him mainly to extended family interactions.[253] He shunned the typical drinking sessions which were so much a part of social life in politics, preferring to sit at home with his wife, where they read to one another. If he did engage in conversation, it was of an intellectual kind.

While shyness in itself is not pathological, it can be argued that in Russell it exceeded normal bounds; yet it did not prevent him from becoming prime minister. Because of his discomfort around others he put up a screen of arrogance, aloofness, vanity, and belligerence, and he often snubbed those who tried to melt his reserve.[254] Such a picture is consistent with social anxiety disorder and even elements of avoidant personality. The significant degree of hostility and rudeness by no means excludes social anxiety.

Russell possessed a somewhat naïve outlook on the world, seeing things in terms of black and white, and having no real skill in achieving compromise or tolerating ambiguity. Perhaps in consequence, his style was to lead from the front rather than achieve consensus; as a result, when things went wrong, he could not count on the support of his colleagues. On many occasions he vacillated and took initiatives not out of boldness but because of weakness and uncertainty. Parry feels that Russell's personality traits damaged him much more after he became prime minister than before: without a working majority, he was cramped in his style and lacked the skills which would have carried him through. As a result, he quickly became frustrated and petulant, and forfeited support.[255]

Russell was afflicted by prolonged grief after the death of his first wife, Lady Adelaide Ribblesdale, who left him with six children, one of whom was only two weeks old. Russell was "utterly prostrated, hid himself away completely and thought of leaving public life."[256] He was so shaken that it was some time before he returned to the House. Thereafter he became more solitary and only went out with his children. His grief continued for at least two years. When he proposed marriage to Lady Frances Eliot, he met with rejection and wrote back to her saying that she was quite right in her decision, that he deceived himself that she might give herself to a person of broken spirits, and that he needed to return to public business despite his sense of misery, which even the children could not drive away.[257]

Lord Russell showed high levels of shyness and social avoidance, but for all that he confounded the odds. Shyness affected his personal and business relationships, and perhaps rendered him a weak leader. Other elements of his personality, such as selfishness, vanity, imprudence, recklessness, belligerence, childishness, and churlishness no doubt played their part too, but some of these traits were likely made worse by anxiety and poor self confidence.[258] Russell exemplifies yet another premier whose career was for a time affected by grief. Information is not sufficient to say whether Russell experienced major depression using current diagnostic criteria.

EDWARD STANLEY, 14TH EARL OF DERBY (1799–1869) *(1852; 1858–1859; 1866–1868)*

Lord Derby was born into one of England's oldest aristocratic families, which traced its nobility back to the 16th century. He thrice served as prime minister — in 1852, 1858–9 and 1866–8. For over 20 years he was leader of the Conservative party, most of which was spent in opposition, and Derby remains the longest-serving party leader in modern British politics. In Parliament he was one of the leading debaters of his day. Politically he is known for emancipating slaves in the British Empire, for passing the Irish Education Act, and for the Second Reform Bill.

Derby was a colorful, impulsive and insouciant man, with interests that went far beyond politics and which were held with every bit as much passion, if not more. His great loves included the turf, game shooting, gambling, philanthropy and translating the classics. Derby owned race horses and became a significant figure in the British race horse world. In this respect, he followed the family tradition, for it was his grandfather, the 12th Earl of Derby, who gave his name to the "Derby" horse race in 1780. Upon his death, Derby left debts of £680,000, mostly from excessive racing expenditure and poor estate management.[259] Derby was also famous for his translation of the Greek classic *The Iliad*, as well as for his philanthropy in promoting social welfare. An additional interesting piece of trivia concerns the fact that his son, Frederick Stanley (later to become 16th Earl of Derby), as Governor-General of Canada, is eponymously remembered by the Stanley Cup, the National Hockey League's equivalent of the NFL Superbowl or FA Cup in English soccer. A love and patronage of sport certainly ran through generations of the Stanley family.

Evidence for Psychiatric Problems

Lord Derby was plagued by painful gout for much of his life, and there are clear suggestions that he was also affected by psychiatric problems to the end. According to Iremonger, he "was a prey to all the ills of the supersensitive, including fainting fits, nervous stomach, neuralgia, rheumatism, and 'gout,' a term which was still employed in his day as a euphemism for mental depression. From that he certainly suffered."[260] Iremonger's allusion to gout as a synonym for depression is interesting for a number of reasons. Firstly, we have seen other statesmen with mental illness who were affected by "gout," such as Pitt the Elder, of whom Dubos wrote, "[William Pitt the Elder] had attacks of insanity which were euphemistically called gout in the brain."[261] Secondly, in the shifting sands of medical terminology, the meaning of words changes over time, and the "bilious fevers" of the 18th century would bear little resemblance to Anthony Eden's "bilious fever" of 1956; even the word "fever" has changed its meaning. One disease may travel historically under a long list of different labels, as is well illustrated by the condition known today as post-traumatic stress disorder. The term "gout" today most probably has a more limited connotation than in earlier times. But nonetheless, Derby did suffer from gout as we currently understand it, and the pain was incessant and at times limited his mobility.

Giving qualified support to Iremonger's claim about depression are the descriptions of Weintraub, which show Derby as completely inaccessible to his colleagues, and paying little attention to government but much to horse racing.[262] In severe depression, one would expect to see a complete loss of interest, so this mixed description of partial loss of interest is more difficult to interpret. Also, as noted above, how much of this behavior was due to gout and how much to depression is difficult to determine, although in later life the separation is more apparent. In 1863, at the age of 65, Derby would doze off at meetings and be in such distress that it was difficult to walk or even stand. He lost interest in politics. "Brooding in isolation" at home, he preferred to work on his translations of *The Iliad*. With the preservation of interest, this sounds more like gout than depression.

Derby's son, Edward Henry, Lord Stanley, made several diary entries which suggest the occurrence of episodic depression. For example, on April 22, 1864, his father was found to be in low spirits, not eating well, avoiding social contact, and consuming too much wine and brandy. Many thought he was not physically strong enough to hold office. Importantly, Lord Stanley pointed out that his father's gout was then under control, so this would not have explained the symptoms. Five months later, on September 2, Derby remained secluded in his country residence, 200 miles from London, preoccupied with translations of Homer which, according to his son, could not be expected to sustain his father's spirits forever. He was clear that such seclusion was not good for Derby's health. It was not until January 1865 that Derby had regained his interest in hunting. Then in late January another flare-up of gout took place. In a diary entry of March 31, 1865, Derby was described as being inexplicably irritable and having developed a marked tremor, which was relieved by alcohol. Could this have suggested alcohol dependence and withdrawal? Between 1865 and his death in 1869 there were further episodes of despondency and withdrawal.

Derby's name has forever been linked with opium, for he conducted and concluded the Opium Wars with China, walking away with the prize of Hong Kong as part of the settlement in 1842. But there are signs that the *taking* of opium became a more personal concern later in life. Bloy notes that Derby "had been stricken by gout. As a means of obtaining relief from the pain, he took opium; there were suggestions the illness and treatment had also affected his mental state."[263] At the end of his second administration in 1859 he was in such bad health that his mental state was affected, quite likely due to the high quantities of opium which had been prescribed.[264] After one particularly bad attack in February of 1868, Derby resigned and effectively terminated his political career. However, good health returned, and on March 1 he was described as "wonderfully recovered," in excellent spirits and speaking with a strong, clear voice. As he entered the last year of his life in 1869, he again secluded himself and saw few people, although apparently being content with this way of existence. In his final days he was semi-conscious due to the large amounts of opium administered for pain.[265] As he neared death on October 29, 1869, surrounded by his immediate family, his young grandson said that he was sorry for his grandfather, to which Derby replied, "Grandpa is very sorry for himself," and that he was "bored to exhaustion"—words that capture the emptiness of his final years, or possibly the effects of chronic opium prescription.

Hawkins refers to Derby's depressive tendencies, both in his personality and in the form of more obvious clinical episodes. By 1847 a pattern had emerged of a man whose energy and activity was considerable in the first 6 to 8 months of the year, to be followed in the fall and early winter by depression, irritability, despair and flare-ups of gout. Naturally the Parliamentary and racing seasons stirred Derby's sap, and by September there was less going on; gout played a part, but it is unlikely that his depressions could be fully explained by these factors. A genetic influence was probably at work, in that both of Derby's sons experienced episodic depression, and his father, the 13th Earl of Derby, an introverted and scholarly man, developed prolonged depression in his old age.[266] The tendency for Derby's depression to worsen in the early winter suggests the possibility of seasonal depression — or seasonal affective disorder, as it is now termed.

Derby inherited and passed on his family's genetic vulnerability to depression and undoubtedly suffered from the illness, including when he was prime minister. Whether from depression, pain or excessive opium use (medically prescribed), his mental state seems to have made him unfit to function, and he eventually resigned. Cromwell has noted the long periods of illness in Derby's life, that his attacks of gout often occurred at crucial political moments, and that his demeanor suggested to many a progressive desire to retreat from the political limelight.[267] The distinction between gout and depression is sometimes unclear, and it is possible that each may have fuelled the other. Gout would make him depressed, while depression could have produced excessive alcohol intake, which in turn could have provoked attacks of gout. Stress could have aggravated both. Of interest in this regard is recent work showing that allopurinol, a drug used for gout, is effective for bipolar disorder. A large clinical trial demonstrated better anti-manic effect when allopurinol was added to lithium, a standard treatment for mania.[268] Perhaps gout and bipolar disorder share a common pathology in some ways, and being at risk for one is associated with risk for the other.

Conceding depression, Saintsbury's account of Derby deserves to be acknowledged:

> But he could always see the humour [of it], and this ... is one of the greatest and rarest gifts of a statesman.... It protects a man almost entirely from that risk of being worn down by nervous exhaustion which has proved fatal to some great statesmen.... It gives him strength to bide the fiercest brunts, as Lord Derby showed in his early struggles with O'Connell. It protects. It gives him patience to endure those periods of disappointment and inaction.... It protects him from the approaches of sycophancy.[269]

Saintsbury goes on to say, "If, as it does perhaps, it carries with it the danger of seeing things too small, it frees its possessor from the still greater danger of seeing them too large." This last comment is consistent with Owen and Davidson, who noted that a sense of humor is one factor which protects a powerful leader from the error of hubris, as well as being a recognized component of resiliency.[270]

GEORGE GORDON, 4TH EARL OF ABERDEEN (1784–1860) *(1852–1855)*

Lord Aberdeen was prime minister between 1852 and 1855. Better suited to peacetime leadership, it was his misfortune to be premier during the Crimean War, which began with a series of unforeseen calamities and did not go well for Lord Aberdeen. Eventually he resigned following a defeat in the House of Commons, to be succeeded by the hawkish Lord Palmerston. Aberdeen had great difficulty in managing the strong personalities in his cabinet, perhaps due in part to the cumulative effects of unresolved grief, as described below. Outside of politics, Aberdeen was a scholar of Greek studies and archaeology, and was elected president of the Society of Antiquaries. He acquired an interest in forestry, planting 14 million trees on his large Scottish estates, whose improvement he supervised.

Aberdeen remains one of the more overlooked prime ministers.[271] Serial bereavements mark him as one of the more tragic figures in British politics. Even by the standards of the time, where life was short and death in childhood common, Aberdeen's losses went far beyond reasonable expectation. He lost his father and mother when he was aged 7 and 11, respectively. His chief political mentor (Pitt) died when he was 22, to be followed six years later by the death of his beloved first wife Catherine. He was left to raise three young daughters, all of whom died before they reached the age of 21. Aberdeen and his wife also had one stillborn son. Aberdeen remarried and lost his second wife after 16 years, as well as their daughter, who died one year later.

He could never speak of his losses and was given to periods of gloomy lack of interest. The effects of so many deaths turned this one-time man of adventure, who was quite active in the London social scene, into a cold recluse, unable to project himself in public.[272] Jenkins described Aberdeen's "lonely childhood and grief-ridden second twenty-five years" underlying the following self-expression written to a friend: "You look for interest and amusement in the ... world and the spectacle it affords; now I cannot express to you my distaste for everything of the kind...."[273] I have had enough of the world ...

and would willingly have as little to do with it as is decent." In 1845, Aberdeen informed Peel that he had no wish to enter the House of Lords again. Iremonger observed that Aberdeen was affected at times by a "nervous tic," headaches, noise and confusion, and nocturnal spasms following the death of Robert Peel, one of the few people to whom Aberdeen felt close. She believes that his guilt over the Crimean disaster was so great that he possibly suffered "some form of breakdown," which went unnoticed on account of his stoicism. In 1854, Aberdeen told a friend that he felt as if every drop of blood shed was to rest upon his head, and he lived forever with this feeling.[274] While in some ways things improved after he left office, Aberdeen was still described as bad tempered, quarrelsome and with a face like thunder.[275]

Aberdeen was devoted to his first wife, Catherine. Her death from tuberculosis in 1812 after seven years of happy marriage was a loss from which he never recovered. His biographer son, Arthur, said the sunshine went out of his life forever. Aberdeen's observance of mourning for the next 50 years has been considered abnormal even for the times, where prolonged observance of mourning customs was common, and made it difficult for his second marriage to prosper.[276] For more than a year he was subject to visual hallucinations of Catherine, and kept a journal in Latin of these experiences. Iremonger believes that in Aberdeen we see one of the "more dramatically extreme reactions to bereavement caused by childhood deprivation."[277]

Aberdeen may not have met all the necessary criteria for either definite complicated grief or major depression by the defining criteria of today's diagnoses, and he was clearly able to function at a high level in politics (otherwise it is doubtful he would have become prime minister). However, he was seen as weak and distant, and he failed to hold together his cabinet. With the responsibilities of raising three young daughters, all of whom succumbed early to tuberculosis, Aberdeen was often in conflict as to his first duties — politics or family — and at times he would enter long periods of withdrawal from political life. There is no doubt that his frequent preoccupations with grief, anticipating death and having to care for terminally ill relatives hampered his effectiveness in politics. Aberdeen's cumulative bereavements froze his ability to express feelings, which is seen in complicated grief and in severe depression. Aberdeen's cousin, the poet Lord Byron, is known to have suffered from manic-depressive disorder, but there is no evidence of this in Aberdeen. He might best be seen as showing features of dysthymic disorder, a term which refers to chronic low-grade depression and irritability, often lasting for several years. However, we do not know the extent to which his depression lifted, and it is possible that recurrent brief depressions occurred rather than one long, unbroken state. Lifelong chronic headaches, which started in 1813 after

Aberdeen's carriage overturned and left him with a concussion, were also a problem.[278]

How he was able to reach the heights he did is hard to explain, but it speaks to certain undeniable strengths which outweighed his limitations (though they did not prevent poor leadership). Chamberlain is of the opinion that this shy and sober man projected himself poorly to the public, that he was not well suited to the cut and thrust of adversarial politics, and that he would perhaps have been happier as a scholar and reforming landlord.[279]

HENRY JOHN TEMPLE, VISCOUNT PALMERSTON (1784–1865) *(1855–1858; 1859–1865)*

Viscount Palmerston was a jaunty, supremely confident, and brash figure who was famous for his Don Juan–like relations with women, earning him the moniker "Lord Cupid."[280] Perhaps for one who, as legend has it, was descended from Lady Godiva, this is no surprise. He was one of the more colorful characters of 19th century British politics: at the age of 80 he appeared in court, accused of adultery. Palmerston's rebarbative manner also earned him the moniker "Lord Pumicestone." He lived a long and vigorous life, enjoyed riding and hunting, remained in good health at least into his sixties, and was a firm believer in the salutary benefits of exercise. He died in office at the age of 81, his last words reputedly being, "Die, my dear doctor, that is the last thing I shall do."

Evidence for any mental illness is limited to Post's assessment of "marked" psychopathology and the fact that Palmerston eventually became worn out by the stress of office; he "was frequently tired, and suffered bad headaches, gout and boils."[281] While Post does not back up his assertion with detail, his authority and qualifications cannot be overlooked and thus suggest that there is a good basis for his opinion. Iremonger rates Palmerston along with Lloyd George, Gladstone and Melbourne as showing extreme ("suicidal") recklessness in the Kingdom of Venus, but there is little to suggest bipolar disorder, other than Bagehot's reference to Palmerston's "over buoyant" behavior in 1858, where he exhibited unwarranted rudeness, made an inappropriate cabinet appointment which suggested impaired judgment, and made several other appointments which Bagehot thought were "un-administrative mistakes."[282] Might this speak to possible bipolar tendencies? There is little else in the way of earlier support. In the absence of more information, Palmerston cannot be considered to have experienced mental illness or personality disorder.

BENJAMIN DISRAELI, 1ST EARL OF BEACONSFIELD (1804–1881) *(1868; 1874–1880)*

Early Years

Benjamin Disraeli was born on December 21, 1804, and died April 19, 1881. His father, Isaac Disraeli, was a distinguished author. Disraeli was mostly educated at home and did not attend university, an unusual path for one destined to become prime minister. Although baptized into the Anglican Church at the age of 13 (but never diligent in observing a particular religious faith), Disraeli's Jewish ancestry was another obstacle in the way of his political ambitions at a time when racial and religious prejudices were strong. Disraeli was directed by his father into the legal profession, with the expectation that he would practice as a solicitor, a course of action which met with resistance on the part of Benjamin, who gave up practicing law at 21 and turned his hand to writing. Disraeli's first novel, *Vivian Grey*, was an autobiographical account of a young man's childhood and efforts to rise in politics, written when he was 24. *Vivian Grey* became an instant success and went through several printings. (It is also believed that the word "millionaire" was first printed in this book.) By the time he was 30, Disraeli had written 4 novels, three of which were completed in less than 3 years. In his novels, perhaps Disraeli reveals an awareness of human complexity and psychological insight which served him well in dealing with his own neurotic ways.

It was on the heels of such prolific creativity that Disraeli's political ambitions began to take shape. After a series of failed attempts, Disraeli was elected Member of Parliament for Maidstone in 1837. Within four years he had managed to antagonize his prime minister, Sir Robert Peel, by suggesting that Peel appoint him to a ministry. Such overt self-promotion did not find favor with Peel, and Disraeli's feelings of rejection turned to harsh criticism of his leader, which eventually played a part in bringing about the collapse of Peel's administration.[283] Disraeli's Parliamentary career went from strength to strength, and culminated in two terms as premier — in 1868 and from 1874 to 1880.

Evidence for Mental Illness

Notwithstanding the success of *Vivian Grey*, it was poorly received by literary critics whom Disraeli respected. Such rejection put him in a "tailspin of depression ... [and] nervous breakdown," followed by a "less dramatic but long-lasting depression" with sadness and lassitude.[284] The public humiliation, as it was perceived by Disraeli, caused him to leave for Egypt, where he stayed for some time until he recovered.[285] Disraeli's sensitivity to slights was to rupture more than one friendship.[286] There were suggestions of oversleeping, a symptom recognized in depression of the rejection-sensitive type, sometimes referred to as *hysteroid dysphoria* or atypical depression.[287] Other depressive symptoms which affected Disraeli included depersonalization (i.e., a feeling that the self or parts of one's body are unreal), palpitations, fatigue and inability to sustain attention, producing a condition he referred to as "the great enemy."[288] As often occurs in severe depression, Disraeli withdrew socially, closeting himself in his room and "forgoing altogether the *deliciae* of society."[289] His family came to worry whether Disraeli would lose his mind and possibly his life. It seems that Disraeli's state of depression lasted for about five years, from age 22 to 27.

This may not have been Disraeli's first encounter with depression, for there are strong suggestions that he had already experienced depression, with school anxiety, as early as 11 years of age.[290]

Shortly before writing *Vivian Grey*, Disraeli had amassed large debts from foolish investments and poor business judgment. To make good these debts, he attempted to establish a newspaper, carrying on "frenetic" correspondence with lawyers, journalists and architects, and taking a number of "exhausting" trips to Scotland to find an editor. Even Disraeli's partner, the publisher John Murray, complained of his "unrelenting excitement," and after four months of intense activity, Disraeli referred to being "utterly exhausted in body and mind."[291]

There is reason to think that Disraeli's depression was of the bipolar (manic-depressive) variety. He described the "frantic, almost mad, composition" of the autobiographical *Vivian Grey*, who commenced writing before noon, working in a frenzy with racing thoughts that were too quick for his hand, and as he finished each page, he threw it on the floor.[292] He "was amazed at the rapid and prolific production," which left him exhausted. This state of exhaustion was then punctuated by pacing and a need for wine, which restored him to further writing. Not until after midnight would he retire to bed, only to awaken early next day, drink more wine and then continue on his book. Under these frenetic yet focused conditions, *Vivian Grey* was finished in a few days.

In keeping with this characterization is Lord Derby's remark many years later that Disraeli showed a "tendency to extremes of alternating excitement and depression."[293] Recklessness in business, in extramarital relationships, in gambling and extensive debts all caused problems. His affair with Lady Sykes caused consequences more serious than the usual problems associated with a torrid affair.

As is often the case with bipolar disorder, problems can be compounded by alcohol intake. As a young adult, Disraeli made frequent and enthusiastic allusions to drinking, which went beyond what would have been considered normal for the time,²⁹⁴ and headaches and hangovers affected him throughout his life; in 1872 he was "still capable of magnificent feats of imbibing."²⁹⁵ When invited to join the Austen family on a trip to Italy, the 22-year-old Disraeli replied that he would be pleased to do so, but that it was necessary to inform them of his excessive drinking habits.²⁹⁶ On another occasion, when he returned from Egypt, Disraeli's sister was concerned about his drinking.²⁹⁷ To establish if bipolar disorder exists, the doctor would typically ask about a family history. It is known that Disraeli's father probably experienced depression, but we lack information whether he was also susceptible to mania or hypomania.²⁹⁸ Curiously, Isaac Disraeli developed depression at about the same age (i.e., in his twenties); it lasted three years and was accompanied by lassitude, despair, poor self-esteem and lack of nervous energy, best understood at the time as a psychological disorder. Isaac had been a rebellious boy who showed a "poetic" temperament. Acknowledging the general lack of information, what little we know is consistent with a bipolar type of depression: early onset, lassitude and "rebellious" temperament.

Iremonger considered Disraeli an "attention seeker to end all attention-seekers ... insatiable in love ... aloof, isolated, reserved, hypersensitive, subject to depressions," and that "no man could have been as reckless as he."²⁹⁹ Yet, for the most part, Disraeli overcame the serious disruptions of youthful depression and hypomania. How was he able to achieve this? How did he eventually outgrow the more extreme manifestations of his disorder? An "indomitable will, fanatical energy, refusal to accept defeat" and "astounding drive" may have protected Disraeli in this respect.³⁰⁰ It is also possible that he used writing to convert depression into something more positive, as with Winston Churchill, who found painting and writing to be good antidotes for the "black dog" of his depression.³⁰¹ Many of Disraeli's novels were deeply autobiographical, and through this medium it may have been possible for him to assimilate and control his more severe melancholic tendencies. His contented marriage to Mary Ann Wyndham Lewis may also have been a stabilizing influence. Disraeli is alleged to have said, "Happiness is a choice that requires effort sometimes," and it was always something he had to work at. In this respect, he had much in common with his rival, William Gladstone. Very likely, Disraeli succeeded in meeting his narcissistic needs for fame, adulation and success in his relationships and in politics, and this put some distance between him and his depressions. Disraeli's fear when he was depressed was that he would be unable to do anything that would mark him out from the crowd.³⁰²

Thus, while Disraeli's youth was scarred by quite severe depression and probably hypomania, as he grew into maturity these demons did not affect him to the same extent, although they never left him entirely. Disraeli may have suffered from winter depressions. In 1850, when he was 46, he wrote to his sister that he was suffering "a fit of the old illness, which the fall of the leaf brings ... a sort of equinoctial attack — a great sluggishness and debility."[303] Partial to sunshine, he was "ultimately killed by the east wind."[304] Also, after the arduous sessions in Parliament, when Disraeli returned to his country residence in the fall, it appears to have taken him longer than normal to bounce back and regain his energy. Thus, at the time of the equinox Disraeli experienced greater perturbation of mood.

Summary

There is no reason to doubt the occurrence of depression, probably bipolar in type, and it seems fair to conclude that Disraeli suffered from bipolar II disorder, which tended to worsen in winter. The most severe of Disraeli's depressions took place before he entered politics and may have been connected with his frustrated professional quest and rejection as a writer. There is also the interesting possibility that some depressive symptoms were aggravated by the treatment, digitalis, which was given by his doctor.[305] (Digitalis is medicine given for heart failure, but seems to have had other applications at the time. Used in excess or inappropriately, it can produce unwanted psychological effects.) Disraeli's sensitivity to rejection was perhaps greater than average, yet neither this nor his depression prevented him from reaching the "top of the greasy pole," as he put it. Perhaps bipolar qualities drove him to the top and kept him there for a long time. He enjoyed the good graces of Queen Victoria and remained at the top of the pole, at least as Leader of the Opposition, until his death in 1881 at the age of 76.

WILLIAM EWART GLADSTONE (1809–1898)
(1868–1874; 1880–1885; 1886; 1892–1894)

William Gladstone was born December 29, 1809, and died on May 19, 1898, at the age of 88. His entire life was one of remarkable productivity and immense energy; there was no gradual fade into the sunset years — he resigned from his fourth and final term as prime minister at the age of 84, and even after that remained active. He was unquestionably a giant in British politics throughout the Victorian era. Gladstone entered Parliament in 1832, five years before Queen Victoria ascended the throne, and departed the political scene only seven years before her death in 1901. Not for nothing was Gladstone known as the Grand Old Man, often abbreviated to "GOM."

Psychiatrically, Gladstone has remained an enigma, and the complexity of his case makes this one of the longer entries in the book. The presence of psychopathology is clear, but its nature has not been well defined. Felix Post has categorized Gladstone as showing "marked" psychopathology on a four-point scale of severity, which ranged from none-mild-marked-severe; but, unfortunately, he failed to provide any additional information or give a source reference to support his assertion.[306] Crosby has offered an interesting analysis of Gladstone mainly from the perspective of coping and stress-response theory.[307] His scholarly assessment concludes that Gladstone was engaged in a constant vigil to control an exceptionally volatile nature with propensities to engage in risky behavior. However, Crosby adopts no diagnostic position and leaves unanswered the question of what, if any, psychiatric disorder his subject may have had.

Gladstone was often affected by stress, and interactions have also been observed between the different aspects of his psychopathology, which will be described below. For example, Matthew wrote, "Illness would often strike Gladstone at times of stress," and that he was "prone to tension," with stress-induced symptoms such as tightness in the chest and diarrhea, both of which are hallmarks of anxiety. Gladstone's sexual escapades and self-flagellation would also be provoked by stress. As Matthew noted, episodes of nervous indisposition would fully remit, attributed in large part to Gladstone's "resilience," which, among other things, took the form of a regular evening diary entry.[308]

Leading biographers and diarists indicate that Gladstone had a family history of depression, drug addiction, and, quite possibly, mania and psychosis (i.e., periods when there was loss of touch with reality, such as experiencing hallucinations or delusional, unfounded, beliefs). Gladstone himself experienced at least 15 depressive episodes, many of which were preceded by elation, and he engaged in extraordinarily risky and somewhat ambivalent "rescue" relationships with prostitutes. There are allusions to overspending, excessive anger ("vehemence" as it was called) and pressure of speech (i.e., rapid rush of words reflecting a whirlwind of thought), all beyond acceptable norms in the eyes of his contemporaries. While examples will be given, it should be said that, as far as mania goes, biographers repeatedly stress his remarkable powers of concentration, as well as his generally successful efforts to recover from setbacks by turning to work, family or vigorous physical exercise, which goes against the case for severe bipolar disorder to some extent. Moreover, his ability to maintain a diary for his whole life, containing around 25,000 entries, speaks to a sustained discipline which would be difficult to maintain in the throes of extreme mania. Therefore, it is unlikely that he succumbed to the greater extremes of bipolar disorder, but milder manic (i.e., hypomanic) forms of illness are distinctly possible, and his temperament is quite in keeping with this notion.

Family History of Mental Illness

A review of what is known about Gladstone's family history of mental illness can be extracted from the rather cursory yet revealing descriptions of Gladstone's contemporaries and later biographers.

Gladstone's father, Sir John Gladstone, was a successful businessman, trading with North America and owning sugar plantations in the West Indies. He established a strong mercantile presence in Liverpool, which was to last for much of the 19th century. For this and other works, he earned a knighthood. Sir John's overbearing and controlling ways may have been too much for his wife, who became a "perennial invalid," traveling from one place to another in a futile quest for good health; and William's diary entries would often say tersely, "Mother ill."[309] The nature of her illness is unclear, but one possibility could be that Mrs. Gladstone suffered from what has variously been called neurasthenia, somatoform disorder, chronic anxiety and/or depression.[310]

Gladstone had been close to his sister Helen, but, like William, she had not found it easy growing up with their formidable father and eventually developed a serious opium abuse problem. In 1845 Gladstone journeyed to Baden-Baden to help his sister, who was residing there in very poor health. He wrote to his mother that Helen had drunk 150 drops of laudanum (an opiate drug) and was in danger of death. Fortunately she rallied but, according to Gladstone, was "poisoned much in body and, more in mind, by the use of that horrible drug."[311] On another occasion she barricaded herself behind the locked door of her room and drank a bottle of eau de Cologne. Helen had a long list of lovers, was "unstable" and had to be restrained by the Lunacy Commission in 1846. The presence of an opium-related disorder is clear, and an alcohol-related disorder is also possible. Her serial unstable sexual relationships and compulsory legal commitment into a psychiatric hospital raises the possibility of bipolar disorder, but this remains conjectural without more information.

William's brother, Robertson, appears to have suffered from mental illness. Lord Stanley wrote that in 1857 "Robertson Gladstone is on some points hardly sane," describing a paranoid speech which he had given on behalf of his brother, an aberration which, according to Lord Stanley, was later explained by his "showing signs of mental disturbance, and [being] under medical care."[312] Robertson was head of the family business but let control pass to an exploitative associate, much to the distress of William. Worse still, Robertson had over many years allowed one of the family properties to fall into decay, ultimately leaving William Gladstone with massive repair costs. While we cannot be sure about the nature of Robertson's disease, we do know that it required medical treatment and was associated with a declining ability to manage everyday affairs.

Evidence for Depression

According to Magnus, Jenkins, Crosby and Matthew, Gladstone is reported to have experienced episodes of sadness, insomnia or exhaustion, sometimes lasting for several months, in 1836–7, 1840, 1845, 1850, 1857, 1867, 1869, 1872, 1873, 1874, 1876, 1882, 1884–5, and 1892. On almost all occasions there had been a precipitating stress, and it appears to be the case that Gladstone made a full recovery from each episode, as described below.

1. Unlike several other prime ministers with a history of mental illness, and who displayed neurotic or academic problems in their schooldays, Gladstone acquitted himself well at Eton and at university. His first episode of clinically significant depression appears to have been at the age of 26 in the early part of 1836 when, following his mother's death and the rejection of his courtship by Caroline Farquhar, he was seen to be "extraordinarily feeble" in his Parliamentary performance, which was attributed to his "emotional distemper."[313]

2. Further misfortune was in store for Gladstone in 1837. A second rejection, this time by Lady Frances Douglas in November 1837, was hard to take. Compounding his disappointment in love was the fact that two of Gladstone's brothers had married during this time, acceptance of which was grudging on the part of Gladstone, who found cause for complaint about their choices of spouse. It also appeared to Gladstone that his political career was going nowhere. To deal with his distress, he asked his father to send him to the West Indies to tend the family plantations, a request which was denied. His diary of 1838 contained many references to moods of discouragement and despair, "oppression and pain." On one occasion, after receiving compliments from his Parliamentary colleagues for a successful speech, he was unable to savor the joy, writing, "Isolated from love and my greedy heart unappeased by a thousand consolations, I am half insensible even in the moment of delight to such pleasures as this kind of occasion affords."[314] In June of that year Gladstone's diary still mentioned daily sadness, "inward trouble" and being "perpetually restless and depressed." On one occasion, while attending a funeral, he even considered suicide, although how seriously is unknown. Thus, for much of 1838 Gladstone was in the grip of a troublesome and persistent depression, unable to feel pleasure or brighten up when things were better (e.g., being able to accept a compliment). The inability to brighten up in response to positive environmental cues, and the loss of ability to experience

pleasure, are core features of depressive illness. Gladstone also described "restlessness" in the context of depression. Given the case for bipolar disorder, the possibility of mixed symptoms of mania and depression at the same time will be considered later.

Crosby makes the important observation that Gladstone was able to find his own way out of depression on many, if not all, occasions. He was comforted that "active duty" helped see him through the 1838 depression, as well as many to follow. In his capacity to turn to work, Gladstone was better able to cope with the setbacks which met him along the way. At the same time, it must be asked if this was always healthy, since at times his activity was described as "strenuous" and pathological. For example, as chronicled below, after Jessy's death and his ensuing profound grief, Gladstone returned to his "rescue" work with London prostitutes, about whom Gladstone became obsessively preoccupied.[315] Such behavior again fits with the profile of bipolar disorder.

3. Magnus refers to a depressive episode in 1840, perhaps triggered by the poor reception of Gladstone's book *Church and State*.[316] He was noted to be tardy in fixing the study of his new London home and to think seriously about withdrawing from public life, as he would often do in future periods of depression.

4. A brief but intense depression occurred in 1845, after Gladstone had resigned from Peel's cabinet over a disagreement about funding the Catholic Church in Ireland by means of the Maynooth grant to support a training seminary for priests in the town of that name. Since Gladstone had previously supported this grant, many found his resignation hard to understand. It is likely that personal factors were of some importance, for Gladstone's sister, Helen, was at this time struggling with opiate abuse, and he felt compelled to visit her after she had dismissed her companion for trying to stop her drug-taking habits and for not answering letters sent from home.[317]

5. In 1850, Gladstone was laid low once again from depression brought on by the death of his young daughter Jessy and some political setbacks, one of which concerned a doctrinal dispute in the Church of England. While Gladstone was not responsible for the dispute, he became so worked up about its consequences that he was "plunged for many months into a mood of black depression."[318] To cope with his stresses, Gladstone took his family on a long trip to Italy, but throughout he was noted to be "peevish and out of sorts," argumentative and quick to take offence.[319]

6. Crosby notes an episode in 1853 when the stress of preparing and presenting the budget induced physical exhaustion and "nervous strain"; in April 1853, Gladstone recorded feeling "a good deal overset" and took a "blue pill" for his symptoms. Whether it was the pill or the illness, he felt even worse

the next day and eventually was ordered to bed by his doctor. In such a vein he continued throughout the summer, after which his health took a different turn with the appearance of erysipelas (a skin infection), which required prolonged bed rest.[320]

7. Another depression occurred in 1857 following the death of Gladstone's sister-in-law. As Magnus expresses it, "Private and public grief ate deeply into Gladstone's mind and for some months he was deeply depressed."[321]

8. After Gladstone lost his Parliamentary seat in Oxford in 1865, he entered another spell of depression, with thoughts of escaping from politics.[322]

9. Allusion is made by Magnus to a "mood of deep depression" in 1867 when Gladstone was front-runner for leadership of the Liberal party. It is unclear how long the depressions of 1865 and 1867 lasted, or how they affected Gladstone. Jenkins fails to mention them in his comprehensive biography, although he noted the peculiar and inexplicable failure of Gladstone for over a year to visit the family retreat in Wales, which had always been of such high importance.[323]

10. Two years later, in 1869, Gladstone introduced a bill to disestablish the Church of Ireland and appropriate its extensive funds, which provoked considerable resistance in Parliament. Gladstone's impetuosity ("emotional reaction") and "rash determination" were seen by his supporters as jeopardizing passage of the bill. Although a compromise was fashioned, Gladstone was driven by these events into another state of "nervous exhaustion." Crosby sees this as a pattern, in that whenever Gladstone could not enforce obedience on his peers, and the opposition became intractable, then he developed symptoms of mental distress.[324] No mention is made as to whether this episode resulted in medical treatment, "rest cures" or the like.

11. A more disruptive episode of depression occurred in 1873 and 1874. Gladstone's relationships with Queen Victoria started quite well but deteriorated over time, while the queen's regard of Disraeli grew stronger and stronger. A sense of the chemistry between Gladstone and Victoria is captured by the queen's comment that she always felt that when Gladstone spoke to her, it was as though he was addressing a public meeting — there was little rapport. During the early 1870s, Gladstone was attempting to create a broader role for the Prince of Wales as Viceroy of Ireland, proposing that he remain there for five months a year, and that he should take over some of his mother's ceremonial duties in London — a delicate assignment to be sure, and one which, unfortunately, gave much offence to the queen. In the mistaken belief that he was doing the right thing, Gladstone remained headstrong in persisting with this quest, despite being advised to let the matter drop. By

1873 he felt thwarted on all sides and was "completely disheartened" at his failure to "bring about an altered attitude on the part of the Royal Family."[325] An observer at the time, General Ponsonby, commented on how much Gladstone had changed, that he was looking back and not ahead ("no keenness about future measures"),[326] giving way, and showed a "want of interest in the political future which was not like his old self."[327] The queen wrote to Gladstone that she had never seen him so "agreeable."[328] While agreeability is usually considered to be an endearing quality, in this case it more likely goes along with the passive compliance of a man in the throes of depression, which he was. As Magnus says, he was "profoundly depressed and afflicted with a deep sense of failure."[329]

Initial political differences between Gladstone and the queen turned into personal animosity, and for much of 1872–3 he became preoccupied with these matters, finding it hard to control his "natural vehemence" and again thinking about quitting politics. Gladstone appears to have been in a state of prolonged tension, which "began to provoke minor faults of temper and judgement in the conduct of his private as well as in that of his public life."[330] Among these errors in public office were his efforts to bypass normal procedure and take short cuts in ways which were hard for his colleagues to understand, all accompanied by high-handed arrogance.[331] His friends became concerned that Gladstone was suffering from signs of overwork and strain. His decision to dissolve Parliament was taken impulsively in the midst of depression brought on by the stress of his daughter's wedding, the preparations of which exhausted him.[332] Although at the time he was under medical care for "general exhaustion,"[333] the queen refused to accept his resignation, and Gladstone's government limped along for another 10 months until an election was called, which he lost to Disraeli. He told Queen Victoria that his downfall was the greatest expression of public disapproval that he could ever remember, and that he again wished to retire because of old age. The mood of depression which had settled on Gladstone during this period lasted much longer than usual.[334] During the last 10 months of Gladstone's first administration he made a series of mistakes, largely attributable to exhaustion. One example was Gladstone's decision to appoint himself to the onerous office of the exchequer, a move described as "crassly foolish for a prime minister at the limit of his reserves."[335]

12. Between 1882 and 1885 there were more periods of depression and insomnia. On December 16, 1882, after returning to his country home for Christmas, he began to experience lack of sleep and low morale. While there was no clear precipitant, Gladstone had just relieved himself of the burden of the exchequer, and at times of (relative) relaxation he was also vulnerable. For instance, in 1881, after completing the Irish Land Bill, he wrote, "A sharp

and long continued labour ... the heaviest I have ever had: it will I think be followed by a severe fit of lassitude."[336] Matthew believes there were some trigger factors, including Mrs. Gladstone's insomnia, the thwarting of the GOM's retirement plans, arguments with queen and colleagues over a government reshuffle, and anxiety about what to say at the forthcoming January Midlothian campaign.[337] This bout of insomnia lingered, and by early January of 1883, with only 2 to 6 hours of sleep at night, he started to obsess about the problem and summoned his doctor, Dr. Clark, from London, which was 200 miles distant from his home at Hawarden. Dr. Clark advised him to postpone his Midlothian campaign in favor of a rest cure in the south of France, which quickly restored him to better spirits for a while.

13. By December of 1883 he was overcome once more by severe insomnia, leaving him with only 1 to 2 hours sleep at night. Matthew believed this was brought on by the stress of the Seats Bill negotiations and a painful dispute in his cabinet about Egyptian finance. This time the Christmas vacation trip to Hawarden restored his sleep to normal.[338] One point of view holds that this and other of Gladstone's illnesses were "understandable reactions after periods of intense strain," and that he showed a remarkable capacity for recovery,[339] implying that they were nothing more than normal, understandable stress reactions. Even if this is true, it should not blind us to the fact that major depression and bipolar disorder can be provoked by "understandable" stress. However, Gladstone's breakdowns were not always of long enough duration or of sufficient severity to merit the label of "major depression."

14. 1885 was to prove another difficult year. In January the governor-general of Sudan, General Charles George Gordon, was trapped in Khartoum and killed by Madhi insurrectionists on the 26th of the month. The news was received with deep dismay in Britain, and responsibility for this hero's death was placed at the feet of the GOM, whose moniker was for a time reversed to MOG, reflecting a perception that Gladstone was the "Murderer of Gordon." Again Gladstone's health broke down, and he took to bed with multiple symptoms of diarrhea, anxiety, and skin and voice problems. Magnus refers to the "mood of deep depression" that had been preceded by momentary elation.[340] Throughout most of 1885 Gladstone was plagued by a variety of health concerns, including trouble with his voice, which was put down to laryngeal catarrh. It is unclear how long the episode lasted.

15. Gladstone was in his fourth administration during the 1890s, by which time he had passed the age of 80. During the autumn of 1892 an impasse concerning the British East Africa Company and its finances brought Gladstone into conflict with Rosebery, and he again became "exceedingly depressed,"[341] lost interest in public affairs, withdrew from social engagements, and could not summon up enough energy to deal with Irish Home Rule leg-

islation, a cause which had always been so close to his heart. By November he had emerged from his despondency and was working on the Home Rule Bill.

Gladstone undoubtedly experienced multiple episodes of depression throughout his life, some of which were sustained and moderately severe, others of which were more in the nature of brief stress reactions. Sometimes they were interlaced with anxiety and its physical symptoms, and at other times by separate medical problems. The main question at this point is to ask whether Gladstone simply had depression or if it was part of a bipolar disorder. The clues to sorting out the differential diagnosis will be described. There is also the strange persistence over many decades of unusual encounters with prostitutes and courtesans, which could easily have put his career in jeopardy. Whether or not these were manifestations of his mood disorder will be considered.

Evidence for Bipolar Disorder

Consideration of Gladstone's temperament suggests the presence of cyclothymic features. Even at the young age of 21 the GOM was aware of his excitable temperament and that he feared the result of letting his emotions get the better of him.[342] Jenkins observed that "Gladstone's metabolism enabled him to move with bewildering rapidity from disturbingly frequent bouts of prostration to displays of almost manic energy."[343] One of the qualities which made Gladstone pre-eminent, in Jenkins' opinion, was his tremendous physical energy, which even exceeded his widely acknowledged intellectual abilities. Another was the "commanding force of his not always limpid words."[344] In the eyes of others, he was "dictatorial, irritable, impulsive, and lacking in judgement and tact."[345] Interestingly, Jenkins highlights Gladstone's "extraordinary capacity, however heavy the press of official burdens, to get on with postponable tasks."[346] This capacity for prompt action in areas which could easily be put off is consistent with decisiveness, which can be good, but also with rapid reaction to impulses or lack of reflective capacity, which can sometimes be bad, as seems to have been the case with the prime minister, since Crosby refers to extensive evidence that Gladstone was a man of "great volatility and passion,"[347] indicating that control over anger remained a lifelong problem.

Beyond the manifestations of temperament, there were abnormally manic moods that took the form of exuberant energy, pressure of speech, inappropriate and excessive anger, and possible overspending. Increased sexual preoccupation is also a feature of mania/hypomania, and this matter needs to be addressed, too, but analysis of the diagnostic significance of Gladstone's sexual behavior is complicated because it is hard to demonstrate that such episodes were short lived and therefore part of a hypomanic swing.

His enormous energy is shown by incessant tree-felling on his country estate, which came close to being denuded over the years. He continued to engage in this activity until he was 82, finding that it helped concentrate his mind on the present—focusing on the point on the tree where the next axe blow should fall, an activity which today would perhaps be considered a form of mindfulness. At 75, he climbed the highest peak in the Cairngorms, at 4300 feet, a 20-mile excursion which took over seven hours. Yet sometimes his activity would better be thought of as part of hypomania. For example, when he was staying with the queen in Scotland, as soon as he arrived he excused himself to bed with stomach problems; yet within a week he was able to complete a 33-mile walk in a day over very rough terrain.[348] In 1866 he found time to write a paper on *Ecce Homo* while in a state of "extraordinary mental excitement" when he reputedly invested heavily and unsuccessfully in mining speculations and was nearly ruined financially, and when many feared he would lose his sanity. It was his intention to read this paper at a religious meeting, but his friends dissuaded him in view of his condition.[349]

In 1881, Gladstone visited Lord Derby, who, as described by Jenkins,[350] found in Gladstone's speech "a copiousness and abundance of detail.... I have heard nothing like his eager and restless volubility. Nobody would have thought he had cares on his mind, or work to do. His face is very haggard, his eye wild." It is probable that there was more to it than simple enthusiasm, for on a second visit two years later Derby observed a tendency for Gladstone to drift away from the topic: "He began by saying that he wished to discuss some pending questions with me: but after the first five minutes he seemed to forget them & wandered off into a general dissertation on politics ... and leading up to nothing in particular." He went on to opine:

> For the first time, a suspicion crossed my mind that there is something beyond what is quite healthy in this perpetual flow of words — a beginning perhaps of old age.... He left us at 3 for Hawarden: at the last moment there was a scramble & bustle about missing or forgotten luggage, & in the end he went off with a greatcoat of mine, his own being lost. I imagine his & Mrs. Gladstone's domestic arrangements to be incoherent.

While advancing age could be the explanation, Gladstone was only 72 at the time and had many good years ahead. Given the whole context of Gladstone's temperament and life history of mood disorder, it is more probable that Derby was describing a hypomanic episode. We can understand this as part of a bipolar episode if it is kept in mind that some months earlier, worn out by the Egyptian crisis, Gladstone had noted an "increase of disinclination to my work, and disposition ... to scamp it." He lamented having to "remain on the stage like a half-exhausted singer, whose notes are flat, & everyone perceives it except himself would be of no good anyone." He complained of "inability of brain, to face legislative work."[351]

There were many outbursts of excessive anger, which were either inappropriate in their intensity or inexplicable in terms of context. Vincent referred to a prediction by Gladstone's doctor in 1864 that he would die insane and that "an excessive irritability has appeared in him on various occasions, and especially in the Spring of 1857, when he attacked Sir G. Lewis on a financial question of no great moment, with bitterness rarely equaled in Parliament."[352] Lewis himself described the outburst as "rabid," and there was consensus that such vehemence went beyond the bounds of proper Parliamentary behavior.[353] What made the attack even more puzzling was the fact that Gladstone and Lewis were friends, and that Gladstone had mentored his colleague over fiscal matters. In 1867 Gladstone again "los[t] his temper as usual" in Parliament.[354]

Concerning reckless or imprudent spending, Derby noted in 1866 that stories circulated about Gladstone making large purchases of china, which he collected but sold when times were rough. Such spending drew disapproving cries from Mrs. Gladstone, but her husband would take no notice. The abnormal character of Gladstone's spending habits is suggested by Derby's conclusion that it contained a "germ of insanity."[355] Gladstone also showed poor judgment in his investments, according to Jenkins, who said that he was "rarely a cautious investor." He gambled and lost heavily in some railway stock. His judgment was also questioned over Egyptian bond holdings at a time when Britain had territorial designs and was deeply involved in a military campaign in that country. Indeed, these holdings comprised 37 percent of his total portfolio.[356]

Drugs and Stage Fright

Gladstone's anticipatory fear of giving speeches in Parliament has received little attention, but it is on record that he would often take laudanum in his coffee before addressing the House of Commons; he found it gave him relief and may have "sustained his self-possession during the period of speechifying." Lord Randolph Churchill likened Gladstone's speeches to the taking of morphia: "The sensations ... are translucent; but the recovery is bitter."[357] Given Gladstone's self-righteous condemnation of England's "national iniquity" towards the opium trade with China, and his deep disapproval of his sister's opium habit (that "horrible drug"), the contradiction between public posture and personal behavior in this paragon of morality is striking.

Gladstone's Sexual Activities

Increased activity directed at pleasure or reward is common in mania or hypomania, as manifested, for example, by heightened sexual activity. Here Gladstone's work with prostitutes and his personal attraction to several of them, as well as to courtesans, deserves a close look. At first sight it would fit well into the case for bipolar disorder, but its persistence for several decades on a more or less continual basis presents something of a problem; and this side of his life is obscured by Gladstone's religious zeal to "save" women, as though he had a duty to do so. Certainly his zeal in wanting to reform prostitutes was shared by many at the time, including the Duke of Wellington, for this was a popular Victorian cause. Thus it is more difficult to distinguish between meta-explanations (i.e., it was culturally normal) versus simply describing the behavioral phenomena (i.e., it was part of a psychiatric syndrome). Unfortunately, the "phenomenology" is not as clear as with the other bipolar features reviewed above. One way to understand Gladstone's rescue work is that it provided a morally acceptable compromise between his strong libido and his punishing conscience. Gladstone was no Disraeli or Palmerston, for with such a strong super-ego, any extramarital affairs would be out of bounds, yet by "performing good works" he could still give vent to his sexual energy.

While there is no incontrovertible evidence of extramarital sex in the usual sense of the term, it is likely that Gladstone was sexually aroused by some of his encounters with prostitutes. In some cases (e.g., Mrs. Laura Thystlethwaite) his intimacies pushed the concept of platonic love to the extreme.

Late in the 1820s, Gladstone first took an interest in pornography and prostitutes, and at the same time commenced self-flagellation after engaging in pornographic activities.[358] In the 1840s, through a church connection, Gladstone became involved with work to reform destitute women, some of whom were prostitutes. This reform work soon expanded to prostitutes regardless of their personal circumstances and was again followed by self-flagellation. In one form or other this behavior continued until the 1880s. At times his encounters with prostitutes occurred frequently, with over 120 taking place during 1852–3. In 1851 he set up 12 meetings with one particular woman, Elizabeth Collins, in a 3-week period. Sometimes he would go to considerable lengths to find Ms. Collins if she wasn't on her regular beat. Of Elizabeth Collins, Gladstone said she was "lovely beyond measure," and that, of his feelings towards her, he was "surely self-bewildered."[359] On July 25 he excused himself early from a meeting with the U.S. ambassador to find Ms. Collins, with whom he spent two "strange, questionable" hours and upon return home flogged himself. Indeed, he used the lash three times in ten days after meeting Collins. Self-flagellation continued at least until 1859, being noted by Gladstone in his diaries with a special symbol.[360] At times the flagellation was so severe that it left scars on his back.[361] While the movement to reform prostitutes received the church's full support, it is doubtful if they would have condoned some of Gladstone's other dealings with these women.

On one of his nighttime excursions Gladstone was pursued by a man attempting to blackmail him. Instead of trying to hush things up or escape, Gladstone brazenly marched the man to a police station, pressed charges and arranged for the media to keep it quiet.

Naturally, many rumors abounded, such as Gladstone requesting a prostitute to strip naked, sit on his knee and have intercourse.[362] The veracity of these is not established, but they are no more far-fetched than his known pursuits, which, in themselves, strain credulity. Friends remonstrated with him to no avail. Indeed, a feisty Gladstone told them of his need to act in this way for the good of his health![363]

His relationship with Laura Thystlethwaite was somewhat different, in that she was not a prostitute to be rescued but was referred to as a "courtesan" in her youth and eventually married Captain Thystlethwaite, a man of violence and complex sexuality.[364] Gladstone first met her in 1864, and they developed a strong attraction.[365] By 1869, Gladstone and Mrs. Thystlethwaite were enjoying considerable intimacy, intense correspondence, dinner meetings, gifts and visits to the theater, which continued until well into the 1870s. Through Mrs. Thystlethwaite, Gladstone was introduced to spiritualism, séances and the Society for Psychical Research, moving in these circles for about two years. Gladstone was blind to his friends' efforts to dissuade him from associating with Mrs. Thystlethwaite. Despite being close to the edge, Gladstone managed to avoid doing himself any damage before he eventually cooled on the relationship. He did visit her in April 1894, two weeks before her death.

From the perspective of psychiatric assessment, the question is to decide if Gladstone's sexual activities were (a) a normal expression for a man who was often away from his wife, or (b) pathological. If the latter, then was it part of a hypomanic picture or a primary paraphilia (i.e., sexual deviation) or both? Available information, when taken *in toto*, seems to suggest a degree of the pathological. The strong element of risk, poor judgment and derivation of sexual pleasure points to bipolarity, but, as mentioned earlier, it was not exclusively episodic, which would be expected with the waxing and waning of high and low moods. Chronic hypomanic states can occur, as in the case of the composer George Frederick Handel, so this is a possibility, albeit rare and unlikely.[366]

As defined in DSM-IV, paraphilia refers to a condition of recurrent, intense, sexually arousing fantasies, urges or behaviors involving nonhuman objects, suffering or humiliation to oneself or one's partner, or children or other non-consenting persons, lasting over 6 months.[367] It is possible that Gladstone exhibited features of sexual masochism, which is coded as 302.83 in DSM-IV. Hesitancy is prudent, however, over the issue of "suffering" if he avowed it to be good for his health, but the frequent and persistent flagellation must have caused some distress, and others were concerned about his conduct. If the purist is unconvinced about this label, then at least one can settle for the category of paraphilia not otherwise specified (302.9).

Summary

Taken as a whole, historical evidence strongly suggests that Gladstone met the criteria for bipolar disorder, with numerous depressive episodes, some of which were preceded by short periods of elation. These periods began early in adult life, continued until his death at 88 and were mostly triggered by setbacks in romance or politics, or by grief. They were at times sufficiently troublesome for Gladstone to obtain medical care and/or retire from work with "rest cures." Underlying his mood disorder was a volatile temperament, strong passion, recklessness and proclivity to abnormally intense anger. Like many other prime ministers, Gladstone was sometimes troubled by public speaking anxiety, for which he took opiates to calm his nerves.

Offsetting the pathological elements of his nature were compensatory qualities of great self-discipline, amazing physical vigor into old age, widespread interests, the ability to quickly bounce back when down, an assertive, commanding manner in formal oratory and charm as raconteur on more informal social occasions. For all his deviant sexual ways, Gladstone enjoyed a rock-solid marriage of over 60 years, and cultivated a strong family bond with his wife and many children — visits to Hawarden were always restorative. He was known for remarkable powers of concentration, and, unlike many of his colleagues who put in long hours in Parliament and occasionally fell asleep, he was forever awake and alert to what was happening in the chamber. The diary which Gladstone kept for most of his life must have been a trusted and helpful friend. A commitment to exercise surely muted the impact of his depressions, as it is known that regular exercise has antidepressant effects.

What other conclusions can be drawn? His story illustrates, once again, that having a major psychiatric disorder is not incompatible with effective political leadership. Unlike some premiers, such as Rosebery, Baldwin and MacDonald, whose illnesses reduced their stamp, Gladstone was able to serve four terms in office and to span a 60-year career in Parliament. He was a colossus. Slater has proposed three ways in which character trait (and perhaps other psychopathology) can affect working capacity: (a) it may hamper the individual but not prevent success; (b) it may have no effect; or (c) it may have some positive effect in furthering creative work.[368] The balance of evidence would suggest that Gladstone fits into the third category; i.e., by coping with his volatile, cyclothymic, driven temperament and its more severe eruptions into mania or depression, he learned to effectively manage himself. To be sure, there were dips in the road, and there is no discernable benefit attached to his paraphilia. Overall, the greater outcome was a positive harnessing of potential flaws to the service of his political career. In this regard, he joins the ranks of Abraham Lincoln and Winston Churchill. If Gladstone had not been the man he was — prone to depression, hypomania and volatility — would he have achieved such greatness? Gladstone's psychopathology played itself out on the stage as a "Tennysonian mixture of religion, sex, and patriotism, each element both stimulating and moderating the others to produce a soul in great tension but in balance — a mixture whose balance Gladstone only just maintained, and which conditioned all his public and private actions and thoughts."[369] Birds of a feather flock together, and, interestingly, Gladstone and the depression-prone Tennyson developed a strong affinity for one another. It was partly due to Gladstone's encouragement that Tennyson accepted elevation to the peerage after initially declining an offer from the queen.

ROBERT GASCOYNE-CECIL, 3RD MARQUESS OF SALISBURY (1830–1903) *(1885–1886; 1886–1892; 1895–1902)*

Robert Arthur Talbot Gascoyne-Cecil was the second son of the 2nd Marquis of Salisbury. He was born February 3, 1830, and died August 22, 1903, having been three times prime minister. His cumulative 14 years' tenure in office makes him one of Britain's longest-serving premiers. Besides his political interests, Salisbury was a champion of science, had a great interest in farming and installed a chemistry laboratory at home.

Robert Cecil was a frail child, prone to episodes of depression and sleep walking. He was unhappy at school and was described as a moody, nervous, bad tempered, unsociable boy for whom school was a "nightmare."[370] His father complied with Robert's request to leave Eton at the age of 15. The boy's fragile emotional state persisted into adulthood, and Cecil's doctor prescribed a voyage to Australia, South Africa and New Zealand in 1851 when Cecil was 21 years old. At first things seemed no better since he was overcome by the physical demands of walking up Table Mountain in Cape Town, having to turn back with headaches and palpitations. By March 1852, after arriving in South Australia, Cecil seems to have picked up considerably, switching his energies from introspective theological readings to what was going on in his environment, and to be much more engaged in vigorous exercise, all of which were recorded in his journal, by that time a much "more lively" record.[371] Physical and nervous exhaustion had departed, at least for a while.

Cecil returned from his trip in May 1853 and immediately set about a career in Parliament, being elected without contest for the constituency of Stamford later in the year. His early impact in Parliament was undistinguished, and he had some difficulty with the stress of political life, as well as conflicts with his father. The 2nd Marquis had always been disappointed over Robert's lack of interest in "manly" pursuits, like hunting, shooting and contact sports: he had little time for the country rambles and botanical activities to which Robert was drawn. So in 1855 he created the opportunity for a military commission for his son. Shortly afterwards, Robert's health again broke down, and he wrote to his father:

> With my wretched health it is hardly enough that I can do this [prepare for a political career] as it is: with any other regular duties it will be impossible and must be abandoned.... It is the peculiarity of my complaint, that it lays me up and makes me incapable — sometimes for days — without any sort of warning; and that House of Commons work exposes me to these nervous attacks.

A second letter followed in which Cecil admitted his unsuitability for military duty, firmly declining his father's offer. His shocked father was left to rue the fact that Robert was prey to what he called "nerve storms" and, even worse, was willing to talk about them openly.[372]

The family doctor, Dr. Acland, was approached by Robert's father, and he wrote of Robert as follows:

> He was of a very weakly habit, incapable of great fatigue and prone to excessive nervous exhaustion; and as a consequence of these things he requires great care lest on the one hand he should be over-fatigued, or on the other, by too much yielding, be led into the habits and health of a hypochondriac.

Dr. Acland went on to express confidence that Robert was capable of making up his own mind as to what he could and could not do.[373]

While Robert achieved some mastery over what was called his "febrile" temperament, it was only partial, for he remained subject to "nerve storms" and "black glooms" throughout his life.[374] These attacks were characteristically precipitated by worry or exhaustion, and accompanied by depression of spirit and bodily lassitude.[375] A return to Eton many years later in connection with arranging his sons' education provoked an episode of depression, which was so bad that his wife insisted that she alone was to make all future trips to the school. By nature he was solitary and shy towards others, even to the point of reluctance in consulting his cabinet colleagues.[376] In keeping with this propensity, he disliked any public appearances, and loathed recognition or receiving compliments, the hallmarks of exaggerated social anxiety.[377] Short-sightedness was another problem which likely gave rise to much self-consciousness.

As with so many other prime ministers, grief made its impact. Salisbury's wife, Georgina, who had been the mainspring of his life and career, passed away in November 1899. It is said that he never recovered from this blow and that he resigned from office three years later broken-hearted.[378] There was also some evidence that for two years before her death Salisbury was overcommitted with the unusual duties of both prime minister and foreign secretary, positions which he held concurrently. In March 1898 there were rumors that he was suffering from depression and "brain fag," which rendered it impossible for Salisbury to maintain his dual roles. Five months later, Salisbury was described as a "tired Titan ... shadowed with grief."[379] His wife had undergone an operation, and her poor health dispirited the prime minister. It was thought that many of the foreign policy problems arose from conflict between Salisbury and Queen Victoria, who was unusually obstinate in a way which called to mind the behavior of her predecessor, King George III.

Offsetting Salisbury's neurotic tendencies was the strength he drew from deep religious convictions, his marriage and in directing his thoughts to public and political matters rather than his own problems.[380] Salisbury's life took a turn for the better when he became heir to the Marquisate on the death of his older brother in 1865; a happy home life and fulfillment from politics also lifted his spirits. In 1868, Robert's father died, leaving Robert as 3rd Marquis of Salisbury: the worst days were over, and there is no record of subsequent incapacitation from nervous breakdowns, although the tendencies were always there, such as a heightened sensitivity to noise and touch when he was exhausted, and being "subject for most of his life to severe mental depression," although just how severe was not made clear.[381] In old age he became obsessed by the belief that he had fallen short of his moral standards.

Disraeli paid tribute to Salisbury's courage when he said to Lady Gwendolen Cecil, "Your father is the only man of real courage that it has been my lot to work with."[382] Courage is a core aspect of resiliency, and it enables people to surmount many obstacles. Perhaps it helped Salisbury to overcome his tendency to depression, fear and weakness, and gave full play to his many talents as a statesman. It has been said that "the incalculables of his greatness are the disasters he averted from Britain and the whole human race by wise statesmanship. Disasters have come in plenty after his guiding hand had been removed."[383] Salisbury experienced repeated episodes of clinically significant depression and/or anxiety which diminished with age. They seem to have been worse in his childhood and teenage years, but one episode in his twenties was severe enough to require medical treatment. High levels of social anxiety were present, although it is doubtful whether he met criteria for social anxiety disorder. Despite these lifelong tendencies, Salisbury was able to either overcome or suppress them and achieve great success.

ARCHIBALD PHILIP PRIMROSE, 5TH EARL OF ROSEBERY (1847–1929) *(1894–1895)*

"Rosebery's government was quickly lurching from one mess to another, while the prime minister suffered a form of nervous breakdown, exacerbated by the morphine he took to cope with insomnia. Within 18 months he had departed."[384] Much was expected of Lord Rosebery, yet he proved to be a most ineffective leader. His story is one of squandered talent and wasted opportunity. How could a man, born with a silver spoon in his mouth, who lived in such splendor that even his wealthy friends were left in awe, have "blown it," as they say?

Childhood

Rosebery was born Archibald Philip Primrose and took the title of 5th Earl of Rosebery on his grandfather's death in 1868. His childhood was marked by the early death of his father when Rosebery was 3. Unfortunately, his mother, Lady Dalmeny, lacked any warmth towards her son, favoring instead Rosebery's younger brother Everard. Rosebery's father, in contrast, held great affection for Archie, and the little boy's grief upon his father's death lasted for several months. So severe and prolonged was the reaction that family members grew alarmed, but he finally recovered, albeit as a more reserved and sensitive child than he had been previously — traits that were to stay with him for the remainder of his life. After Lady Dalmeny remarried, Archie became even more reserved.[385]

Rosebery received little affection from his family except for the close bond with his sister Connie, who had also been rejected by their mother; Connie and Archie kept up a lifelong correspondence. Rosebery performed acceptably at Eton College and then Oxford University, which he left before graduating. His early departure from Oxford came about when he purchased a racehorse in violation of University rules and refused to give it up. Like Lord Derby, the turf became one of his great passions; but unlike Derby, Rosebery could boast successful ownership of three Derby winners.

Rosebery's Personality

A number of accounts offer insight into Rosebery's character and proneness to mood swings. As a child, Lady Dalmeny saw him to be "affectionate ... so sensitive that a harsh word throws him into a flood of tears ... nor is he, like his sisters, one instant crying, the next laughing — he is some time recovering from a burst of sorrow," a characteristic which remained for the rest of his life.[386]

Iremonger described Rosebery as "lame, inept and panic-stricken" in his love life.[387] She noted that, despite being a gifted speaker, he was tormented by nervousness before and during speeches, regardless of how successful they were. She characterized him as perverse, bad-tempered, solitary, aloof, and given to desolation as reflected in the following lines he wrote on his 28th birthday about the years ahead:

> The years to come that break upon thy dream
> How cold they glitter, like a grove of spears;
> How sharp their points, how sinister their gleam.

Other accounts mention his reticence, inconstancy, hesitancy, lack of stamina, haughtiness and self-doubt as a leader.[388] Rhodes James described the young Rosebery at age 25 as moody, cynical, apprehensive and indecisive. Yet he put on a good mask with his wit, erudition, aristocratic polish, good manners and apparent confidence, so that "the admiring audiences of his public speeches had no notion of the immense trouble and the mental anguish which had preceded these triumphs, nor of the acute nervousness — almost amounting to terror — with which he inwardly confronted a large gathering."[389] For one who has been described as "the most dazzling speaker of his era," this talent was purchased at a high cost, indicative of the anguish that sometimes lies beneath the smooth polish of compelling oratory.[390]

Mixed in with these character flaws was ambition to reach the top and a relish of power, which was offset by a proclivity to shrink from struggle. This tug of war, combined with his proud, sensitive and introspective nature, made him ill equipped to take advantage of the opportunity to lead his country. The question arises as to the origins of Rosebery's ambition. His friend Lord Hamilton wrote:

> R[osebery] has always been a puzzle to me, though probably I know him almost better than any one else.... My belief is — and Henry Primrose shares it — that R has a genuine dislike ... of public life; that he loves seclusion; that he is not really ambitious — whatever ambition he had was buried with his poor wife; that he has been totally unable to realise the importance of his own position; and that he thought his only chance of escaping finally from

public life was to cut himself adrift now, or else it would (or might) be never.[391]

Rosebery's wife was surely the dynamo in his political career, providing him with self-assurance and resources to compensate for his own deficiencies of character. As for Rosebery, his temperamental unsuitability for leadership was pithily expressed by Churchill: "Toughness when nothing particular was happening was not the form of fortitude in which he excelled."[392]

Career Highlights

Rosebery took his seat in the House of Lords in 1868 and aligned himself with Gladstone and the Liberal party. In 1881 he became undersecretary of state for Scotland but resigned in 1883 when he was persuaded that Gladstone would not devote adequate time to Scottish problems (Irish Home Rule taking much greater priority). After an extended period of travel in America and Australia, Rosebery returned to Britain and was appointed Lord Privy Seal and next, in 1886, foreign secretary in Gladstone's third administration. He was reappointed to this office in 1892 in Gladstone's fourth and final term. Rosebery became prime minister upon Gladstone's resignation in 1894 after the Irish Home Rule Bill had again been defeated in the House of Lords. The new prime minister immediately antagonized his party in his first speech by advocating an imperialist policy and shelving the question of Irish Home Rule, which, in his opinion, should be determined at England's convenience. This went against all that Gladstone had worked for on behalf of Irish independence and was a most unwise move, since the Liberal party depended on the support of Irish Members of Parliament to stay in power. Rosebery was unable to control his fractious colleagues and failed to build any meaningful consensus. Effective legislation became difficult, and in July 1895 his party suffered the largest electoral defeat in British history. Thus came to a quick end Rosebery's "transient and embarrassed" leadership, which was summed up by Tacitus' phrase *"capax imperii, nisi imperasset"*—he was worthy of the empire until he became emperor.[393]

How could a man who showed so much promise, and who was targeted by Gladstone and others for future leadership, have been such a failure? Gladstone himself offered three assessments of Rosebery following his defeat in 1895:

    i. He is one of the very ablest men I have ever known.
    ii. He is of the highest honour and probity.
    iii. I do not know whether he really has common sense.[394]

What could this lack of "common sense" be all about? Much of the explanation must lie in Rosebery's personality and anxiety, and the complicating factors of severe, unresolved, grief.

Evidence for Mental Illness

Rosebery suffered from sleep problems and depressive tendencies long before the loss of his wife. In 1880, following an attack of scarlet fever, he went into a 6-month period of fatigue ("prostration") and inability to take part in public life. In his words, he endured a state of "complete depression and exhaustion." He also wrote to Mrs. Gladstone about insomnia, the first time he is known to have made reference to this complaint. The prime minister thought Rosebery was "low about himself." For these problems he received medical care, being prescribed rest and avoidance of official duties.

In 1882 he renovated an old castle (Barnbougle) to serve as a private retreat on the Firth of Forth, where the "stillness of the waters were conducive to sleep." He would repair alone to Barnbougle to be among his books, while his wife and children would remain in nearby Dalmeny Castle.[395] Although insomnia was present from time to time in his early life, this was mild compared to its intensity after the premature death in 1890 of his wife, Hannah, from typhoid fever and renal failure.

At the time of their marriage in 1878, Hannah was believed to be the wealthiest woman in Britain as heiress to the de Rothschild fortune. Hannah was devoted to her husband and was his main driving force. Although her money was one factor, it was arguably of lesser significance than her emotional support and ability to read people, politics and opportunity better than her husband. Her energy in the Midlothian campaign was a good example, and this successful re-launching of Gladstone back onto the political scene may have been one of the first stage-managed, media-crafted manipulations of public opinion in modern democratic politics. Without Hannah, it is doubtful if Rosebery could have carried off this campaign successfully.

Rhodes James observed, "It is impossible to exaggerate the shattering effect which [the Countess'] death had on Rosebery."[396] It was the greatest personal tragedy of his life, and he never recovered from it. His friends were shocked at the deep depression which set in and from which he was slow to recover, just as his mother had noted when, as a child, he would experience sorrow. Even in an age which indulged in prolonged elaborate mourning rituals, Rosebery's behavior seems excessive, as witnessed by the ways in which he perpetuated the memory of his deceased wife. For some years he insisted that his children be dressed in black, and for the remaining 39 years of his long life, Rosebery conducted his correspondence on black-bordered notepaper. As with Miss Havisham in *Great Expectations*, life in many ways came to a standstill when Rosebery lost his spouse. Like the jilted Miss Havisham, who stopped the clocks just prior to her wedding once she realized that marriage was not to be, and continued wearing her wedding dress for the rest of her days, Rosebery stopped his emotional clock when his wife died and never accepted the reality of life without his partner. Hannah's bedroom remained exactly as it was when she was alive, never being occupied again, and he would from time to time add books to her library until his death. Hannah's death "drastically accentuated the gloomy — indeed, almost morbid — side of Rosebery's nature" and "revived his love of solitude ... it effectively destroyed what ambitions he had ever possessed."[397] In October 1891 he wrote, "The sole object of my ambition has disappeared with the death of my wife."[398] During 1891 and 1892, Rosebery's insomnia became a serious problem, along with more general depression. He withdrew from life, had little to do with his friends, and, as late as 1894, wrote that he had not dined out for four years and thought he would never do so.

By 1892 he had partially recovered, at least to the point of returning to office, and a colleague noted him to have "recovered his usual spirits.... He is still restless ... but he is again alert, ready and *suivi*." On the surface, Rosebery appeared competent in handling meetings and delivering speeches, but in fact he was not well — indecision, unhappiness, and constant insomnia haunted him. He was still having numerous dreams of Hannah, which contributed to further melancholy and suggests a prolonged grief reaction, by now 2 years in duration. In 1895 he confided that unremitting insomnia made him think about suicide as an option.[399]

Rosebery pressed on, despite persistent depression. Not only did people fail to grasp the full extent of his psychological problems, but, mindful of his box-office drawing power, they still acclaimed him as Gladstone's heir apparent; he was viewed as a political moderate who could bring his party back to the center after prolonged squabbles and splits over dogma.[400] As it turned out, he left a devastating legacy and bore considerable blame for his party's eventual demise as a major force.

Prime ministerial burdens proved beyond Rosebery, and his health declined further, reaching its lowest point in his long life (except for the final days forty years later). So bad was his insomnia that he took to carriage rides at night through the London parks. His doctor prescribed morphine on a regular basis, and there is some evidence that he also took cocaine, at that time an acceptable drug. Yet a third drug, sulphonal, was given. Sulphonal is an alcohol derivative which tends to work slowly and produce side effects the next day, such as drowsiness, dizziness, unsteadiness and mental side effects.

Davenport-Hines wrote:

> The Earl of Rosebery relied on sulphonal to cope with the strains of being prime minister.... If he takes "Sulfonell," he sleeps fairly well; and he is much less depressed.... Later he seems to have used cocaine to enliven his public appearances. "Rosebery made rather a curious speech the other day in the

House of Lords," Lord George Hamilton gossiped. "I am informed, by those who watch him, that the impression is he takes some drug before speaking, which makes him brilliant for the moment, but exceptionally flabby and invertebrate for the remainder of the day. He has got very big, and looks very much like the fat boy in Pickwick."[401]

Drug-taking was clearly out of hand and, for all that it enabled him to get through his speeches, did him no good. Like other leaders (e.g., Lord North and U.S. President Taft), Rosebery may have also coped with stress by overeating.

Devoid of self-confidence, he would lose his way during speeches, stumble over his lines, and even fall into silence mid-speech. Such lapses could be attributed either to his underlying depression or to the side effects of drugs. Who knows how the stew of sulphonal, cocaine and perhaps morphine would affect his speeches? He would suffer as long as three weeks without proper sleep. His doctors worried that he might die and were not averse to prescribing ever higher doses of morphine in hopes of giving him the sleep he lacked. His conduct in office was at times strange, as, for example, during the 1895 general election when he took an extended yachting trip in the Scottish islands.

A *cause célèbre* erupted in 1895 which lead to allegations of Rosebery's homosexuality. In the trial of Oscar Wilde, who had conducted an affair with Lord Alfred Douglas, an accusation was made that Rosebery's government was hounding Wilde to cover up the prime minister's supposed homosexuality. Although the best research offers no good basis for the allegations, the attacks on his name were additional stresses for a man who could barely keep things together.

Rosebery's political career essentially came to an end with his electoral defeat in 1895 and resignation as Liberal party leader in 1896. Although attempts were made at political revival, either by Rosebery or by others, they amounted to little, and he came to be known as the "Flying Dutchman" of politics, a ghostly vessel floating about the ocean without anchor or port.[402] Even in less demanding tasks than those he faced as prime minister he was unable to meet the challenge. In 1907, for example, he chaired a select committee to address reform of the House of Lords, and in the discharge of this duty he was physically unequal to the moderate workload, liable to fits of discouragement, hypersensitive to criticism and unable to keep his fellow committee members focused — in short, he "made a very bad chairman."[403] Yet as late as 1916, Lloyd George and King George V were keen for Rosebery to join the cabinet, but he declined the offer.[404]

Fate had another cruel blow in store for Rosebery when, on November 17, 1917, his son Niall was killed by a stray bullet, the last shot fired after Turkish troops had surrendered their position near Gaza. Niall had been particularly close to Rosebery, and the loss was devastating. One year later Rosebery suffered a stroke from which he made a full recovery of his mental faculties but not of his physical health. As he grew older, he "sunk in sad and silent meditations," according to John Buchan.[405] His health declined and he entered a coma on May 20, 1929, dying on the next day. His last wish was to hear the music of the Eton Boating Song, a song which reminded him of his schooldays — the gramophone record was played, but it is not thought that he was able to hear it. Thus came to an end the life of a man who, in the words of Bernard Shaw, "never missed a chance of missing an opportunity."

The Paradox

For a man so unsuited to political leadership, it is puzzling that Rosebery set his sights on supreme political office, even more so since he had no need to seek an income. No doubt this was partly determined by a strong family tradition of public service and his own education at Eton and Oxford. He must have considered himself equipped to deal with the stresses and strains of politics. His skills in communicating and his talents as an orator turned him into an inspirational icon, and the public acclaim and hero-worship which he received would be reinforcing. Although a great deal has been made of Hannah's ambitions on behalf of her husband, it is more likely that she adopted Rosebery's aspirations and helped put them into practice more effectively than he could have done alone. After her death, Rosebery's personality and mental condition were not up to the task — his isolated, aloof manner shut him off from other potential sources of strength, including the possibility of remarriage. In his impacted grief he could never move on. What was left was a man of great vulnerability: over-sensitive to criticism, unable to consult others or work towards consensus, moody, and racked by severe lack of sleep. Depressive withdrawal could last for months or years, and there are hints of excessive anxiety (for example, when it came to giving speeches) as well as hypochondriasis. All of these problems would shake his confidence and make for a heavier burden of office, which he accepted without conviction. The prescription of addictive drugs that produce untoward psychological side effects created a new set of problems and rendered him an even less effective prime minister. It is perhaps fortunate that there were no major world crises during the administration of this incompetent and jingoistic leader: his impact on the yet-to-come Boer War was minimal, and by the time of World War I he was a spent force.

Shortly before he died, Rosebery offered his own interesting explanation of where he went wrong — he put it down to hubris.[406] While he might not stand out as one of the more obvious examples of this character trait, it is rare for a hubristic person to actually acknowledge it. Perhaps he was in some ways correct, and his tendencies in that direction would not have served him well in the long run.

ARTHUR BALFOUR (1848–1930), 1ST EARL OF BALFOUR *(1902-1905)*

Arthur Balfour was born in Scotland on July 25, 1848. His father was a Scottish Member of Parliament, and his mother, Lady Blanche Gascoyne-Cecil, was the daughter of 2nd Marquis of Salisbury and brother to Robert Cecil, the 3rd Marquis. Balfour was therefore nephew to the man who immediately preceded him in office and owed much to his uncle for the progress of his own career. It has been said that the phrase "Bob's your uncle" derives from the Marquis having paved the way for his nephew to succeed him as leader. Balfour therefore "had it made."

Balfour: A Man of Many Parts

Balfour is well known for the 1917 Balfour Declaration in which, as foreign secretary, he laid out the blueprint for today's state of Israel. Other more unusual aspects of Balfour's life bear mention. For example, it is rare for a prime minister to have studied parapsychology or to have served as president of the Society of Psychical Research (SPR), which is dedicated to showing that humans survive death. It is also unusual for a prime minister to have written seminal books on theology, but these achievements also belong to Balfour's curriculum vitae. He enjoyed a long association with the SPR as vice-president between 1882 and 1892, as president from 1892 to 1895, and again as vice-president from 1895 to 1930. An interest in spiritualism ran in his family, for his brother was president of the SPR from 1906 to 1907. Balfour conducted many psychic "sittings" with a Mrs. Willett.[407] As to his theological and philosophical writings, he authored at least four books, of which *The Foundations of Belief*, written in 1895, was widely read and highly regarded. He was invited to deliver the prestigious Gifford Lectures in 1914, and these lectures, entitled *Theism and Humanism*, remain in print today. The renowned 20th century theologian C.S. Lewis acknowledged that Balfour's second Gifford Lectures, *Theism and Thought*, were for him among the most influential books.[408]

In 1904, Balfour was elected president of the British Association for the Advancement of Science. Scientific and medical research continued to be important causes to Balfour, who, as Lord President in 1926, did much to provide funding for the newly formed Medical Research Council, an organization which today is among the chief funding sources of medical research in the United Kingdom.

Balfour as Politician

Balfour was first elected to Parliament at the age of 26 and eleven years later accepted office as chief secretary for Ireland in his uncle's cabinet. Salisbury subsequently appointed him leader of the House of Commons. Upon his uncle's resignation, Balfour became prime minister and served in this capacity from July 1902 to December 1905. Among the achievements of his administration were the passage of the Irish Land Purchase Act, which made it easier for tenants to purchase land, and active cooperation with President Roosevelt to settle the Russo-Japanese War. He worked effectively to shore up national defense by establishing and chairing a Defense Committee. On the education front, his administration saw passage of the Education Act, which provided state aid for voluntary schools, as well as establishing a number of new universities.[409] Because of his failure to maintain party unity over fiscal affairs, he resigned from office in December 1905. However, he was far from finished with politics and held many important posts over the next 20 years, including foreign secretary between 1916 and 1919. In 1921 he represented Great Britain at the Naval Limitation Conference, and in 1925 joined Stanley Baldwin's cabinet, a post he held until 1929. He was ennobled as Earl Balfour in 1922.

Balfour's Personality and Mental Health

Balfour never recovered from the death of his fiancée, May Littleton, from typhoid fever in 1875, and he remained a bachelor his whole life. He acquired a progressively more chilling distance from others, estranging himself from many of his former friends, and was known for being unusually aloof.[410] It was also after May's death that he became interested in spiritualism.

Others described him as languid, sparing in his energy, and late to rise from sleep. Yet underneath was considerable inner strength, and he was an ardent tennis and golf player (he even wrote a chapter called *The Humours of Golf*).[411]

As a young man, Balfour was very sensitive and "inclined towards sentimentalism and even hysteria," which changed into callousness and self-control as he grew older.[412] Begbie wrote, "In public he is ready to shake the whole world by the hand, almost to pat it on the shoulder, but in private he is careful to see that the world does not enter even the remotest of his lodge gates."[413] Lloyd George likened his place in history to "the scent on a pocket handkerchief," and Iremonger referred to the "lunar desolation" of a soul which refused to totally commit itself publicly or privately to anyone or anything.[414]

As with many other future leaders who were educated at Eton, Balfour was unhappy there, being solitary and not strong enough to play football, while weak eyesight excused him from cricket. According to Iremonger, during his thirties, Balfour was "plunged into horrible depressions or oppressed by a sense of failure and poisonous self-doubt."[415] Of the grief he experienced after May's death, note has been made. He was again to undergo prolonged grief when his brother Frank died in a mountaineering accident in 1881, leading to a reaction of "black depression" which persisted for at least 2 years.[416] Beyond this we have no further details of major psychiatric illness; thus we conclude that Balfour may have experienced at least two periods of depression related to grief, from which he recovered, and which seem not to have compromised him as a politician.

SIR HENRY CAMPBELL-BANNERMAN (1836–1908) *(1905–1908)*

Sir Henry Campbell-Bannerman was born (as Henry Campbell) and raised in Scotland, where his father was a prominent businessman and local politician. "CB," as he was known later in life, became a partner in the family firm, was elected to Parliament as member for the Stirling District Burghs in 1868 and continued to serve that constituency until his death in 1908. Between 1899 and 1908 he was leader of the Liberal Party. Upon Balfour's resignation in 1905, CB took office and received a Royal Warrant giving his appointment the official title of prime minister, although this term had long been used informally without ever being officially sanctioned. Until then, the "official" names had been first lord or first minister of the treasury.

CB was 69 when he became prime minister. In office he was regarded as undistinguished, lackadaisical, reactive and ill-focused in relations with his cabinet — genial, unenergetic and a non-thruster.[417] Perhaps his major achievements were holding together a party which had been in danger of splitting, promoting reconciliation in South Africa after the Boer War and paving the way for the great Liberal Party reforms and votes for women.[418]

Campbell-Bannerman's Health

Campbell-Bannerman was seriously troubled by cardiac disease during the latter part of his term, suffering a number of heart attacks after the death of his wife in 1906. It is believed that his poor health was brought about by a mixture of physical and mental stresses. During this time, government could only continue because CB delegated heavily to Asquith, who served as unofficial prime minister.[419]

There is no evidence of mental illness before his premiership, but the peculiar relationship between CB and his wife Charlotte in all probability affected his abilities as prime minister. It has been said that her ambitions for him far exceeded his own ambitions, so he may never have reached that height without her drive.[420] Campbell-Bannerman's relationship towards Charlotte has been described as "uxorious," and there was a clear and pathological degree of mutual dependency for this childless couple.[421] Charlotte Campbell-Bannerman is reputed to have been chronically depressed.[422] She was described as

> a shy woman who suffered from ill-health for most of her life.... As a result of her illness [probably diabetes] she was overweight and this exacerbated her lack of self-confidence and dislike of London society.... She was heavily dependent on her husband, but her influence over him was considerable; he often referred to her as his 'higher authority'.... Throughout their lives they were inseparable companions.... When she became critically ill she would not be nursed by anyone except her husband. He exhausted himself sitting with her during the nights, although he had his duties as prime minister. CB was broken by her death in 1906 and he died just over a year later.[423]

Iremonger asserts that Charlotte was exacting, possessive and a great drain on the strength CB needed to fulfill his public duties.[424] She writes:

> Henry continually sacrificed the nation's business to her convenience, spending three months every year in Scotland and two abroad, to Marienbad, where she went annually for cures. He would refuse to return if the crossing was too rough for her, and public engagements, Cabinet meetings, and late business in the House suffered from his unusual sense of priorities.

The Party Whips would be exasperated when meetings had to be cancelled or postponed at the last minute on account of Charlotte's illness.[425] He saw her as having infallible judgment.[426] During Charlotte's terminal illness, CB spent 6 months sitting up at night tending to her needs. Charlotte insisted her bedroom door always be kept open so that Henry could respond to her (incessant) calls. CB bore a degree of guilt over his behavior and in July 1906 wrote to the king, "I have deeply felt for some time the neglect of my duty implied in my absence day after day. My wife however is so ill and weak that I cannot leave her for long. I am profoundly sensible it is not right."[427]

When Charlotte died on August 30, 1906, her husband was "not only miserable, but absolutely broken, far more broken than I realized at the time," according to his private secretary. For a while he even considered stepping down from office but recovered sufficiently to continue. While CB put on a brave face and welcomed the distraction of conversations and walks with friends, he would at times be found upstairs by his private secretary with his head in his hands, sobbing. In Spender's words, while he "bore himself bravely, he was nevertheless mortally stricken and the seeds of his own fatal illness were sown."[428] Five weeks later CB had the first of several heart attacks and on April 22, 1908, died at 10 Downing Street, two weeks after resigning office. It is Iremonger's view that CB died of grief, and Asquith, in his tribute to Campbell-Bannerman, referred to the sad domestic trial which darkened his days and dealt what proved to be a fatal blow.[429] The medical diagnosis was "blood pressure combined with cardiac asthma, and liability to develop rather alarming symptoms owing to his constitution having been undermined."[430]

Five months a year away from work, and the keeping of strange hours when he was at home, all on behalf of his ailing wife whose judgment he thought was infallible: hardly an auspicious recipe for good leadership of one's country, and it is no surprise that CB is seen as "lackadaisical" and "unenergetic." Following Charlotte's death, his grief was overwhelming and terminal. The best psychiatric term to use might be "adjustment disorder unspecified" (coded as 309.9 in DSM-IV), incorporating elements of a "partner relational problem" (V61.8 in DSM-IV) and "bereavement" (coded as V62.82).[431]

HERBERT HENRY ASQUITH, 1ST EARL OF OXFORD AND ASQUITH (1852–1928) *(1908–1916)*

Asquith served as Liberal prime minister from 1908 to 1916. He was born into a middle-class family but eventually married into wealth through his second wife, Margot Tennant. His career has been described as "one of almost unbroken success from his schooldays onwards ... and now [at the beginning of 1912] for the past three and a half years prime minister of England in a period of immense difficulty, stress and strain which he had surmounted with extraordinary adroitness."[432] It was Asquith's misfortune to preside over his country when World War I broke out, as his talents were more suited to times of peace than of war, and ultimately, in 1916, he gave way to Lloyd George.

Asquith graduated from Oxford, established a successful practice as junior barrister and then entered politics as member of Parliament for East Fife in 1886. Gladstone was impressed with the young Asquith and in 1892 offered him the post of home secretary, which he held until 1895. His party was then out of power for 10 years, during which time Asquith returned to his law practice while remaining as a member of Parliament. Another opportunity to return to the Cabinet came in 1906 when the Liberals were returned to office and Campbell-Bannerman offered Asquith the post of chancellor of the exchequer. Campbell-Bannerman died in 1908, leaving Asquith as his successor.

Asquith's administrations were known for reforms such as the Old Age Pension Act, the Finance Bill, which achieved a degree of wealth redistribution, and the 1911 Parliament Act, which curbed the power of the House of Lords. Much of the foundation for the welfare state was laid down by his government. He also moved along the process of Irish home rule, although its establishment was delayed by the outbreak of World War I. In the early phase of the war, Asquith for a while appeared to enjoy some success as a leader, but with the accumulation of problems and internecine squabbling, he decided to form a coalition government.[433] Difficulties arose, including a failure to anticipate the Irish Easter Rising, problems with conscription, shortages of shells, the disastrous Dardanelles campaign and catastrophic losses at the Somme offensive. His leadership was increasingly questioned by the opposition Conservative Party. In December 1916 his erstwhile colleague Lloyd George split and, following Asquith's resignation, formed a new administration with the Conservatives. Asquith retained his seat until the 1918 election, when he failed to gain re-election. In 1920 he was returned for the Paisley constituency, only to lose his seat again in 1924. In 1925 he was elevated to the peerage as Earl of Oxford and Asquith, and remained leader of the Liberal party until 1926, when he was replaced by Lloyd George. In the last years of his life Asquith wrote a number of books to provide income to himself and his family. He died in 1928, having seen his once dominant party exit forever from the stage of British politics as a meaningful force.

Asquith's upbringing is notable for the fact that his father died when he was 8 years old, and "effective family life perished with him."[434] For three years the Asquiths continued to live in Yorkshire in modest circumstances, with Asquith's mother becoming a chronic invalid. At the age of 11 he was sent to live with an uncle in London in order to attend school there. In 1870 he won a scholarship to Oxford and later became president of the Oxford Union.

Mental Illness in the Family

At the age of 25, Asquith married his first wife, Helen Melland, who bore him four sons and a daughter. Helen died from typhoid in 1891, but Asquith had already started an affair with Margot Tennant, whom he eventually married in 1894 and who bore him two more children. Many of his children achieved success, two becoming peers and one a leading film director, yet almost all of his seven children experienced mental illness. Raymond, the oldest son, was subject to the depression "from which all of Helen Asquith's children suffered at times of stress in their lives."[435] Asquith's second son, Herbert ("Beb"), developed shell shock, from which he never recovered. Problems with alcohol then supervened, and by 1937 Beb was no longer able to continue work as a writer. A third son, Arthur ("Oc"), received severe wounds in battle and never recovered from either the physical or mental strain of war.[436] Violet (Bonham-Carter) went through at least one episode of prolonged insomnia, "hysteria" and barbiturate overdose, and was described as being emotionally unstable.[437] From Asquith's second marriage, his daughter Elizabeth and son Anthony ("Puff") both became alcoholics. Elizabeth's drinking ruined her health. Puff, a famous film director, went through a 6-year period of excessive alcohol intake and was laid low from his work by this problem for at least two years.

Asquith's Problems with Alcohol

The fact that all his children suffered from some type of mental illness would suggest that Asquith himself would be a prime candidate for psychiatric disorder, as indeed is the case. The man who never went by any constant name at home, being variously called Herbert, Henry and H. H. Asquith, is best known to posterity by the uncomplimentary name of "Squiff," in reference to his liking for alcohol (from Asquith derives the colloquialism "squiffy" to describe the state of inebriety). Iremonger also sees him as prone to deep depression.[438]

Was Asquith an alcoholic by today's standards? In other words, would he have met the criteria for alcohol abuse or alcohol dependence? For alcohol abuse, drinking must lead recurrently to one or more of the following: failure to fulfill major obligations (e.g., poor work performance related to alcohol), putting self or others at risk (e.g., being drunk while conducting business), legal problems, or social or family problems due to drinking. Asquith most probably would have met this criterion, even though one biographer believed that Asquith was never an alcoholic, largely based on the fact that his alcohol intake was less than that of Churchill, a very high threshold indeed![439] But Clifford reports that Asquith would regularly drink to cope with the strain of the many crises attendant on his job, and by such drinking he had abused his body for years. To the point at issue, for several years friends were concerned that his drinking problem was "serious."[440] His close associate, Haldane, warned Asquith in 1904 about his champagne consumption. In 1907 he was described as "a character deteriorated ... by the free use of wine which he cannot carry." In 1909 another colleague observed that Asquith has "been drinking during the last week or two pretty hard." Churchill commented in 1911 that Asquith's performance in the House of Commons was best before dinner, "— but thereafter..." suggesting a decline in Parliamentary performance after his dinnertime drinking. Indeed, Churchill's comments came on the heels of an episode when Asquith appeared on the front bench too drunk to speak in a debate about the Parliament Bill. It is likely that this was no isolated incident, since Asquith had a reputation for swaying on his feet in the Commons.[441]

The personal and professional stresses on Asquith in 1911 were considerable. Family worries stemmed from the fragile emotional state and depressions of his wife Margot and daughter Violet. On the national front, Asquith had to contend with fierce struggles over the budget, House of Lords reform, Irish home rule, suffragette demands and miners' strikes. In this setting, a family friend who had lunched with Asquith wrote to her sister: "The PM kind, extremely cordial — but how he is changed! Red and bloated — quite different from what he used to be. He gave me a shock. They all talk of his overeating and drinking too much. I am afraid there is no doubt about it."[442] In fact, during April 1911 his doctor had already ordered him to substantially reduce his alcohol intake, yet by October he was still drinking heavily or in ways which were injurious, and some years later he was still drinking to excess. One anecdote describes Asquith downing several large glasses of brandy on a visit to Field Marshal Haig at HQ in France in 1916, then becoming unsteady, yet still able to keep a clear head, read the map and discuss the war situation.[443]

Given the evidence that colleagues felt it necessary to address his drinking over a seven-year period, and that he appeared drunk and incoherent for a Parliamentary debate, it's likely that Asquith would qualify for one of the four criteria. There is always the risk that uncomplimentary judgments about a politician's drinking are motivated by partisan interests. While there was an element of this in Asquith's case, it is not an adequate explanation. Similarly, while the argument can be made that Parliamentary life was, to an extent, a "culture of booze,"[444] it would merely serve to facilitate the abuse of alcohol "on the job" by those prone to such problems. This culture has undergone considerable change in the last 30 years. One MP said that members "used to be capable of drinking a bottle of wine over lunch but those occasions are now rare. Annie's Bar used to be full very often but now I'm sure half of the members don't even know where it is." Another politician stated, "The big drinking days of MPs have gone. I think that's good for democracy — it's not good for tired and emotional MPs to be voting on policy."[445] This was just as true in Asquith's day as it is now.

Romantic attachment to Venetia Stanley enabled Asquith to reduce his intake of alcohol, and by 1914 it was observed that all he took for dinner was a whisky and soda and glass of port.[446] Thus, when in 1914 and 1915 Asquith's government passed a series of Acts to restrict access to alcohol where it could possibly undermine the war effort, at least he could keep his conscience clean![447] However, he was again drinking copiously in 1916.

Raymond Asquith's Death and Its Effect on His Father

With his tendency to depression, one particular experience shook Asquith in ways which are hard to measure, yet left an enduring mark.[448] In January 1915 his oldest son, Raymond, enlisted for part-time service in the Queens Westminster Rifles. Feeling the need to make a bigger contribution to the war effort, and despite family opposition, he applied for, and received, a commission with the Grenadier Guards in July of that year. He was sent to France, where he saw action at the front and, on September 15, 1916, was fatally shot at Delville Wood while leading his men over the parapet in the face of enemy fire.

Raymond's death hit Asquith hard. The man who, as prime minister, could survive relentless attacks from the press, who could conduct a war, who could ride through the conflicts of Commons and Lords, Catholic and Protestant, and party infighting, did not have it in him to cope with the loss of his son. This event broke him.[449] Lloyd George wrote that the loss of Raymond "shattered his nerve ... came upon him with stunning effect, and he visibly reeled under the blow."[450] Ten weeks after Raymond's death, this normally stoical man was observed by his wife to weep in the privacy of his bedroom every day.[451] By the end of 1916, "his long premiership had worn him out; he had grown a little careless, even about governmental crises."[452]

By late 1916, in Cabinet meetings Asquith was becoming indecisive, indifferent, distractible and preoccupied with other matters.[453] Sometimes he would even be absent from critically important Cabinet sessions. He had become tired and weary, burned out by incessant stress, which "only a man with Asquith's iron constitution could have stood [the strain] so long." Riddell goes on to write, "Then in September 1916, came the death in action of his brilliant son, Raymond, to whom he was so devoted. It was a terrible blow to Asquith, upon whom ... it left an indelible scar. Such a tragic loss had inevitably a most unfavorable effect upon his capacity to carry on the Government."[454] A number of opponents, including some from within his party, had long sought to remove Asquith from the leadership. When he was at his most vulnerable he succumbed to the sharks circling in for the kill, and on December 5 submitted his resignation. Asquith's Liberal Party rival Lloyd George was appointed successor.

We have little information as to the precise clinical picture of Asquith's grief, but it was widely acclaimed as the "straw which broke the camel's back." It can be presumed that he made some level of recovery to the extent of being re-elected to Parliament, as well as writing his memoirs. But he was perceived in 1920 and 1921 as tired, uninterested and not meaning business. All agreed that Asquith was never the same after losing Raymond, and a visible slackening of his will was noted by his son Cyril. He had been deserted by his former allies in Parliament, and by turning on Lloyd George, he was to be censured by his own party, being saved from more humiliation when he had a stroke. Asquith himself said after Raymond's death that all pride he had in the past and hope for the future had largely been invested in him, and that "now all of that is gone."[455]

Summary

Herbert Asquith undoubtedly had an alcohol-related problem that affected him in his work. His friends, family and doctor were concerned; he was asked to sharply reduce drinking yet was unsuccessful in doing so. We do not know whether alcohol affected him in a gross sense, as it may have done for Harold Wilson, but there is always the possibility that his judgment was adversely affected, despite Haig's assurances to the contrary. In trying times he was far from the top of his game. He did not rise well to the challenges of wartime leadership but achieved more in peacetime. He was beset by personal stress, mental illness in his children, and profound grief, and after 1916 was burned out.

DAVID LLOYD GEORGE, 1ST EARL OF DWYFOR (1863–1945) *(1916–1922)*

As the "man who won the war," David Lloyd George was a legend in his time. After World War I, the "Prime Minister of Europe" was seen as a heroic figure "in a way without parallel in the long roll of British Premiers."[456] Lloyd George was "clearly one of the makers of the modern world," and his legacy was far-reaching."[457] Yet he suffered a slow, terminal decline from exalted power in mid-career, while remaining in Parliament for another 20 years.

Lloyd George subordinated all other causes to his omnipotence, and by virtue of his ruthlessness and single-mindedness was successful in achieving this goal, but could not hold on to it for long.[458] For his flair, combativeness, and unashamed pursuit of power at all costs, he has few rivals. In many respects he can be compared with Winston Churchill; but of the two, Lloyd George "was more fun," while Churchill "was perhaps the greater man," according to Lord Beaverbrook.[459] He reached the peak of his achievements during and shortly after World War I, but for another quarter century was a man without a party, excluded from any major political office yet always managing to stay in the news. Some have seen this as the inevitable nemesis which afflicts those who, like Lloyd George, "commit the crime of arrogance" and who "fell and never rose again"—the payback for hubris.[460]

Lloyd George almost certainly suffered from mild to moderate mental illness, with Post even judging him to have "marked" psychopathology.[461] Ludwig believed that he suffered from depression, while Iremonger referred to Lloyd George's tendency to develop stress-related psychosomatic illness and recurrent depressions.[462]

Did Lloyd George Suffer from Depression?

The period between late 1912 and early 1913 was a low point in his life, and persistent depression seems to have occurred following the Marconi shares scandal in 1913. At around the same time, his long-standing marital difficulties were exacerbated when he began a relationship with his daughter's tutor, Frances Stevenson, which lasted for the rest of his life and lead eventually to Frances becoming his second wife.[463]

Hard on the heels of problems in his personal life, Lloyd George unadvisedly invested in stock with the American Marconi company. The manner in which he acquired this stock at favorable rates from the attorney general, Sir Rufus Isaacs, whose brother had sold them the shares, made many people uneasy. The British government was at the time negotiating a profitable deal with the British arm of Marconi to build telegraph stations throughout the Empire. Naturally, Lloyd George's actions gave rise to possible serious impropriety, and a formal enquiry ensued. Lloyd George escaped punishment (mainly because the committee of enquiry hewed to party lines), but his reputation was damaged and the whole experience took a big emotional toll. Owen said of Lloyd George:

> He fretted, talked of little else, would suddenly break off conversation on other matters and walk away, or stand in moody silence, brooding on the shadow that had fallen across his life.... He needed every one of them [his friends and secretaries].... He lost weight, lost vitality, fell ill again, and his black hair grew grey, the lines began to mark his face.... A great life poised on the edge.[464]

These symptoms lasted for several months, but by his acquittal in late summer of 1913, Lloyd George had found his feet and was "in a dangerous mood and looking for trouble."[465]

Other periods of depression occurred, such as in 1922.[466] By contrast, Owen gives Lloyd George a clean bill of health during his term as prime minister, at least as far as depression is concerned, but other, less severe episodes of distress may have occurred during this time.[467]

Depression followed the sudden death of his young daughter Mair in 1907. Lloyd George's grief was so severe that it "almost destroyed him," and his secretary, Willie Clark, was worried about the possibility of suicide. This grief reaction was severe, if short-lived, although certain aspects of it never went away.[468] In her diaries, Frances Stevenson expressed a belief that she supplanted Mair and helped Lloyd George (whom she referred to at the time as "C") to thereby cope with his grief. She writes:

> It is just two years since C. & I were "married," and our love seems to increase rather than diminish. He says I have taken the place somewhat of Mair, "my little girl whom I lost" as he always calls her. He says I remind him of her & make up a little for her loss. I always wanted to make this loss a little lighter to him, and he seems now to be able to speak of her with less pain than he used to.[469]

Lloyd George's Neuritis: Was It Psychosomatic?

More difficult to evaluate are the numerous physical symptoms which affected Lloyd George at times of stress, and for which his doctor, Lord Dawson, would prescribe rest cures. One of the earliest of these attacks struck him in 1896 when he was the subject of public contumely for his (unsuccessful) campaigning on behalf of the Cymru Fydd, a Welsh nationalist league. Following this defeat, perhaps compounded by financial problems and being named in a paternity suit, he suffered from nervous exhaustion, which became "a feature of his career at times of extreme crisis."[470]

Other similar episodes occurred. After 72 days of acrimonious debate over the Finance Bill in 1909, Lloyd George appeared with his arm in a sling, a victim of "neuritis." In 1911 even more bitter conflicts erupted over the health insurance bill, leading to an attack of "clergyman's throat," which gave rise to rumors of more serious illness, such as tuberculosis, a possibility which caused some degree of worry to Lloyd George. Although it exists in the International Classification of Diseases under the code number of 784.49, clergyman's throat is a rare diagnosis nowadays. It was regarded as an occupational disorder related to excessive speaking and "voice-strain," and was commonly believed to be an inflammatory condition of the throat in the 19th and early 20th century. However, at least one text noted that in its early stages it was "a purely nervous affection, being unattended with any organic change."[471] The condition was often accompanied by the feeling that a foreign body was present in the throat, a symptom not dissimilar to *globus hystericus*, which is sometimes found in anxiety or depression. We cannot be certain what caused Lloyd George's "clergyman's throat," falling as it does into a gray area between genuine organic change from overuse of his voice and psychological stress. Iremonger's account would suggest that speaking anxiety was more of a problem than we might suppose in this "Welsh magician of the silver tongue," who was known for his fiery oratory. On more than one occasion he was overcome with nerves before a speech, and he would refer to the coal dust in his throat. Once, quite late in his career, he buckled at the knees and was unable to rise to his feet to second a motion of condolence on the Belgian king's death. "His voice and throat often let him down."[472]

In 1913, Lloyd George was caught up in the Marconi affair and, as noted above, became depressed. In May of that year he attributed an attack of leg pain to his customary nervous reactions to stress, present since childhood.[473] An attack of neuritis took place in December 1916 around the time Lloyd George was appointed prime minister, and he had to retire to bed for a few days — a rather unusual way to celebrate such an achievement, to say the least.

During the disastrous battle of Passchendaele in September 1917, he once again succumbed to stress symptoms, as described by Jones.[474] Lloyd George treated his generals with contempt, while the generals distrusted their prime minister. Lloyd George's courage, according to Jones, "never fell lower than in these months," and he became "restless, agitated, wishing to close down the campaign in Flanders haunted by the mounting casualties, harassed by domestic politics and press criticism. On 6 September he went for a fortnight to his Welsh home in Criccieth, suffering from neuralgia."[475] While "neuralgia" now refers to pain caused by nerve damage or inflammation, in the past it carried a somewhat broader connotation — to embrace psychological problems — and would, perhaps, be a counterpart of today's terms for somatic ("physical") distress, such as fibromyalgia, conversion disorder, pain disorder or other somatoform disorder. Interestingly, in a detailed account of neurasthenia at the time, Burton-Fanning noted that pain, neuritis and throat symptoms were all associated with neurasthenia.[476]

In 1921, as he endured "one perplexity after another," and with "crises chasing each other like the shadows of clouds across the landscape — Miners, Unemployment, Repatriation, Silesia, and as always Ireland," he enjoined his friend Bonar Law to swap places with him. He went on to say, "I have had a temporary breakdown — at least Lord Dawson assures me — much to my disappointment it is only temporary...."[477] Here we see the great man actually hoping for more prolonged indisposition.

The next year, when Lloyd George was no more than a titular head of his coalition administration, and with his leadership now in danger, he wrote to Frances Stevenson, "It is difficult to rest with all these crises hurtling about your head. I have had today a return of those neuralgic pains that worried me."[478] Loss of prestige, loss of dignity and loss of control were all very real, and it was in this context that his neuralgia flared up.[479] Perhaps his illnesses were the expression of an inability to control the problems coming at him — quite the opposite of his blazing self-assurance which, a few years earlier, caused him to believe that only he could lead his country to victory. This interpretation finds agreement in the words of a contemporary, Lord Buckmaster, who wrote that Lloyd George was nowhere near as well as he claimed following his rest in Scotland: "Since 1919 ... it is remarkable to see what a change these few years have effected in the man. To me it seemed as though the inspiration he once possessed was gone and I found myself talking to a man uneasy in manner and trying rather to evade events rather than control them."[480]

In subsequent years he consulted with Sergei Voronoff, a controversial doctor who was blacklisted by most of his contemporaries. Among other things, Voronoff achieved notoriety for his claims about the rejuvenating effects of testicular transplants. He conducted many such operations, as well as prescribing a range of tonics, vitamins and the like. Lloyd George "was a willing recipient of [his] hormones and vitamins."[481]

Personality: Bipolar Features?

Lloyd George's personality has been described as "hypnotic ... he could charm a bird off the bough," "mercurial," "changeable," and "bullying."[482] He "did whatever it took to get his way," whether being "conciliatory, generous, seductive, and reasonable with colleagues; but, if that did not work, he could become furious, threatening, and vengeful. And when being frank and open did not bring about the desired results, he could be deceptive and manipulative."[483] While these traits may be found to some extent in many politicians, Lloyd George was more generously endowed in this regard. At his best, he was "a minister of astonishing capacity, speed of thought, and inspirational power," exemplified during his tenure at the Ministry of Munitions in 1915.[484] At other times, when he was beaten down by uncontrollable crises, he lacked vitality and was ready to hand over office to Bonar Law.

Iremonger drew attention to Lloyd George's extreme recklessness and how so many biographers were surprised that he could have so often risked so much for so little.[485] Lloyd George supposedly had multiple and indiscriminate extramarital affairs; in this regard his taste was "catholic," although Morgan doubts if it was quite so free ranging.[486] Nevertheless, his questionable judgment in these matters is surprising, as such behavior was quite against prevailing societal values, in particular the narrow-minded nonconformist "religious right" whom he represented. It had not been so long since the Irish politician Parnell was brought down for similar conduct.

In matters of money, Lloyd George showed poor judgment, most notably over the Marconi shares, and at other times in his life. Maybe this was due partly to his dislike of paperwork and inattention to financial detail.[487]

Jones remarks on how Lloyd George would begin the day "born fresh every morning. He would arrive in the Cabinet room with his batteries fully charged, with ideas which he wished discussed ... he issued a whirl of lightning instructions. Waking early, he had read the official memoranda and telegrams ... at his bedside, and had devoured the newspapers of all colours."[488] On becoming prime minister, he said he was the most miserable man on earth, but this gray mood was quickly replaced by frenetic activity which allowed him to say he had put a "month's work into yesterday" and that the king was "amazed" how quickly he had assembled his cabinet. But "later the strain of the transition told on him and for a few days he was ill."[489] Jones compares Lloyd George, in different ways, to Gladstone and Julius Caesar. Like Gladstone, he possessed an "untiring body subject to an unfailing will"; and like Caesar, he had "self-mastery, self-confidence, inexhaustible energy, intensely practical comprehensive genius."[490] To these comparisons may be added his ability to remain buoyant at the darkest hour, a characteristic which Lloyd George shared with Churchill and which is so important in a war leader.[491]

Conclusions

Lloyd George showed no clear features of fully formed bipolar disorder, but he did manifest some hypomanic qualities and changeable, "mercurial" moods; cyclothymic personality may best account for these patterns. In other words, he belongs to the bipolar disorder spectrum, even without convincing attacks of hypomania. On at least one occasion he experienced a prolonged depressive reaction, as well as several other shorter ones. The etiology of his neuritis, neuralgia and clergyman's throat are uncertain, but their relation to stress was considered to be strong, and several episodes were severe enough to necessitate time away from work. It could either be that they represented a somatoform disorder or mild manifestations of depression, which often presents with mainly physical symptoms rather than psychological ones.

ANDREW BONAR LAW (1858–1923) *(1922–1923)*

Andrew Bonar Law was born in New Brunswick, Canada, on September 16, 1858, and died on October 30, 1923. He was the only prime minister born outside the British Isles.

Early Life

Bonar Law was the son of Reverend James Law, a Presbyterian clergyman. His mother, Elizabeth Law, died in childbirth, and Law was raised by his maternal aunt, Janet Kidston. After Law's father remarried, his aunt returned to Scotland. Reverend Law and Janet Kidston believed that the more prosperous Kidston family could offer the 12-year-old boy superior education and better opportunity, so he was sent over to Scotland to be raised by the Kidstons.

Career in Politics

Law entered business at 16 and became very successful. At 30 he purchased a partnership in a Glasgow financial firm. At 33 he married Annie Robley, and they had five children. The marriage was happy and fulfilling. Law's interest in politics grew stronger as he continued to prosper in business, and he was first elected to Parliament in 1900 at the age of 42. Law was an effective speaker, knew how to drive a hard bargain, and was perceived as honest and fearless. His skills earned him the respect of many, and when the Conservative party looked for new leadership in 1911, Law was chosen. Major issues which preoccupied Law and his party included Irish independence and the tariff question. During World War I he served as colonial secretary in Asquith's coalition government. Following Asquith's resignation, King George V asked Law to form a government, which he declined in favor of Lloyd George, who, in Law's opinion, was better suited to the task. Lloyd George promoted Law to chancellor of the exchequer and leader of the House of Commons. The two men worked well together, with the understated Law restraining Lloyd George's flamboyant, hubristic tendencies.[492]

Bonar Law resigned as Conservative leader in 1921 on the grounds of illness, but by October of 1922 he had recovered and was re-elected party leader, as well as becoming prime minister.

Personality Features

Law's gloomy, pessimistic tendencies illustrate the maxim that prime ministers have come not so much from the ranks of the extrovert, but often from isolated souls with introspective, moody, and hypersensitive traits.[493] Law is invariably described as gloomy and melancholic, along with having a cautious nature and self-deprecating wit.[494] At the time of his election to the party leadership, the Chief Whip correctly predicted that a shining future beckoned for Law, referring to him as "charming to deal with — most thoughtful and kind, melancholy in disposition, witty when moments of relaxation occur, devoted to his family, profoundly convinced of the justice of his cause, of unerring memory, much courage and industry," and that "he ought to go far."[495]

Grief and Depression

Law experienced significant bereavement reactions following the deaths of his wife in 1909 and two sons who were killed towards the end of World War I. Tendencies to gloomy introspection might make a person vulnerable to the effect of bereavement, perhaps reinforced by the absence of any comforting religious belief, as was the case for Law, despite the fact that his father had been a minister. Blake notes how Law was unable to accept death or to recognize over time that death is the inevitable fate of all humans.[496] He had "some curious streak in his temperament which compelled him all his life to dwell with an almost pathological despondency upon the loss of those who were dear to him..... Lacking both the cheerfulness of the pagan and the consolations of the puritan, he was prey to a gloomy despair which threatened for a time to paralyse his whole existence."

Loss of His Wife

The sudden death of Law's wife in 1909 after gall bladder surgery left him devastated, and he never fully recovered.[497] J. C. C. Davidson, who later became Law's secretary, believed that Law constantly felt he had neglected her, and he was "always melancholy with the thought that he should have been less selfish."[498] Law was rescued by two individuals who were brought more closely into his circle — his sister, Mary, and his fellow Canadian friend Max Aitken (later Lord Beaverbrook). Politics served as an antidote to loneliness, and, as others noted after his election as party leader in 1911, "after a long period of depression [he] is rapidly emerging a greater man from despondency..... Pembroke Lodge, the widower's home is wan, cheerless, dejected. Perhaps ... this interval has made him a statesman."[499] With time, and in the face of urgent crises in the government, Law was able to take the advice of his colleague Austen Chamberlain, who exhorted him to return to politics: "It may help you to bear the heavier burden of your private grief by occupying a part of your thoughts with public cares."[500]

Loss of His Sons

Law recovered sufficiently well from Annie's death that he could regain full function in politics, but his world collapsed again in 1917 when both his sons, James and Charlie, were killed in action. Firstly, on April 19, Charlie was reported missing in Gaza. For some time it was believed that he may have been a German prisoner of war. Then as hopes finally dimmed, a false alarm came from the Vatican that he was a Turkish prisoner, giving rise to many letters of congratulation on his presumed safety. In his War Diary, Lord Riddell noted that on May 12 one of Law's colleagues observed him to be looking better than on the previous day, to which Law replied: "Yesterday I was in hell; I thought my boy was dead. Today I am in the sunshine once more; I know he is safe."[501] But it was not to be. This cruel twist had come about due to an error in which the word "not" had been unintentionally omitted when the message was translated out of cipher.

In September, Bonar Law received word that his oldest son, James, had been shot down. James had volunteered as a fighter pilot after having served in what he termed a "safe job" testing machines. Following this second loss, Law was for a time incapable of work and would be seen sitting with a vacant gaze on his face. At the urging of Max Aitken, Law went to France to meet with his son's squadron commander and sat in a plane that his son had flown. He was shown a bullet-riddled aircraft, in which he sat for a while, even asking if he could be flown in it. After this experience Bonar Law seemed to be less gloomy — perhaps it had been therapeutic, and Law was able to resume his duties for a while, never again referring to his loss. It is doubtful if the dark clouds ever left Law as long as he lived.[502] On or about September 27, 1918, Riddell records a conversation between himself and Law, one year after the loss of his sons.[503] In it, Riddell empathized over the hard times Law had endured and acknowledged that, despite all of his difficulties, Law had led the House of Commons with aplomb. Law's tearful reply was recorded:

> It is useless to conceal that I am nearly at the end of my tether. I do my work from day to day because I have certain powers of endurance, but they are growing less and less. You can see the condition I am in. If it were not so, I should not give way like this. Ever since the death of my sons I have been gradually growing worse and worse.

In 1921, due to "exhaustion" and dangerously high blood pressure, Law's doctor thought it necessary for his patient to give up all political activity for at least 6 months. Accordingly, he resigned his position as party leader and retired to France for many months, where he eventually recuperated and, after being given a clean bill of health, returned to politics as prime minister in October 1922. During the election campaign one month later, Bonar Law first noticed discomfort in his throat and problems speaking. He grew progressively gloomy, sad, and exhausted, and his term was cut short by terminal throat cancer in early 1923, his time in office lasting only 209 days.

The question arises as to the nature of Law's temporary indisposition in 1921 and 1922. Could it have been related at all to the developing throat cancer? Was hypertension a sufficient explanation? Might unresolved grief and depression have been at work too? We may never know, but in favor of grief as a partial cause are Law's own words to Arthur Balfour on March 21, 1921:

> I do not think you could possibly quite realize how irksome I have found my work for more than three years. While the war lasted I did not think of giving up but ever since I have longed for release. What, however, brought it to a point is that I had a slight chill the other day and I have been examined by my Doctor. I have felt that as long as it was only a question of my feelings it would be unfair to L. G. (Lloyd George) and perhaps cowardly to run away while the difficulties are so great.[504]

With depression and grief, as with so many other psychiatric disorders, it is not a simple question of recovering or remaining sick; there is a spectrum of distress or impairment, and a large number of people make a partial recovery but with persisting symptoms which can last for years. This applies even with the more effective treatments used today. Quite possibly, Law fell into this category and continued to experience sub-threshold, but still important, symptoms. Apart from the prolonged absences, it does not appear that Law's career was handicapped by his depressions; his modest, uncharismatic, austere and rather gloomy manner was viewed as a welcome antidote to the theatricals of Lloyd George, given the crises of the time.[505] Nevertheless, unrelenting grief left him with darkness, relieved only by the solace of politics.

STANLEY BALDWIN, 3RD EARL BALDWIN OF BEWDLEY (1867–1947) *(1923–1924; 1924–1929; 1935–1937)*

Stanley Baldwin's quick rise from relative obscurity to the premiership was regarded as "one of the most astonishing of modern times," and even after his election as prime minister, a prominent member of his own party confessed that he didn't recognize Baldwin by sight.[506] Over the next fourteen years Baldwin went on to serve three terms of office, during two of which he suffered emotional breakdowns and was unable to function.

Early Years and Family

Baldwin came from an iron manufacturing family whose business had been established in the mid–eighteenth century. His father, Alfred Baldwin, had been head of the firm, was chairman of the Great Western Railway and Member of Parliament for Bewdley from 1892 until his death in 1908. On his mother's side, Baldwin's grandfather was an ardent prohibitionist Methodist minister; and through a maternal aunt, Baldwin and Rudyard Kipling were first cousins. Baldwin had no siblings. His parents set high expectations for Stanley, Mrs. Baldwin exhorting him to be top of the class and his father pushing him to achieve "high honors as a public man." A familial tendency to anxiety is suggested in that Baldwin's father was prone to twitches, was nervous, had an abnormal fear of violence and an excessive fear of thunderstorms. "When the tempest rolled and crashed, this powerful-looking man really suffered pitiably."[507] Stanley Baldwin's oldest son, Oliver, may well have developed shell shock (i.e., posttraumatic stress disorder) as a result of his experiences in the trenches during World War I and as prisoner of war in Armenia after World War I.[508]

Baldwin was educated at St. Michael's School, Harrow and Cambridge University, where he graduated in history and then joined the family business. There he excelled and was seen as a modernizing industrialist. In 1892, Baldwin married Lucy Ridsdale, who bore him seven children, one of whom, Oliver, became a Labour MP. Lucy was known for her "non-conformist probity" and exerted a strong influence over her husband. Their marriage was happy, and Lucy's outgoing manner counterbalanced Baldwin's austere reserve and social discomfort. On one occasion Lucy prevented him from resigning as party leader after he had become depressed in the face of harsh criticism in the press.[509]

Character Traits and Evidence for Mental Illness

Gunther contrasts Baldwin's "John Bull" British solidity and substance with a mystic, puritanical strength of character deriving from spiritual values. He portrayed Baldwin as a man of unshakable convictions who responded to emotion easily and was able to evoke strong feelings in others. Gunther also stated that a familiar criticism of Baldwin is that he "moves slowly, but he *can* move ... is lazy ... sly ... too supine, too passive," but "when really roused, he can make mincemeat of his enemies." On two occasions he successfully fought off attempts to oust him from the party leadership. Baldwin saw himself as of "somewhat flabby nature, always preferring agreement to disagreement."[510] Despite his seeming laziness and flabbiness, by 1922, and no doubt shaped by his reaction to World War I, Baldwin had become messianically convinced that he was God's chosen instrument to heal the nation. Iremonger, Middlemas and Barnes, both credit him with good physical stamina and the mental ruthlessness necessary to "win the game," although under stress much of this stamina and ruthlessness dissipated.[511]

Baldwin and Morbid Anxiety

As a young man, Baldwin was shy, gauche and uncomfortable around women, as well as being worry-prone, isolated and preoccupied with his inadequacies.[512] Dislike of public speaking seems to have been an issue, as he was dismissed from his Cambridge college debating society for never speaking! For twenty years after he entered the family business, no record exists of any public speech; and after he was elected to Parliament, four months passed before his maiden speech. In his first nine years as a member of Parliament he made just five speeches.[513] It is scarcely a surprise that Baldwin remained such an obscurity in Parliament: a streak of social avoidance was apparent in many situations. He thought his antipathy to social gatherings to be a weakness, and all his life he was unable to conceal his misery. As prime minister, he found banquets and big gatherings to be a drain on his nervous energy, so that his wife had to watch him for signs of distress and quickly rescue him.[514] Before a major speech, Baldwin would go pale, sweat would roll off his forehead, and he would feel sick. Unusual facial contortions were present when he spoke in Parliament, and he experienced panic before having to read the lesson in church.[515] Fatigue and exhaustion were frequent companions and usually the first indications of his nervous breakdowns.

Young noted that Baldwin found close relationships difficult, and that he was burdened by the loneliness of the premiership. He suggested that the course of some national events, such as the aftermath of the general strike and the Hoare–Laval crisis, was influenced by his supposed fluctuation between impulsive exertion and nervous relapse.[516] Williamson has taken issue with Young's biography as being unflatteringly tendentious, but its accounts of Baldwin's personality and emotional crises are consistent with other sources.[517]

Anxiety and superstition were constant companions. He was apprehensive of disaster, and a sudden call from Lucy could give rise to "an ashen, quivering figure of terror." He was "sensitive above average, neurotic and somber, with very bad nerves, a severe facial twitch and an abnormal reaction to thunderstorms."[518] Ludwig cited one description of Baldwin as "a bundle of nerves, constantly sniffing at blotting paper or books, snapping his fingers or showing his tension in other ways."[519] He worried constantly, had trouble making decisions, and could not sleep. By 1936 he was under such great pressure that he nearly broke down, and to prevent a complete nervous breakdown, his physician ordered him to take three months off work and total rest. It is likely that Baldwin was experiencing generalized anxiety, with uncontrollable worry, tension, insomnia and restlessness.

Did Baldwin Have Tourette's Disorder?

Beyond his exaggerated anxiety, Stanley Baldwin displayed obsessive, ritualized behaviors. For example, his son wrote of a "severe facial twitch [tic], finger-tappings, repeated throwing and catching of his walking stick, book-smellings and tossings, weird hummings, grunts and snatches of song with their carefully observed sequences, [which] were legendary and clearly recognizable as forms of ... obsessional magic incantations and rituals used throughout the ages as protective devices to ward off evil."[520] Baldwin was superstitious and given to premonition, most notably about the Prince of Wales (subsequently the Duke of Windsor) and what turned out to be the abdication crisis. Whether his rituals were tied to his superstitions is not known, but such a possibility remains. Taken in context of the fact that Baldwin disliked paperwork and avoided making decisions, these highly precise mannerisms appear to have been somewhat counterproductive. The energy which he put into those behaviors could have been put to better use in executing his day-to-day responsibilities as prime minister.

Baldwin very likely manifested a tic disorder. In order to be confident that it met all the requirements for Tourette's disorder, we would need to know that it began prior to age 18 and continued almost every day for a year, with no more than 3 months' freedom from symptoms. In the absence of this information, the safer course would be to assign a "diagnosis" of tic disorder, not otherwise specified (coded 307.20 in DSM-IV).[521]

Depression Prone?

Neville Chamberlain commented on Baldwin's "essential loneliness of spirit, his resemblance to Lincoln, even to his strange physical contortions."[522] Baldwin is said to have been excessively sensitive to bereavement, and after the stillbirth of his first child, Baldwin took the shock harder than his wife, suffering from insomnia for weeks afterwards. "It was a wrench to get himself back to the daily grind of business ... he was very deeply depressed indeed," said his son. It took 52 years before Baldwin spoke about this sad event.

A brief but intense depressive reaction may also have occurred when Baldwin was 39, after an electoral defeat at Kidderminster in 1906, two years before he was successfully elected to his father's constituency of Bewdley.[523]

Thorpe referred to Baldwin's lack of drive and the ease with which he became depressed.[524] Whether this contributed to his failure to adequately confront Hitler and prevent the ensuing march to war is a question for debate, but his innate pessimism about what government could achieve would not have served him well in dealing with Hitler. In Churchill's opinion, Baldwin's conciliatory attitude gave Hitler the impression that Britain would not fight if attacked and did more than the much reviled Neville Chamberlain to permit the course of events which paved the way to "the most unnecessary war in history," although it is an open question how much Churchill's assessment reflects accurate vision versus personal antipathy. Baldwin at least deserves credit for overcoming skeptical opposition in preparing an effective radar-based fighter air defense which was essential to success in the Battle of Britain in 1940.

An interesting contrast can be made between how Churchill and Baldwin, both of whom were prone to depression, stood up to the dictator. Certainly Baldwin lacked Churchill's pugnacity and may not therefore have shared Churchill's clear vision about the danger of Hitler in the 1930s; or perhaps he had the vision but failed to act with enough resolve. In favor of the latter, Baldwin was reported by a contemporary to be one of the first to see the direction of events in Europe—as early as 1935—when he said in a speech that Britain's frontier has become the Rhine, but then "he stayed put."[525] While Churchill and Baldwin both experienced depression, they were not kindred spirits, and on one occasion, when Baldwin took time to name his defense minister, Churchill quipped, "Baldwin has to find a man of inferior ability to himself, and this Herculean task requires time for its accomplishment"![526] Later, Churchill was to say, "I wish Baldwin no ill, but it would have been much better if he had never lived."[527]

It is clear that Baldwin underwent a number of what was called "nervous breakdowns" in 1923, 1929 and from 1936 to the end of 1937. As noted earlier, this lay term does not map directly onto any current diagnostic categories, but can usually be taken as evidence that, in plain language, something is wrong psychologically—that a "clinically significant" psychological state has developed that either creates distress or interferes with normal functioning. Most commonly, a "nervous breakdown" would correspond in today's terms to depression, anxiety or an adjustment disorder. In Baldwin's case, the episodes were of sufficient magnitude that he either took medicine or was ordered by the doctor to take several weeks of "complete rest."[528] These extended periods of withdrawal from office disrupted efficient government and lead to confusion over interim leadership, as well as delays in making important decisions. Even when he returned to work, his mental state left him unable to focus on the business of government.[529]

Towards the end of his second administration, between 1924 and 1929, the prime minister "hardly seemed interested enough in his job to keep a grasp on things, succumb[ed] to inertia, to muddle, to bad advice."[530] And he presided over a "series of blunders" in foreign policy, an aspect of the premiership which interested him very little.[531] Concern was expressed that Baldwin was "lethargic and unwilling to think seriously about future policy."

As mentioned by L'Étang, serious and persistent mood changes in a political leader can escape notice of his closest associates who may fail to appreciate the torment which is produced.[532] As an example of the latter, he quotes Baldwin, who wrote, "The usual pangs are upon me. My inside is a mess of cold rumbling fluidity; my brain is costive. Faith is dying; hope is dead.... I am raglike, sad and helpless, [and my] "mental debility is indescribable."

Of his third term, from 1935 to 1937, Thorpe had this to say about Baldwin's psychological state: "Essentially, Baldwin was a much more neurotic and insecure character than his public persona would have suggested, a fact testified to by his nervous breakdown in the summer of 1936, when he spent three months out of politics, and by the fact that every year he needed to disappear for a month to Aix-les-Bains for rest and recuperation, isolated from politics except for the Davidsons."[533] A major crisis erupted in 1936 when King Edward VIII announced his intention to marry a twice-divorced American woman, Wallis Warfield Simpson. Since the king was head of the established church, which disapproved of divorce, this posed a serious constitutional crisis. Baldwin is generally seen as having handled this difficult situation well. Not long afterwards, and less than two years after his landslide election win, Baldwin retired — "when he wanted to go and in a blaze of glory."

Summary

Stanley Baldwin was born with a genetic predisposition to anxiety. He was unusually fear-prone, depression-prone, over-reactive to bereavement and most likely had a tic disorder. His episodes of depression might best be accounted by the DSM category of "mood disorder not otherwise specified."[534] What is missing in these assessments is firm knowledge of the full symptom picture when he was depressed; but lack of interest, low mood, lethargy, and insomnia comprise four out of the five required symptoms for such a diagnosis, and he endured all of these. Although his attacks of depression seemed to last for at least two weeks, narratives fail to indicate if all of the symptoms occurred at the same time. We do know, however, that they incapacitated him and lead to time away from work. From the clinical management standpoint, most people would think of treating a depressive episode which produces great distress of impairment of function, regardless of the number of symptoms.

For the phobic symptoms, we lack information as to whether Baldwin invariably experienced anxiety every time there was a thunderstorm, and if he himself viewed this as an excessive fear, both of which would be required to meet criteria for specific phobia. So it would be more appropriate to consider this condition as "anxiety disorder not otherwise specified" (DSM-IV code 300.00).[535] Biographical information provides enough details to support a fully emergent social anxiety disorder (300.23).[536] His general tendencies to excessive worry fit the picture of generalized anxiety disorder, with all the required criteria being present (300.02).[537]

Baldwin's "legendary" grunts, mannerisms, vocalizations, stereotypical movements and facial tics are consistent with tic disorder not otherwise specified (307.20), and, as mentioned, Tourette's disorder remains a possibility.[538]

Baldwin himself said, "The Englishman keeps his nervous system sound and sane," and yet his attempts to convey that steady unflappability were scarcely a success; an American journalist's observation that "the real Baldwin ... is taut, passionate, complex, as though within him stormed a chaos" is closer to the mark.[539] On three separate occasions, during tempestuous times in Europe, Britain had as prime minister a man who gave way to stress in the form of anxiety, was obliged to take long periods off work, and almost certainly was not able to give his best to the difficult tasks he faced.

JAMES RAMSAY MACDONALD (1866–1937) *(1924; 1929–1935)*

Ramsay MacDonald was the first Labour Party prime minister, although this the significance of this achievement was subsequently blighted when he was seen to betray socialist principles by leading a coalition National Government in 1931. He is, however, acknowledged for his legacy as an important democratic socialist writer and leader, and in establishing the credentials of his party in government. His political life has been characterized as exciting, unprecedented, dramatic and tragic.[540] Part of the tragedy includes mental decline in the last years of leadership, which left him unable to function. However, even before that, MacDonald was subject to depression.

Brief Account of His Career

MacDonald was born in the small fishing port of Lossiemouth, Scotland, on October 12, 1866, the illegitimate son of working class parents. MacDonald had no contact with his father and was raised by his single mother. At age 8 he came under the influence of his local schoolteacher, the Reverand James MacDonald, who provided critical mentorship for the young Ramsay, encouraging him to be ambitious and following his pupil's progress for many years into adulthood.[541] At 22, Ramsay met Keir Hardie, the great socialist leader, and in 1895 stood unsuccessfully as Member of Parliament for Hardie's newly founded Independent Labour Party. With encouragement from his wife, MacDonald ran again in 1906 and was elected MP for Leicester. In 1911 he became chairman of the Parliamentary Labour group, but resigned from the post in 1914 over disagreement with his party's support of the war. Indeed, he received considerable vilification for his opposition, which was seen in the media as traitorous. Despite this and other setbacks, MacDonald eventually rehabilitated himself with his party and became the first Labour prime minister in a short-lived 1924 administration. His party was re-elected in 1929, and he returned to office as Labour prime minister until 1931, when he formed a coalition National Government, which lasted until 1935. Although he commanded a large Labour majority at the time of the coalition, domestic policy was heavily influenced by his Conservative partners, Baldwin and Chamberlain. He grew increasingly isolated from his former Labour colleagues, who could not forgive what they saw as his betrayal. In 1933 and 1934, MacDonald's health deteriorated to such an extent that his leadership began to falter — at a time when fascism in Europe was threatening international security. In 1935 he ceded office to Baldwin and subsequently lost his Parliamentary seat in a 1936 election. He was later elected back to Parliament for another constituency. Owing to declining health, his doctor recommended a sea voyage to promote his recovery, but this proved to be his last journey, as he died at sea on November 9, 1937.

Evidence for Mental Illness

During his mid–40s MacDonald suffered three bereavements within a short time. In February 1910 the MacDonalds' four-year-old son, David, died of diphtheria. MacDonald's mother, Annie Ramsay, then passed away eight days later. In July of 1911, Ramsay's wife, Margaret, died of blood poisoning. It is widely conceded that MacDonald never fully recovered from losing Margaret. At any event, he neither remarried nor maintained significant personal relationships outside those with his children. As he put it, "I have no close friend in the world," and his own Parliamentary private secretary had never seen anyone so aloof or inaccessible as MacDonald.[542] In losing Margaret, Ramsay MacDonald lost a special woman who is immortalized on her statue in Lincoln's Inn Fields as having "brought joy to those with whom she lived and worked." Margaret was a children's social worker, and she is depicted on her statue holding out her arms to nine small children.

Twenty-five years later, when asked why he had not remarried, Ramsay is alleged to have said that his heart had been in the grave since his wife died.[543] Marquand said that there is no reason to believe the memories had diminished to any extent by the 1930s, suggesting the persistence of grief, which, as noted previously, proved the undoing of other political leaders.[544] MacDonald reportedly experienced bouts of depression and isolation after his bereavements, and again between 1929 and 1931.[545] The loss of Margaret deprived MacDonald of his main cheerleader and source of self-esteem. By later alienating his Labour colleagues, he cut himself off from remaining support, a factor which might have increased the risk of depression during stressful times. Other health problems, such as glaucoma, began to assert themselves in the early 1930s and complicated the picture.

MacDonald's personality has been characterized as oversensitive, shy, hypochondriacal, arrogant, irresolute in times of crisis and avoidant of making decisions that would cause controversy. His hypersensitivity was described as "almost feminine," in accordance with the gender stereotypes of the day, which held men to be tough and in control of their emotions, and women to be touchy and excitable. He felt criticism acutely and had a curious power of retaining the memory of an attack "long after its consequences have completely disappeared."[546] These character flaws were offset by more positive traits of commitment, adherence to principle and thoughtfulness.

From Depression to Dementia

More destructive than depression was MacDonald's progressive decline into dementia during his third administration. Park has suggested that the decline of MacDonald's effectiveness as a leader paralleled the decline of his health, beginning as early as 1930, when he was still head of the Labour government.[547] He was already described then as being "senile" and "inadequate" by Lafore.[548] After acrimonious Parliamentary debates in 1931, MacDonald twice collapsed and was sidelined for several days. In September 1931 an observer noted that the prime minister tended to vomit when under great nervous strain.[549] Park's assertion that these episodes were "hysterical" or "psychosomatic" are supported by MacDonald's own diary entry of January 19, 1933, in which he wrote, "The depression has been one of the blackest & has affected everything.... The strain is at last telling on me, & I am feeling as though [in the] last few weeks I have crossed the frontiers of age. I walk as an old man, & my head works like an old man's.... How long can I go on?" Similarly, in 1932, after undergoing eye surgery for glaucoma, his convalescence was prolonged due to depression — or "brain fag," as his physician called it — and for which he gave MacDonald a "tonic," or in today's terms, the equivalent of an antidepressant drug.[550]

Poor sleep is a feature of depression, and it is therefore telling that MacDonald was plagued with this symptom throughout his life when under stress. In early 1933 he noted in his diary that he had a "weary night, sleepless and worried." A short time later he wrote, "At night my mind is like a pool which seeks to be quiet but is stirred by springs at the bottom." Then some months later he wrote, "Cannot shut eyes to fact that am unusually depressed and no wish to talk ... decidedly older and of diminished vigour." In January 1934 he was prescribed sleeping medicine.[551]

The progressive decline of MacDonald's cognitive facilities is well known, and its onset appears to have taken place between 1931 and 1933. In November 1931 he wrote, "Worn out and work impossible.... But really head would not work. So depressing."[552] Is he here describing depression or the early signs of failure to think clearly and to reason, either from dementia or depressive pseudo-dementia? More overt signs of dementia began to appear in 1933, such as decline in memory, slowing of thought and intellectual function, and impairment of speech. Whereas in the past MacDonald had effectively infused his speeches with a flair for the dramatic, lofty language and a liberal use of subordinate clauses, he began to lose the ability to use these techniques and came across as forced and histrionic; with the use of mixed metaphors, he lost his way in confusion and anticlimax. "Occasionally the results were comic.... More often, they were merely embarrassing."[553] On one occasion a speech turned into a "long and confused rigmarole of incoherent irrelevancies, which left his hearers in all parts of the House quite unable to follow him." For a while the term "MacDonaldism" entered the vocabulary to denote confusion of thought or lack of clearness. As Winston Churchill put it, "The prime minister has the gift of compressing the largest number of words into the smallest amount of thought."[554] His private secretary commented that MacDonald was increasingly indolent and guilty of dereliction of duty. In a diary entry of 1933 the premier mused, "I surely cannot be well or I have got old suddenly." He began to lie awake at night worrying any time he had an upcoming Parliamentary speech, and after a bad performance he would unrelentingly go over the memories. In 1934 he said, "To speak now is a great effort ... and in the development of the argument I get more & more confused."[555] Sadly, and without any understanding of the reasons for his declining faculties, the media scorned him for his gaffes. Marquand believes that MacDonald stayed on as prime minister two years longer than he should have, and that when he left office, his reputation was in ruins.[556] MacDonald's friend Arthur Salter was of the opinion that by 1933 the prime minister was "no longer in a mental and physical condition to be capable of the continuous and exacting responsibilities of high office."[557] One blunder followed another: he signed off on a key defense paper which he had not read and confessed afterwards that "it is rather odd that I cannot be protected ... against such mistakes."[558] It is likely that MacDonald's deteriorating brain function put him, his government and his country at a serious disadvantage in dealing with Hitler and Mussolini. At the Stresa conference MacDonald failed to take action on the briefings he had been given about Mussolini's planned invasion of Ethiopia, never even raising the matter for discussion. Worse still, he rambled so badly in discussion that his interpreter couldn't understand what he had said and was therefore told to make up a speech for him. MacDonald began to dress inappropriately and had to be protected from the press in case he did even more damage. Shortly after returning home from Stresa, MacDonald tendered his resignation.

Conclusions

Ramsay MacDonald began life in humble circumstances. Drive, fortunate mentoring and a deep commitment to the principles of democratic socialism allowed him to progress steadily along the political path, ultimately becoming Britain's first Labour prime minister and the first from working class origins. By nature, MacDonald was aloof, shy and arrogant, highly sensitive to criticism and lacking in self-assurance. After three bereavements in 1910 and 1911 he was grief-stricken and is believed never to have fully recovered from the death of his wife. From these losses and later rejections, he experienced quite severe bouts of depression and anxiety, with hypochondriacal tendencies. By 1933, signs strongly suggested the development of dementia, which progressed to the point where he was unable to provide competent leadership and almost certainly was ill-equipped to deal with the situation in Europe. He overstayed his time in office, and when he finally retired, his reputation was in ruins. Ironically, he handed over power to Stanley Baldwin, who had his own struggles with depression and was obliged to retire for similar reasons. Strangely, for all his incapacitation, MacDonald again sought re-election and was returned to Parliament—a poor reflection on the parliamentary system. The course of his political career is a reminder to monitor the mental health and competency of leaders, and to identify and take appropriate action when things begin to get out of hand. Otherwise, there is potential for untold harm, either by errors of commission or, in MacDonald's case, by errors of omission.

NEVILLE CHAMBERLAIN (1869–1940) *(1937–1940)*

The name of Neville Chamberlain is forever associated with the policy of appeasement. Rightly or wrongly, on his shoulders is placed much opprobrium for Britain's lack of preparation for war and its early reverses in the "phoney" war of 1940, which lead to the rapid plummeting of his reputation from hero to disgrace. Chamberlain was no war leader, and he quickly resigned under pressure in favor of Churchill.[559] It has been said of him that "No prime minister ... was ever temperamentally less suited to war ... unsuited even to employing the kind of tactics which ... might have averted war."[560] But despite this, there has been some rehabilitation of his reputation."[561]

His talents were better suited to social reform and home affairs than to standing up to Hitler.

Like Baldwin, Chamberlain was born into a prosperous Birmingham manufacturing family. Chamberlain's father, Joseph, became Lord Mayor, then Member of Parliament and a cabinet minister. His brother Austen also served as Member of Parliament, becoming chancellor of the exchequer, foreign secretary and Conservative party leader. Neville entered politics later in life. As he explained in 1900, he had no wish to follow his brother into politics and even confessed reluctance about giving speeches in the general election campaign: "I am speaking as often as my nervousness and laziness permit me (which is not much) but I haven't begun to think of politics as a career."[562] Chamberlain was first elected MP at the age of 49 after pursuing a career in business for over 20 years. During this part of his life, Chamberlain encountered major failure and financial setback in his efforts to grow sisal in the Bahamas, but thereafter returned home and became successful in manufacturing. Like his father, he entered local politics in Birmingham, becoming Lord Mayor in 1915.[563]

After election to Parliament, Chamberlain made an immediate impression from the back benches and began his rise up the party ranks. Between 1923 and 1931 he was minister of health, and between 1931 and 1937 he served as chancellor of the exchequer as well as *de facto* prime minister during Baldwin's illness. In 1937 he replaced Baldwin and continued as prime minister until 1940. For a while after the Munich agreement, Chamberlain was regarded as a savior against war, but things quickly turned sour, and his reputation collapsed as the situation in Europe came apart. At the time of his resignation in May of 1940 he already had advanced bowel cancer and died 6 months later.

Chamberlain's Character

Chamberlain has been described as shy, bashful, aloof, isolated and given to displays of hubris — all qualities with which we are now familiar in the roll call of prime ministers. He was sanguine, proud and sensitive; in fact, some thought he was too sensitive for politics. He was driven by duty and possessed a keen awareness of the social responsibility that went with wealth. These qualities in his character went hand in hand with self-reliance, the ability to plan carefully and a good grasp of detail. Somewhat surprisingly perhaps, Chamberlain was known for his "formidable presence in the cabinet," and a "take charge" approach to the running of government when he became prime minister.[564] To quote Crozier, "His mastery of government business was prodigious."[565] Unfortunately, once he became prime minister, some of his undesirable traits became more prominent, including intolerance of criticism, the desire to take control, a rigid belief in the correctness of his view and isolation from his Parliamentary colleagues.[566] Chamberlain's hubris may have damaged his leadership abilities at a crucial time.[567] Physically, Chamberlain possessed great stamina until the last few weeks of his life and at 60 could outpace younger men on hikes. He always slept well.

Chamberlain's Mental Health

There is reason to believe that Chamberlain was susceptible to recurrent depression. Iremonger notes Chamberlain's isolation as a youngster, lack of intimate friends and proneness to long silences. After his failure in the Bahamas, he was "weighed down with guilt" and blamed himself for losing £50,000 of his father's money, even though his father took it in stride.

In 1917, "once more he was thrown into one of those abysmal depressions which attacked him periodically all his life," the occasion this time being his failure as director general of national service.[568] Chamberlain looked at the prospect of advancing age and thwarted ambition. "He agonized at his increasing age. After a few weeks, and with the support of his family, his depressed state of mind had begun to lift and Chamberlain saw the way forward for his climb up the greasy pole." Just as he was recovering, a cruel blow lay in store for him, however. In December 1917 his cousin Norman was reported missing in action, and his death was confirmed a few weeks later, putting Neville once more "in the depths."[569] Crozier states that Norman's death "undoubtedly also contributed to the depression which followed his unsuccessful directorship of national service. He [Chamberlain] wrote: 'My career is broken. How can a man of nearly 50, entering the House with this stigma upon him, hope to achieve anything?'"[570] Norman and Neville had always been exceptionally close, and it has been said Neville never fully recovered from his grief over Norman's death. From the historian's perspective, it is perhaps important that this loss may have "sowed the seeds of [Chamberlain's] lifelong hatred of war, which would affect him and the nation so dramatically later on."[571]

Feiling draws a contrast between the public perception of Chamberlain as calm, patient and strong through life's ups and downs, and his "sensitive, high-strung, and restless [inner state] ... within [which] the mood was black, and there were depressions to be fought down."[572] At times Chamberlain lamented his inability to keep himself under proper control and would be overtaken by a desire to "flee away and hide myself in a South Sea Island." This was probably more than just metaphor, since, to the end of his life, Chamberlain was uncomfortable giving speeches and disliked the "exhibitionism of elections." He was much more at ease at home or in small, more intimate gatherings. With larger groups he would stiffen up and "intimidate by gruffness, and estrange by reserve." Depression returned in 1924 when, during the 10 months Chamberlain was out of office, gloom took over and he sought help from his doctor, who advised a vegetarian diet. Whether from the diet or spontaneous improvement, Chamberlain again recovered his energy and discarded those transient thoughts of giving up politics for business.[573] Chamberlain's famed self-discipline was helpful as he coped with depression, just as with Gladstone a generation earlier. It is somewhat curious that Chamberlain wrote a chapter on "Personality and the Equipment for Success," in which he championed fixed principles and self-discipline, the elements of which were integrity, judgment, courage, sympathy and patience.[574]

Summary

A combination of qualities was present in Chamberlain, including shyness, and a dislike of public presentation and many of the trappings necessary for politics. However, his discomfort and lack of self-assurance around others did not prevent Chamberlain from bearing a considerable degree of hubris. He has been judged a poor negotiator who was unable to conceal what he knew, and lacking in mental antennae, the power of anticipation and the ability to grasp what was in his opponent's mind. In conditions where it was necessary to engage his opponent at an emotional (visceral) level, he was weak — his forte was when business could be handled at a rational level. There were, of course, assets in his character as well, including integrity, devotion to principles, solicitude for others, good planning ability and the ability to succeed against personal adversity. He was effective in his use of the media.

In the context of professional failure or rejection, Chamberlain was susceptible to recurrent depressions, most of which were brief but sometimes severe enough for him to seek medical help. At such times his confidence sagged and he would doubt his ability to stay the course in politics. It is not stated whether his depressions were accompanied by physical symptoms, like poor sleep, poor appetite, low energy or impaired decision-making. We do know that his encounters with Hitler shook him up so much that he confessed to coming "nearer to a nervous breakdown than I have ever been in my life."[575] There is a suggestion of enduring grief from Norman's death in battle and some evidence of chronic anxiety related to scrutiny, but otherwise nothing to imply that Chamberlain was dogged by unremitting mental illness or crippling depression which interfered with his daily function other than for short periods at most. However, some of his character traits did not serve him well later.[576]

Successful leadership in war calls for different qualities than in times of peace. Degrees of impetuousness, decisiveness, grandiosity and unbridled enthusiasm may be more desirable in war than in peace.[577] Bagehot applauded "the imperious will, the rapid energy, the eager nature fit for great crisis" during war, but pointed out that they were often impediments at other times — "A Lord Liverpool is better in everyday politics than a Chatham."[578] It is therefore no surprise that the ill-equipped Chamberlain was a poor war leader, and it is also no surprise that he was out of his depth with Hitler; he simply didn't have the viscera. His talents were better suited to peacetime domestic politics.

SIR WINSTON CHURCHILL (1875–1965) *(1940–1945; (1951–1955)*

One authority wrote, "You cannot judge the P.M. [Churchill] by ordinary standards: he is not in the least like anyone that you or I have ever met."[579] The man was larger than life. Arguably, more has been written about Winston Churchill than any other British prime minister, and many accounts have described the recurrent episodes of depression which he experienced. Also up for debate has been the question of whether he suffered from bipolar disorder and alcohol dependence.

Churchill was born in 1875, the oldest of two sons. His father, Lord Randolph Churchill, died at the age of 45, possibly from the effects of tertiary syphilis, although this is not absolutely certain. On his father's side, Churchill's lineage can be traced to the first Duke of Marlborough, a hero of British campaigns against the French in the early 18th century. Churchill's mother, Jennie Jerome, was the daughter of an American millionaire. She was not closely involved with her son's upbringing and left Winston to the tender care of his nanny, Mrs. Everest, towards whom the boy developed great affection.

Churchill's childhood and teenage years were unhappy, and at school he was a poor pupil. When he was nine years old he was placed last in class, and his teacher noted him to be "feeble" and poor in composition and spelling: This was not something expected of a man destined to receive the Nobel Prize for literature.[580] He was unpopular with his peers; at the age of 12 he was stabbed by another schoolboy in an art class altercation while others looked on. He was teased and bullied, and would hide in the woods to escape victimization. This picture might evoke the possibility of attention deficit-hyperactivity disorder (ADHD), but apart from a number of popular websites arguing its presence, there is no good scientific or biographical support for this diagnosis. As a teenager, Churchill had pledged to overcome his timid ways and wrote to his mother that he wished to enter the army and expose himself to whatever risks it would bring because "I am so conceited that I do not believe the gods would create so potent a being as myself for so prosaic an ending"—since he, like Disraeli, was "intended to do something in the world."[581] However, gaining entry into Sandhurst proved difficult, owing to Churchill's poor academic skills. It was only after three attempts that he was accepted into cavalry training, which he had chosen over infantry because entrance requirements into the former were less exacting and there was no requirement to learn mathematics, a subject which he disliked.

In a letter from Sandhurst in 1893, Churchill described how he was "cursed with so feeble a body that I can scarcely support the fatigues of the day; but I suppose I shall get stronger during my stay here."[582] In this expression of optimism, Churchill proved to be right, and in 1894 he graduated 8th out of 150 in his class.[583] Churchill's communications reveal a high level of self-awareness that his task was to intentionally build up courage and toughness, and fulfill his sense of mission, and that to do so he would have to overcome deficiencies in his character and physical weakness. Storr proposed that Churchill never wholly conquered the disadvantages which were part of his make-up, but that his entire career was an effort to overcome them.[584]

The Black Dog: Churchill's Depression

Storr referred to Churchill's recurrent depressions, for which, as a remedy, he adopted his own program of "therapy" by painting and writing. In *Painting as a Pastime* he refers to the circumstances under which he took up painting.[585] In 1915 Churchill was forced to resign from his position as First Lord of the Admiralty, bearing responsibility for the disastrous Gallipoli campaign. This left him in considerable mental turmoil: "I had great anxiety and no means of relieving it.... I had long hours of utterly unwonted leisure." He goes on to say, "And then the Muse of Painting came to my rescue" and said to him, "Are these toys any good for you? They amuse some people." Henceforward, the rest is history, and he became a sufficiently accomplished painter to be elected Honorary Academician Extraordinary of the Royal Academy of Art, where some of his pictures now hang. Painting was both a source of fun and a chance for him to play the imaginary part of commander on the battlefield.[586] Who knows but that some of these "mind games" prepared him for the real battles two decades later?

His words on painting give us an insight into how he may have been able to cope with the depressions and rejections which so threatened his well-being. Going further, they suggest how Churchill perhaps integrated the lows and highs of his life to better fulfill his mission as a statesman and inspirational leader. On pages 22 and 23 he has this to say about black and white, which we can see in part as metaphors for his depressions and highs:

In painting, the reserves (using the military analogy) consist in Proportion or Relation. And it is here that the art of the painter marches along the road which is traversed by all the greatest harmonies in thought. At one side of the palette there is white, at the other black; and neither is ever used "neat." Between these two rigid limits all the action must lie.

We may conjecture that, through painting, Churchill came better to find harmony and balance between the blacks and whites of life. He goes on to say that "the true artist is able to produce every effect of light and shade, of sunshine and shadow, of distance and nearness, simply by expressing justly the relations between the different planes and surfaces with which he is dealing." The cultivation of an intuitive capacity to grasp the complete picture may have enabled Churchill to see with greater clarity the threat of Hitler before others were able to do so. By cultivating the ability to blend black and white into shades of grey, Churchill acquired skill in dealing with uncertainty and being able to examine things from different perspectives.

Did Churchill Have Bipolar Disorder?

In 1915 Churchill became depressed, and further episodes occurred, most notably in 1944 and in his old age. But since youth he had been plagued by lesser degrees of depression, recognized initially by Churchill as a medical disorder.[587] Although he was at first prepared to consider taking medicine, he ultimately found his own ways (painting and writing) to overcome the problem, which his daughter referred to as his constant companion.[588] While obviously of value, Storr points out that painting was not an entirely successful self-treatment.[589] Churchill's depressions were accompanied by fears of self-destructive behavior — jumping in front of a train, thoughts about death, and feelings of futility. Towards the end of his life he said to his daughter that he had achieved nothing.[590] Indeed, the last five years of his life were "so melancholy that even Lord Moran [his physician] draws a veil over them."[591]

Some, but not all, of Churchill's depressions appear to have been triggered by rejection or stints in the political wilderness; fulfillment and self-esteem came from being in the arena of political leadership. The need for approval is present in everyone, but for some who are particularly dependent on it, or who easily take slight to what they perceive (rightly or wrongly) as rejection, the risk of developing depression is stronger, as earlier noted by Donald Klein and colleagues.[592] This is not to imply that Churchill would have met all the features of rejection-sensitive depression, but rejection is not uncommon in those who rely on the popular vote to sustain them in office. Therefore one who is sensitive to rejection and prone to depression might be at risk for an episode when they have been turned out of office or lost status, as seen in a number of prime ministers.

Despite the enormity of his achievements, Churchill remained prone to feelings of despair, emptiness and meaninglessness throughout his entire life, as indicated by his daughter's comments late in his life, and in his novel *Savrola*, written when he was 22 years of age.[593] At times, he would brood over these feelings.

Depression: Unipolar or Bipolar?

Was Churchill's depression of the unipolar or bipolar variety? His limitless energy, creative ideas and "immense volatility" suggest bipolarity, and some associates remarked on his "crazy state of exultation."[594] Churchill's chief of staff, General Ismay, described him as a person who could not be judged by ordinary standards, who was either on the crest of a wave or in the trough, highly laudatory or bitterly condemnatory. His moods were "as variable as the April day."

On a website devoted to bipolar disorder, the following descriptions of Churchill are given.[595] Lord Beaverbrook depicted Churchill as "at the top of the wheel of confidence or at the bottom of an intense depression." Tendencies towards belligerence, overspending, enormous energy, prolific creativity and grandiosity were all there in plenty. Belligerence was illustrated by his combative style of interpersonal relationships, his open relish of World War I ("a glorious, delicious war"), and monologues lasting 4 hours. Churchill spent money beyond his means and had to recoup many of his expenses through his writings. His energy was not only enormous — putting in 20-hour work days — but he would expect his staff to fit in with this unreasonable schedule. Churchill's creativity encompassed 15 tons of personal papers and 43 books in 72 volumes, as well as all his other activities, such as painting and bricklaying. As to his grandiosity, he became aware of his special mission as an adolescent (when bipolar disorder often emerges), and "he was notorious for his disdain for other people and their opinions, his unwavering belief in himself as a great man."

While the consensus seems to be that Churchill did not exhibit fullfledged manic episodes, he showed many features of hypomania. To meet the criterion of this disorder, at least 3 from the following list of 7 symptoms must be present for a minimum of 4 days and observed by others: inflated self-esteem and grandiosity; less need for sleep; excessive talkativeness; racing thoughts; distractibility; increase in goal-directed activity; excessive involvement in pleasurable activities with potentially harmful consequences. The difficulty in applying these criteria precisely is that we would require narratives which clearly show that the symptoms occurred together and lasted for at least 4 days; not surprisingly, this level of detail is mostly lacking in biographical accounts. But it is clear that the "essence" of hypomania was present, and that, as described by Goodwin and Jamison, Churchill's cyclothymic nature was punctuated with severe depressions and times of high energy, elevated mood, irritability, impetuousness and questionable judgment.[596] Storr remarked, "All those who worked with him also agreed that he needed the most severe restraint put upon him, and that many of his ideas, if they had been put into practice, would have been utterly disastrous."[597] Among these potentially disastrous ideas we may count his plan to disseminate poison gas over German cities. Fieve's assessment of bipolar II disorder ("mild mania" or hypomania) has some merit, but there is room for debate as to the extent of Churchill's bipolarity.[598]

Assessment of Churchill's mood state is complicated by the possible influence of alcohol and, as he grew older, of senility. But notwithstanding, his underlying personality traits would not have altered and may have been shown in even greater relief by these factors.

Alcohol Problems Too?

There is some disagreement about whether or not Churchill had an alcohol problem. Storr believes he was alcohol-dependent but fails to back up his assertion.[599] Ludwig argues that he suffered from "alcoholism," based on the high quantities which he imbibed.[600] Ponting states, "There is no doubt that he had an alcohol addiction problem."[601] The Churchill Centre takes a more equivocal position.[602] Owen also sits on the fence, commenting that Churchill's inebriated state in the early hours of the morning concerned his wartime chiefs-of-staff; he opines that Churchill was not harmed by his heavy intake yet finds it hard to imagine how Churchill could have functioned. He had, perhaps, become tolerant to the effects of heavy alcohol intake over a 50-year period, a feature which points towards alcohol dependence.[603]

What is quite clear, however, is that his intake was unusual both in amount and in pattern. He took his first whiskey and soda (albeit strongly diluted) after breakfast, and his glass was rarely empty for the rest of the day.[604] At lunch and dinner he always drank champagne followed by several glasses of brandy. In 1924 he wrote to his wife: "I drink champagne at all meals and buckets of claret and soda in between."[605] The extent to which he was impaired by alcohol is unclear, but accounts exist of times when he had difficulty completing a speech in Parliament and had to be lead away.[606] There were several different observations of him "in no fit state to discuss anything — too tired and too much alcohol." For example, at a meeting of the wartime

Defence Committee in 1944, Churchill showed up at this particular cabinet meeting "very much the worse for drink," and the import of his condition could have been catastrophic if it was not for the intervention of his alarmed chiefs of staff.[607] In his inebriated state, Churchill took the decision to commence poison gas attacks on German cities — in violation of the Geneva Convention.[608]

The bottom line seems to be that if we apply the criteria of DSM-IV, for example, then (a) Churchill possibly did develop tolerance, and (b) recurrent alcohol use resulted in a failure to fulfill major work obligations.[609] Neither of these is sufficient to meet the criteria for alcohol dependence or abuse, yet the nature of his behavior when under the influence of alcohol gave cause for concern on at least one occasion. Assessment of his alcohol use is difficult and no doubt obscured by his own tendencies for hyperbole (e.g., the letter to his wife quoted above). Perhaps his quip that "I have taken more out of alcohol than alcohol has taken out of me" indicates that for most of the time he was in control, but the possibility of alcohol dependence or abuse cannot be entirely excluded.

Summary

As with other members of Churchill's family, going back 200 years to the first Duke of Marlborough, Winston Churchill was plagued by recurrent episodes of depression, which he and others recognized as "morbid." Possibly some of these might qualify for "major depressive episode" in today's terminology, while others would qualify for brief recurrent or minor depression: the data aren't sufficiently specific to allow us to decide. He may have experienced episodes of hypomania, although their duration is not mentioned; by general consensus, and at a minimum, he would be considered to show a cyclothymic personality. One would fall short of calling it a disorder, partly for lack of information on the exact chronology of hypomanic and depressive episodes, and also because one could argue that the cyclothymia was what made Churchill who he was, rather than it being the "cause of clinically significant distress or impairment" for any enduring length of time. His alcohol consumption probably went beyond being "normally high" for someone in his station and at times was pathological. In the last years of his life, as he suffered from strokes, evidence of senility and impaired mental function arose (e.g., difficulty with his speeches and in discharging his duties as prime minister); but rather than having Alzheimer's disease, as has been implied by some, he probably had signs of mild multi-infarct dementia.[610] During his second premiership, Churchill's failing mind became so apparent that efforts by his party to persuade him to retire gained momentum. In 1954 he gave a disastrous speech on the nuclear bomb and lost control of the House of Commons. At times his second government of the 1950s "coasted along without him, propelled forward by the efficiency of his top ministers."[611] Growing dissension in the party ranks ultimately lead to his retirement at the age of 81, with an impatient Anthony Eden waiting to take over.

Churchill found his own ways of coping with depression, some more successful than others. Perhaps the most crucial support came from his strong marriage of over 50 years to Clementine. Although he knew his depressions to be abnormal, and, like Macmillan, used the same Scottish term — "black dog" — to describe these dark visitations, he did not think of them in psychiatric terms and would have had no truck with psychiatry as a form of treatment. At times cyclothymia was a deterrent to his (and perhaps others') wellbeing, but at many other times it was the source of courage, vision, creativity and inspirational leadership.

CLEMENT ATTLEE, 1ST EARL OF PRESTWOOD (1883–1967) *(1945–1951)*

As a young man, Clement Attlee had no clear direction in his career; he qualified as a lawyer, but his heart was not really in it. Battlefield experience during World War I played a formative role in shaping his social convictions, and in the early 1920s he decided to serve the underprivileged as manager of a London boys' club. At the same time, Attlee made an impact in local politics, becoming mayor of Stepney and then Labour Member of Parliament for Limehouse in 1922. In the World War II coalition government Attlee was Churchill's deputy. The Conservatives were swept from office in 1945, and Attlee became prime minister, occupying that position for two terms between 1945 and 1951. Under his leadership many welfare state reforms were introduced through an extensive nationalization program.

Attlee was short of stature, very shy, reticent and unobtrusive, and did not possess any great oratorical skill. In reply to King George's approving comment about Attlee's modesty, Winston Churchill quipped that Attlee had much to be modest about. This well-educated, privileged and rather cerebral man was a strange misfit in some ways amongst his militant blue-collar trade union colleagues who formed the backbone of the Labour party, but, surprisingly, he made it work and survived as party leader for many years.

Attlee was stable, methodical and even-keeled, unlike Eden, Macmillan and Churchill, who were all known for their emotional liability or boisterousness. He recalled his family and childhood years as harmonious, and his long married life brought much satisfaction. Despite temperamental shyness and (seeming) lack of assertiveness as a leader, he coped adequately with the stresses of politics and never suffered from mental disorder as far as can be ascertained. In fact, Attlee is one of few prime ministers who was able to turn his modesty, shyness and good nature to advantage, for it has been said that others would go along with his proposals because they didn't want to upset him. Perhaps, after all, humility, shyness and agreeability do carry some biological advantage even at the highest levels of politics.[612]

SIR ANTHONY EDEN, 1ST EARL OF AVON (1897–1977) *(1955–1957)*

Anthony Eden was born in 1897, the third son, and fourth of five children, to Sir William Eden and Sybil Grey. His mother was descended from Earl Grey, the prime minister between 1830 and 1834, and was a relative of Sir Edward Grey, foreign secretary in the early 20th century, who steered Britain into World War I and who was impaired by grief and mental stress at that time.[613]

Eden was educated at Eton and Oxford University, where he graduated with first class honors in oriental languages. Despite initially not having political ambitions, once he entered the fray, Eden's rise was meteoric. He was appointed foreign secretary at the young age of 38 and was to occupy this position on three different occasions in the Baldwin/Chamberlain and Churchill administrations. Eden was regarded as a skillful, patient and successful negotiator who could take credit for several major triumphs, including (a) the Balkan crisis agreement of 1934, after the assassination of King Alexander of Yugoslavia; (b) the Anglo-Egyptian Treaty of 1936; (c) rescuing the European Defense Community and NATO after French obstructionism threatened serious damage to the organizations; (d) the settlement of the Trieste question in 1954; and (e) the signing of the Austrian Peace Treaty in 1955. Not for nothing was Eden hailed as the "Crown Prince" of the Conservative party. With all these achievements, it seems surprising that Eden is mainly remembered for one humiliating black mark against him, an event which lead to his resignation as prime minister and which has bedeviled his reputation ever since: the Suez Crisis. As his *Times* obituary said in 1977, Eden "was the last Prime Minister to believe Britain was a great power and the first to confront a crisis which proved she was not."[614]

Eden's Psychological Problems

Eden's state of mind has been the subject of many books and articles, and it is quite clear that he was unstable, nervous, highly strung and, despite his acknowledged patience as a negotiator, prone to losing control of his emotions at inopportune times. As a leader he failed to delegate, was poorly focused and conducted his cabinet meetings in a frenetic style that others found bothersome. On top of his temperamental flaws, he experienced serious gall bladder problems before, during and after his brief term as premier, which obviously contributed to his shortcomings as a leader. Added to these was a dependence on stimulants and sedatives. In that his gall bladder and drug problems were aggravated by mistakes made by his doctors, a good part of Eden's ill health was sadly of iatrogenic origin (i.e., doctor-caused).

How could things have gone so badly awry after such a promising start? We can address the psychological difficulties by first considering elements in Eden's make-up. He has been described as "a sensitive child," "essentially a shy man," brittle, irritable, nervous, given to "almost hysterical displays," having exaggerated sensitivity to criticism and jealousy, "excitable and temperamental," and a man with few friends.[615]

While the use of these terms can easily be taken pejoratively, they are intended to be no more than dispassionate observations about a person, which could be given to many of us if we look hard enough. Unfortunately, such characteristics are assigned negative valence by society, but they are not meant judgmentally when used in the medical context. The questions to consider are whether (a) they fall within generally accepted limits of normality (e.g., most people have some shyness, many can be moody, some are naturally suspicious, many drink a bit too much, no-one likes criticism, etc), (b) they form a breeding ground for more significant psychiatric illness, such as neurosis, psychosis, drug and alcohol misuse, and (c) they promote or hinder effective problem-solving under conditions of high stress. In Eden's case there is documentation that in 1935, long before Suez, he required medical care and "rest" due to anxiety.[616] Eden had been flying in an unpressurized aircraft between Leipzig and Cologne in turbulent conditions and became violently airsick. His pulse rate slowed to 45, and he came off the aircraft in a state of collapse. He was provisionally diagnosed as having a "strained heart," a diagnosis which was confirmed by a specialist upon his return to London and followed by a prescribed course of "convalescence." In a healthy person of 38, the most likely explanation for what happened was a vaso-vagal reaction brought about by extreme fear. Such a reaction is similar to that found among people who faint at the site of blood or needles, where fear generates impulses in the (parasympathetic) vagus nerve, which slows down the heart and reduces blood pressure, leading to a fainting response. Eden's reaction took place in the context of a stressful extended visit to Eastern Europe, with long journeys, irregular eating, interrupted sleep and endless discussions.

As with diagnoses like "clergyman's throat" and "neurasthenia," the diagnosis of a "strained heart" has fallen by the wayside except as a layman's term. Even during World War I it was recognized that strained heart was part of neurasthenia (or anxiety), found in people with "generally shattered nerve energy ... with exaggerated sensibility," and not usually evidence of cardiac disease in the absence of other changes.[617]

Apart from developing a duodenal ulcer towards the end of World War II, Eden's health remained good until 1951, although he did have one "collapse" at a meeting in 1949. During 1952, Eden became jaundiced, and in April 1953 he underwent surgery for cholecystitis. Unfortunately, during surgery the surgeon is said to have inadvertently injured the bile duct as it exited from the liver, resulting in biliary obstruction, "a schoolboy howler" of a mistake (as it has been described).[618] The effect of this complication was that Eden required two more operations over the next three months, then developed fever and chills in 1954 and 1955 on a total of 4 occasions.[619] Despite obvious embarrassment to the community of British surgeons, Eden's subsequent operations were conducted in the USA at the New England Baptist Hospital in Boston. Persisting fevers resulted in readmission in 1957 for further surgery on his biliary stricture. There followed three years of freedom from symptoms, but febrile attacks due to ascending cholangitis recurred between 1966 and 1967, and again with increasing frequency and severity after 1969. Yet another operation took place in 1970, which was followed by a relatively benign course. However, in 1975, Eden was diagnosed with prostate cancer and died from metastases in 1977. The chronology of this part of Eden's medical history makes it clear that he was badly affected by high fever, chills and weakness in October 1956, as the Suez crisis was building up, and he required emergency hospitalization in London, followed afterwards by a four-week period of rest in Jamaica. Clearly, Eden's gall bladder problems had a major impact on his fitness to conduct business during Suez. There is every reason to believe that Eden was unfit to conduct business at the time he was discharged from University College Hospital, London, in October 1956, as he was still "intoxicated" from the effects of high fever and, perhaps, stimulant drugs. Cholangitis itself can produce moodiness, argumentativeness and paranoia. Eden recognized that in this state he was unable to do a good day's work.

For all this, Eden was said to be resilient and to recover quickly from illness, but the enormity of his health problems and the comparable enormity of stress from Suez overcame his customary resilience.[620] Adding to his biliary problems was a precarious mental state of exhaustion, insomnia and low morale. In February 1956, Eden wrote to his wife, "I am well but was very tired yesterday, so stayed in bed all day." As Owen points out, "This is not the behaviour of a fit man. Lack of sleep and tiredness are too often underplayed when trying to assess the effects of people's health on their decision-making. The following month, in a rancorous debate in the House of Commons ... Eden uncharacteristically lost his temper."[621] Severe fatigue sapped his power of thought, and "tonight's winding up of the debate was a shambles."[622]

He consulted with his medical doctor, Sir Harold Evans, at least ten times between July and October of 1956. Evans prescribed barbiturates for rest and sleep, and Benzedrine, an amphetamine stimulant, to pick him up. Although disputed by Eden's wife, Eden is reported to have said that he was "living on Benzedrine." In January 1957, Evans wrote that he had prescribed two barbiturates, sodium amytal (180mg) and seconal Enseal (90mg), to be taken every night, and Drinamyl (a stimulant in the amphetamine class) to be taken most mornings for several months. Evans felt these treatments to have been "really essential," and went on to say that Eden was suffering from "overstrain and general physical nerve exhaustion," requiring rest, sedation and Vitamin B_{12}.[623] Amphetamine and barbiturate drugs were widely prescribed in the 1940s and 1950s before it was realized that, on the whole, their bad effects outweighed their benefits. It was insufficiently appreciated that both drug classes were addictive, and that they could have undesirable withdrawal effects, as well as untoward mental and behavioral consequences. Barbiturates were sedating and disinhibiting (i.e., they could remove social restraints in one's conduct), and could interfere with mental alertness. Amphetamine drugs have an awakening, alertness-enhancing effect but are also capable of producing aggression, irritability, mood swings, restlessness and rash overconfidence. Higher doses of stimulants can produce paranoia and rage. When the two drugs are combined together, as they were in Eden, their effects are potentiated (i.e., enhanced). Less well recognized is the fact that during Suez, Eden also engaged in binge drinking, which would cloud the picture even further.[624] Eden was clearly under the influence of mind-altering drugs as he went about his daily business of "running the country."

The neurologist and historian Bert Park expresses the very reasonable opinion that Eden was drawn to amphetamines because of

> the physical need to stay awake; the psychological need to combat anxiety, depression, and feelings of inferiority; and the practical need to think clearly and act forcefully. Laboring through the Suez crisis with less than five hours sleep a night, perceiving condescension in the American president and secretary of state, and resolved to send Nasser a forceful message without losing face, the anxiety-ridden prime minister needed a psychological crutch to bolster his self-confidence. Benzedrine offered a ready solution for one who had already been living on his nerves for some time.[625]

There is little doubt that during the Suez crisis Eden was affected by amphetamine, barbiturates and perhaps alcohol in ways which adversely affected his judgment and decision-making capacity, and which caused him to behave in ways which were out of character; it was as if he had undergone a "personality change."

It is unclear at what point Eden started to come under the influence of stimulants, but after 1953 it is possible to see an acceleration of the destructive side effects noted above, and which corresponded to his increase in the medication dose. By the time of his resignation in January 1957, Eden admitted to his cabinet that "During these last five months, since Nasser seized the Canal in July, I have been obliged to increase the drugs [i.e., barbiturates] considerably and also increase the stimulants necessary to counteract the drugs. This has finally had an adverse effect on my precarious inside.... [My doctors] think I would not last more than six weeks."[626]

World War and Personal Tragedy

Like his contemporaries Harold Macmillan and Clement Attlee, Eden saw extensive combat action in World War I and was forever affected by these experiences. Eden originally hoped to enter Sandhurst (the British equivalent of West Point) but was rejected due to poor eyesight. With the outbreak of war, as the Army relaxed its entry requirements, he earned a commission in the King's Royal Rifle Corps. Shortly after arrival in France in June 1916 he learned that his 16-year-old brother Nicholas had drowned when his boat sunk at the Battle of Jutland. Eden went on to fight in the Battle of the Somme and won the Military Cross for his rescue under fire of a wounded sergeant. After the attack in Delville Wood, 394 members of Eden's battalion were killed or seriously injured, including almost all junior officers, which lead to his rapid promotion to adjutant, and later to major, a rank which he attained at the age of 20, making him the youngest major in the British army.

Besides the loss of his younger brother Nicholas, he had learned earlier, before leaving Eton in 1914, that his oldest brother John had been killed in battle in 1914. His second brother, Timothy, was a German POW for 2 years. Compounding these tragedies, Eden's father died in 1915 after a long illness.

Almost 30 years later, war was to claim the life of his son, Simon, who was killed in Burma shortly before the end of hostilities with Japan.

For one given to anxiety and excessive sensitivity, we might expect these harrowing war experiences to produce some degree of post-traumatic stress, but there is little to suggest this was the case, apart from Eden's reminiscence that, after the war, he was unable to appreciate the beauties of the countryside and wondered if he "could ever again see them free from the memory of those other shell-worn trees and ravaged fields with their torn wire and heaped and silent bodies." Intrusive symptoms from his battle trauma apparently persisted for some time. Eden rarely talked about his wartime experiences, but they shaped his defiant and steadfast attitude towards the rise of totalitarian regimes in Europe when, at the time, he was one of few British politicians willing to stand up against them. For his courage, Churchill saluted Eden as "one strong young figure standing up against long, dismal, drawling tides of drift and surrender.... He seemed at this moment to embody the life-hope of the British nation."[627]

Summary

Eden was hypersensitive, and prone to attacks of anxiety and irritability, yet he possessed considerable strengths. As a young adult he weathered the storms of extreme stress during his war service, overcame several tragic bereavements and, two decades later, stood up to the dictators of Europe. As he aged into his sixth decade, and the inevitable prize of the premiership seemed forever to be dangled teasingly by Churchill, he grew increasingly frustrated and petulant. At the same time, his health deteriorated and he suffered gravely from a surgical error on the operating table. Compounding all of this was his growing need for addicting sedative and stimulant drugs, so that by the time he was occupying No. 10 Downing Street as prime minister, he was quite unable to provide sound leadership and made a series of uncharacteristically poor decisions, leading to humiliation and early resignation.

HAROLD MACMILLAN, 1ST EARL OF STOCKTON (1894–1986) *(1957–1963)*

In many ways the dice were loaded against Harold Macmillan, yet his life embodies stoicism over physical and psychological pain and an ability to overcome the odds. Based on his childhood and adolescence, few would have envisioned him reaching such political heights. His struggles over inner demons took up much energy but paved the way for great achievement.

Harold Macmillan was the third son of Maurice Macmillan and Nellie Belles. Maurice was of Scottish pedigree, whereas his mother was born and raised in the United States and came to Europe to study art. Like his contemporary Winston Churchill, Macmillan thus had joint British-American heritage. His father was a remote figure, immersed in his family publishing company, while his mother showed a thrusting ambition which perhaps paved the way for Harold's achievements.

Early Years and War Service

At school Harold was frequently sick, his heart was thought to be "overstrained," and he left Eton College prematurely on account of ill-health. It is believed that Macmillan's lifelong hypochondriacal worries first appeared at this time. After he left Eton, special tutoring was provided, and he won a classical exhibition to Oxford University where, despite his shyness, he distinguished himself by becoming secretary and treasurer of the esteemed Oxford Union; had war not broken out, it is likely that he would have become president. For a man with marked public speaking anxiety, such activity took courage, and it also gave early notice of a leaning towards politics. He graduated in June 1914 and enlisted for military service.

Between September 1915 and September 1916, Macmillan saw extensive front-line action and was wounded three times — at Loos, Ypres and the Somme. These injuries were serious and required prolonged convalescence. The worst wounds were inflicted at the Battle of the Somme in September 1916, where he sustained injuries to his pelvis and thigh; he was lucky to survive and then almost succumbed afterwards to wound infection. For one day he lay in a shell hole in no man's land before being found by a colleague, and then had to make his way "in a state of panic" to the dressing station. During the 24 hours of waiting for help, Macmillan found time to read (in Greek) the copy of Aeschylus' *Prometheus*, which he was carrying. Reading was always Macmillan's way of getting through bad times in his life and showed a capacity to detach from, or "get outside" of, acutely stressful situations.

As a result of his wounds, Macmillan was left with recurrent pain for the rest of his life, and other health problems almost certainly were aggravated by his traumas. Yet war experience left Macmillan the better in some important ways, as it did his contemporary and predecessor as prime minister, Clement Attlee. Both Macmillan and Attlee attributed their "compassion, resilience and perspective" to their war experiences.[628] The effects of war trauma on Harold Macmillan will be discussed later.

Marriage

Macmillan married Lady Dorothy Cavendish in 1920. One son and two daughters were conceived by their marriage, and a third daughter, Sarah, is widely regarded to have been fathered by Lord Boothby, but was accepted as one of the Macmillan children and raised by Harold and Dorothy. While Macmillan was devoted to Dorothy, she was in many ways unfulfilled and in 1929 began a lifelong affair with Macmillan's political colleague, Lord Boothby. The origins of this affair are the subject of speculation, but it is known that, since youth, Macmillan was prone to recurrent depressions and that his libido was chronically low, which could have proved intolerable to Dorothy, who came from a family (the Dukes and Duchesses of Devonshire) whose women were celebrated for their high libido. Added to this concern was the fact that Macmillan was deeply occupied in his dual careers of publishing and politics, often making him unavailable to provide affection and support to his family. In any event, Dorothy's liaison with Boothby was greatly disturbing to Macmillan, who in 1931 "suffered a full-scale nervous breakdown," diagnosed at the time as neurasthenia, leading to several months treatment at a sanatorium near Munich. It is rumored that Macmillan may have made a suicide attempt.[629] Despite the real possibility of divorce, Harold and Dorothy preserved their marriage; and although it improved somewhat in later years, the painful effects of her conduct remained with Harold for the rest of his days.

Psychological problems emerged in all their children. Maurice endured several years of struggle against alcoholism, which he eventually overcame with treatment. The Macmillans' three daughters and a grandson also had drug or alcohol problems, his grandson dying after accidentally ingesting a toxic mixture of drugs and alcohol. Their daughter Sarah died "accidentally" at the age of 40 after years of psychiatric difficulties and hospitalizations.

Macmillan in Politics

Macmillan first entered Parliament as the member for Stockton-on-Tees, an industrial constituency in the northeast of England, which he served between 1924 and 1929. He lost the seat in the 1929 general election but regained it in 1931, retaining it until the 1945 election when he again was unseated. He then obtained the safer Bromley seat from 1945 and retained it until retirement in 1964. For a long time Macmillan remained in relative obscurity, but he came into his own during World War II as Churchill's resident minister at Allied Force Headquarters in the Mediterranean. Through this appointment Macmillan increased his stature within the party and became known as "Viceroy of the Mediterranean by stealth."[630] Following the war, after a period in opposition, he became minister for housing, and then defence, in Churchill's second administration. Under Eden, Macmillan served as foreign secretary and then chancellor of the exchequer. Macmillan became prime minister upon Eden's resignation on January 9, 1957. Macmillan brought the country out of the long shadow of post-war austerity into an economic recovery. It was one of Macmillan's major priorities to lead Britain into the newly formed European Union, but, sadly for him, these efforts were rebuffed by President de Gaulle.

The year 1963 produced Conservative party turmoil via the spy and John

Profumo sex scandals, which made retirement an appropriate course of action for Macmillan. After committing to it, then changing his mind, in early October Macmillan was stricken with a medical emergency. Seemingly, he had delayed telling the doctor about his symptoms for some time, and it took an episode of painful urinary retention to force the issue. While the condition — prostatic hypertrophy (enlargement) — was benign, Macmillan feared the worst and took it to mean he had cancer, which could well have factored into his decision to resign, according to Owen.[631] He resigned as prime minister on October 18, 1963, and retired from the House of Commons at the 1964 general election. Many of his remaining years were spent as chair of Macmillan publishers and a period as chancellor of Oxford University. He also wrote his memoirs and war diaries, which, while being of great interest, remained quite guarded about his personal and family life.

Macmillan's Psychiatric Symptoms

Macmillan was affected by four different kinds of symptom: recurrent depression since youth, anxiety when the center of attention, hypochondriasis and neurasthenia. This is not to say that they were all separate pathological processes, but each will be critically evaluated.

Depression. Macmillan was subject to attacks of what he called "Black Dog," a term which was used in Scotland to describe depression, and which was also borrowed by Winston Churchill. It was "cyclical" and "seasonal," often seen as arising from within as much as from external events.[632] For example, Macmillan said:

> I had it very badly at Eton.... I used to get it when in office, then I'd go to Birch Grove for two days, by myself, read Jane Austen. My wife understood.... [I] didn't want to see people ... it was seasonal ... makes you inward-looking, isolated.... External things like Profumo never really worried me.... It was just the inside feeling that something awful was about to happen — or, sometimes, a great exhilaration."[633]

It is interesting that he acknowledges some feelings of exhilaration, but no other clues exist which might support the idea of bipolar disorder. However, his form of depression could be at the distant (i.e., low) end of the bipolar spectrum, less severe than bipolar II disorder.

Typically, Macmillan would deal with these attacks by withdrawing into the world of Jane Austen, Anthony Trollope or other comforting literature, a device which he used to help get through the terrifying 24 hours spent in the foxhole during battle. The "black dog" episodes would last a few days at a time. His low level of interest in sex would be compatible with depression, as this is a well recognized symptom of the disorder, but its constancy over many years suggests another origin (discussed below). The rumored suicide attempt and need for prolonged hospitalization in the 1930s at a low ebb in his fortunes is also compatible with, but not firm proof of, depression. After World War II, when he was in the political wilderness and still dealing with marital difficulties, his memoirs repeatedly refer to a state of melancholy, futility and disillusionment.[634]

Horne notes that 1960 was a bad year for Macmillan, with the collapse of the summit meeting, and problems with de Gaulle, Africa and the economy. 1961 and 1962 were even worse — Macmillan's older brother died of cancer, and he and his family had to vacate No. 10 Downing Street for urgent repairs (and the temporary accommodation was found to be unsatisfactory). In mid–1961 he contracted a viral infection which persisted for some time and left him "old and depressed" after a one-month rest cure had failed to do the trick. Even the queen expressed worry about his health, and in October he was "seriously contemplating resignation."[635] Interestingly, he complained that the doctor's pills made him depressed. Among these prescriptions was a medicine called Veganin, which is still available in many parts of the world, and contains paracetamol (a pain reliever and antipyretic), caffeine (a mild stimulant and possible additive to the effects of paracetamol) and codeine (a narcotic pain reliever, which can have other untoward effects on the nervous system). At this time he also imbibed more alcohol, although in general he was abstemious in his drinking habits.

Despite an upturn in his fortunes during 1962, including the successful Test Ban Treaty among the nuclear powers, he became increasingly troubled, with complaints of lassitude and flatness, and displayed less resilience than usual. He was beginning to "get very tired ... lose his grip" and become "much more fatigue[d]," and one of his ministers commented that Macmillan "drooled and wasted time.... He was hardly sensible; so often the trouble with a man when his powers are failing."[636] Although prostate enlargement might account for some of these changes, depression was almost certainly a partner in crime.[637]

Relief from the pressures of office afforded no protection against the black dog, which kept barking as Macmillan grew older. He endured the deaths of his wife Dorothy in 1966, his daughter Sarah in 1970 and his son Maurice in 1984. Horne notes the extent of his melancholia, fatalism and loneliness in the 1980s. Macmillan's health deteriorated, with the development of blindness, gout, shingles, pleurisy and aggravation of pain from his war injuries. He found reading difficult and, in the opinion of his family, "died of boredom. Life was no longer fun."[638]

Anxiety, Neurasthenia and Hypochondriasis

Speech Anxiety. Macmillan readily acknowledged his nervousness before having to give a speech and his "perpetual terror of becoming in any way conspicuous."[639] This, too, is a form of exaggerated social anxiety, which can impede a person in fulfilling their life goals or cause unbearable distress if they do expose themselves to the feared situation. While it did not prevent Macmillan from reaching the top of the political ladder, on many occasions his extreme pre-speech nerves interfered with his well-being, and it is instructive to see how hard he made himself work in studying the mannerisms of successful orators in Parliament, like Lloyd George. From them he learned a lot and overcame his lackluster efforts and ineffective posturing to become a highly skilled speaker himself. As Horne notes, "Having studied performances from the backbenches for so many years, and having received the advice of real professionals like Lloyd George and Winston Churchill, Macmillan had by now come close to perfecting the art of dominating the Commons."[640]

In describing how he felt when he made his maiden Parliamentary speech in 1925, he said it was "as alarming as any experience except for 'going over the top' in war."[641] Before his 1956 budget speech he spent the morning in bed, unable to eat, finding that "the nervous strain of these speeches seems to get worse as one gets older."[642] In this he was correct, for on a tour of Africa in 1960 he had to make several unplanned bathroom stops for abdominal problems before giving speeches, and on at least one occasion was taken to the toilet where he vomited.[643]

Macmillan's anxiety before speeches was above and beyond what most people would consider normal, especially for such an accomplished speaker; it was greatly distressing but never disabling. He admitted and dutifully faced up to his fears, did the right things by studying the masters and accepting their advice, and became a master of the art himself; yet he never lost his anxiety.

Neurasthenia, Hypochondriasis and Possible Post-Traumatic Stress Disorder. Neurasthenia was a fashionable diagnosis during the late 19th and early 20th centuries. It literally means "weak nerves." The diagnosis has long since disappeared from the practice of western medicine, although it still exists as a diagnosis in ICD-10, under the code of F48.0, and continues to be used quite frequently in some parts of Asia; it even responds to antidepressants.[644] The label is something of a "catch-all" but refers to a disorder of easy fatigability after only minor effort, whether mental or physical. It also embraces symptoms of anxiety and physical symptoms, so a degree of hypochondriasis is sometimes seen. In order to avoid the stigma of having a mental illness, this somewhat more "physical" diagnosis would have been more respectable, and may be the reason that Macmillan's depression in 1931 was so labeled. Using the same terminology as Macmillan's doctors, Horne believed that Macmillan's post-traumatic eczema in 1944 was also of neurasthenic origin.[645]

Among its various meanings, neurasthenia was also an alternative name for what is today referred to as post-traumatic stress disorder (PTSD), and many returning veterans of World War I received this diagnosis.[646] Almost all the officers who were hospitalized at Craiglockhart War Hospital in Edinburgh towards the end of World War I received this diagnosis, including the celebrated war poets Wilfred Owen, Robert Graves and Siegfried Sassoon, all of whom are believed to have suffered from PTSD. Little attention has subsequently been paid to the relationship between neurasthenia and trauma, but in one study of earthquake survivors, my group of researchers at Duke and colleagues in Taiwan have observed a rate between 11 and 24 percent for neurasthenic-like syndrome 10 months after the earthquake, so there may indeed be a relationship between trauma and neurasthenia.[647] We should therefore consider if there is any evidence to support the possibility that the "neurasthenic" Harold Macmillan actually suffered from PTSD, either partial or complete.

A positive history of depression or anxiety is known to increase the risk of PTSD following exposure to trauma, and Macmillan was positive on both counts. He undoubtedly experienced several major traumata during military service, as well as a later life-threatening air crash with burn injuries during World War II. The worst of these traumata appears to have been at the Battle of the Somme, where he feared for his life ("I was absolutely terrified ... very frightened") and experienced panic at the time of the event.[648] From studies after the 9/11 New York terrorist attacks, we have learned that having a panic attack at the time of the trauma is a potent risk factor increasing the likelihood of developing PTSD.[649] We do not have documentation that Macmillan experienced the recurrent intrusive memories or nightmares of battle, but there is some possibility that he showed "psychic numbing" or loss of the capacity for intimate feelings — in that he seems to have developed a lifelong disinterest in sex and kept a tight rein on showing his true feelings. In addition, he remained aloof from people and was reluctant to reveal his real self, which are the kinds of behaviors associated with another key symptom of PTSD: detachment or estrangement from others. These symptoms never seem to have resolved and may have contributed to the loneliness which characterized much of his later life. As to the last class of PTSD symptoms (increased arousal), it is difficult to know their extent — there would have to be irritability, exaggerated startle reactions, insomnia, poor concentration or increased vigilance (watchfulness). While many of these were described at different times, they could have been related to PTSD, depression, pain from pelvic injuries from the war, other anxiety or medical problems.

PTSD is often accompanied by guilt for surviving when others died, which haunted Macmillan for many years and which imbued in him a sense of obligation to "make some decent use of the life that had been spared to us."[650]

One essential aspect of PTSD which apparently did not affect Harold Macmillan was the presence of avoidance symptoms. Rather than tending to avoid reminders of the war, Macmillan saw in the "great experience" of war much that was positive.[651] He saluted the courage of many brave comrades, acquired an undying respect for courage in others, and identified with the underprivileged in society. The camaraderie and the striving for perfection to which he was exposed in war became a "good working rule for civilian life."[652] Reminiscing in his old age, Macmillan said that war "was all great fun, I enjoy wars; any adventure's better than sitting in an office."[653] In politics, he was more readily attracted to former warriors as friends and counselors than those who had not fought in battle.

So all in all, Macmillan may have experienced a degree of post-traumatic stress in his distancing, detachment and survivor guilt—a topic for further enquiry. Illustrative of this contention is his description of neurasthenia in 1931 as being "rather a battered feeling ... the same kind of experience after Loos or after the Somme. But I was younger then, and had (I suppose) more resilience."[654] However, he lacked the all important avoidance symptoms which arise from fear of the event. Instead, as he noted, Macmillan was able to harness considerable positive energy from his "battering," from which he grew and obtained clearer focus in his life. It was perhaps in his personal life that he paid the highest price.

SIR ALEC DOUGLAS-HOME, LORD HOME OF THE HIRSEL (1903–1995) *(1963–1967)*

Alec Douglas-Home was born in 1903, inheriting the name Lord Dunglass in 1918, then the Earl of Home in 1951, which he renounced to become prime minister in 1963, whereupon he took the name Sir Alec Douglas-Home. In 1974 he acquired his final title of Lord Home of the Hirsel. As is clear from all this, Douglas-Home came from a landed aristocratic background, and his appointment as prime minister so late in the 20th century—60 years after the last titled aristocrat had occupied 10 Downing Street (Lord Salisbury)—made him a rather anachronistic figure. While he was well respected, his upper class background made it hard for most of the electorate to identify with him, and he was not returned at the 1964 election.

Alec Douglas-Home is not known to have experienced any form of psychiatric disorder, and his overall health was good, except for a severe bout of spinal tuberculosis in 1940 which necessitated surgery and a 2-year period of immobility.[655]

HAROLD WILSON, LORD WILSON OF RIEVAULX (1916–1995) *(1964–1970; 1974–1976)*

Harold Wilson won election as prime minister a total of four times, albeit with very narrow majorities in three of them. He served as premier between 1964 and 1970, and again between 1974 and 1976, before resigning abruptly. His resignation took most by surprise, and his voluntary retirement from office was quite unusual in that most other leaders were removed either by electoral defeat or internal party rebellion. Wilson's mental health almost certainly played a key part in his decision, as he became increasingly compromised during the final phase of his leadership by stress and early dementia, despite his relative youth, for he was only 60.

Jenkins considers Wilson to be the dominating British politician between 1963 and 1976, and while neither leaving any ideological legacy nor being particularly inspirational, he was "a very considerable servant of the state" who "kept the government on the rails over difficult stretches." Perhaps Wilson's biggest contribution was holding his party together over the fiercely disputed matter of whether Britain should join the European Community, as he negotiated terms for entry.[656]

Wilson's Mental Health

Three problem areas can be identified with respect to Wilson's psychological health during his final term between 1974 and 1976: (1) difficulty coping with stress, which produced a variety of symptoms, chiefly worry, gastrointestinal problems, proneness to eye infections, insomnia and acute anxiety; (2) the end result of many years of heavy drinking; and (3) failing memory, concentration and confabulation (i.e., making up details to cover gaps in memory), all of which have been chronicled by Owen, Ziegler, Pimlott, Jenkins and Ludwig, among others.[657]

Stress and Anxiety

With respect to stress and anxiety, Wilson had two serious airplane accidents — the first in 1947, which appeared to have left no lasting scars, and a second in 1974 after an aborted landing, which resulted in acute anxiety ("heart flutter"), frightened him, and then resulted in numerous visits to his doctor for tiredness, "psychosomatic" stomach pains (which he experienced before difficult or stressful meetings) and eye infections when under pressure. Despite his doctor's judgment that Wilson was "a very tough cookie in medical terms," we should consider the possibility that this assessment downplayed the role of stress on Wilson's mental state, as well as the effect of his increasing need for alcohol and his declining memory.[658]

"The ceaseless grind of routine matters, the pressure of working at a desk where every buck was bound eventually to stop" was starting to get on top of Wilson by 1974, just as he began his final administrations.[659] Other manifestations of stress which became apparent in his final term of office included insomnia and stomach pains before painful confrontations. Anticipatory worry before Prime Minister's Question Time in the House of Commons began to prey on his nerves in a way it had never done before.[660] The many seemingly insoluble problems filled him with "embittered despair."[661] Pimlott remarked that Wilson talked and worried a lot about his health, and that there was "no sparkle left."[662]

Use of Alcohol

Wilson was known as a "vigorous toper" who filled his brandy glass "and quaffed it as though it were ale."[663] In 1960, some years before he became prime minister, Wilson's colleague Crossman thought his drinking was no greater than that of many politicians, although another colleague, Hugh Gaitskell, believed that it was excessive.[664] However, by 1964, when he became prime minister, his intake had increased, and brandy, which hitherto was his drink of choice as "an occasional stimulant," had now "become a need." Worryingly, much of Wilson's drinking took place when he was alone; it was less a form of socialization than a way of dealing with stress. Episodes of intoxication, however, were few and far between.

During 1974–1975, Wilson became increasingly isolated as problems built up, including the IRA terror campaign, unilateral declaration of independence in Rhodesia, inflation, the state of the British currency, a struggle for the heart and soul of the Labour Party and the behavior of his long-serving political secretary, who made a "deplorable" impression on others and reduced Wilson's standing in Whitehall.[665] In this somewhat bleak setting, Wilson turned increasingly to alcohol. His doctor, Joseph Stone, supposedly prescribed alcohol to strengthen his patient's metabolism, but as Ziegler suggests, it is doubtful whether Stone was aware of the amount of brandy Wilson consumed (nor is it likely that he would have approved of it). The prime minister needed brandy before most meetings, and civil servants would frown on his solitary drinking during ministerial meetings. Later he gave up brandy to lose weight but replaced it with five pints of beer a day — hardly a good trade-off. Ziegler claims that a steady intake of high quantities of alcohol over the years damaged Wilson's health.[666]

Dementia

By 1974, Wilson was observed to lose his famed sharpness of memory and to make regular errors when referencing dates or figures. Sometimes he was unable to follow a train of thought, and confabulation was noted by at least one doctor who had occasion to be with Wilson. (Confabulation is the term used to describe the habit of covering up memory gaps in speech by making up or guessing at details and is regarded as a sign of brain damage.) Allied to these changes, Wilson gave the impression of being tired, listless and unable to generate any fire or enthusiasm. He "lost all capacity for original thought ... and found difficulty in improvising even a routine constituency speech." On at least one occasion he lost control of a cabinet meeting, letting it lapse into a disorganized tangle. While he could still conduct the orchestra most of the time, he was surely aware of these changes, and for a person who had taken pride in his excellent memory, "to be at a loss for words or to grope for a statistic was ... a blow to his confidence."[667]

A neurological study of the unscripted exchanges that took place during Prime Minister's Question Time by Garrard suggests deterioration of Wilson's Parliamentary speeches by the time of his final administration.[668] Subtle linguistic changes are among the first signs of Alzheimer's dementia, often appearing before anything else. Garrard demonstrated that, compared to the mid–1960s, Wilson's speeches showed a decline in the use of certain words that had previously made his speeches distinguishable from others in Parliament. Garrard's theory could readily explain why Wilson developed such anxiety before Question Time in the House, where answers must be extemporaneous and unscripted. In such circumstances, when concentration and memory are slipping away and one cannot rise emotionally to the challenge, anxiety would be an understandable reaction.

In later years, Wilson's dementia worsened, and on a speaking tour in the U.S., during an arranged meeting with former president Carter, he forgot who Carter was and why the two were meeting. He was unable to adapt to the five-hour time change; he kept waking in the middle of the night, expecting breakfast to be served and to set out on his appointments of the next day. This pattern of confusion as to day and night is a feature of dementia. As a result of these problems, Wilson ceased his lecture tours, and as the years passed, his capacity to concentrate diminished even further. It is generally believed that Wilson was suffering from dementia by this time, although whether as the result of alcohol or Alzheimer's disorder cannot be said with certainty.[669] His health deteriorated, and he developed bowel cancer in 1980, for which a series of operations were necessary. A doctor at the time recorded how Wilson's memory of things past was excellent, but for recent happenings it was very poor — a classical sign of dementia.[670]

Summary

Harold Wilson was in good health, perhaps even robust health, until his first period as prime minister, when his intake of alcohol started to increase. Wilson's increasing consumption from 1960 onwards, and even more so after 1964 when he became prime minister, suggests a deficit in his ability to cope with the heavy stress of office. He had few other outlets, remained somewhat solitary, was given to paranoia, and had difficulty handling the kind of confrontations which would be expected to occur from time to time. Wilson was described as having a bunker mentality and marked political insecurity.[671] While there may have been some justification for Wilson's paranoia, surely his mental decline must have amplified it beyond a reasonable level. The evolution of his mental illness between 1964 and 1976 reveals progressively more "psychosomatic" symptoms, more frequent visits to the doctor, and uncharacteristic anxiety in situations which had not proved bothersome previously. In addition, Wilson drank to excess and in a way which was inappropriate, and witnessed the steady decline of his cognitive functions. There was no watershed, like a stroke, trauma or other sudden change, just a gradual erosion of those skills and faculties which are so critical to providing good leadership.

Making sense of this from a diagnostic point of view, it is important to keep in mind that late-onset anxiety is rarely due to a primary anxiety disorder (which typically starts early in life) but is more likely to be caused by some other process, perhaps an early result of dementia, hastened by high stress and the toxic effects of alcohol. Wilson's decision to give up power voluntarily and without any pressure (other than the pleadings of his wife) was unusual; as Tuchman said of Solon, it is rare for a statesman to voluntarily walk away from power, and bespeaks a degree of wisdom or at least good common sense.[672]

SIR EDWARD HEATH (1916–2005) *(1970–1974)*

Edward Heath was prime minister between 1970 and 1974. Heath was one of the few Conservative prime ministers who did not hail from a background of privilege and wealth; his father was a carpenter, then a master-builder, and his mother a maid. Heath had "risen to the top against heavy odds by a combination of effort, intelligence and idealism."[673] He is perhaps best remembered for successfully negotiating the United Kingdom's entry into the European Community after previous rebuffs by President de Gaulle. Heath was Conservative party leader for 10 years and fought four elections, winning only one. His period in office did not last long and "ended in spectacular disarray and high drama created by the oil crisis, the miners' strike, the imposition of a three-day week in industry, and the decision to call an election on the issue of who governs Britain, which the government lost."[674] The three-day work week ranks with the general strike, the Blitz and Callaghan's "winter of discontent" as among the unforgettable low points in 20th century Britain.[675]

Heath's Health

Other than sustaining relatively minor combat wounds during World War II and being hospitalized for jaundice in 1959, Heath remained fit and healthy.[676] He was moderate in alcohol consumption and a non-smoker; he even banned smoking at his cabinet meetings, an unpopular move at the time but, in retrospect, perhaps an enlightened decision. Regular exercise, competitive sailing and music were important outlets for him.

Heath's mental health took a knock during the miners' crisis and around the time of the three-day week in 1973 and 1974. As described by Campbell, he became slow, overweight, ponderous, indecisive and silent, and lost his quickness of mind. His voice was hoarse, he appeared droopy-eyed and puffy-faced. Things had reached a point where Heath was putting off potentially troublesome appointments because "such was his condition that his staff liked to limit any potentially tricky problem to one a day."[677] One acquaintance who had not seen him in a few years was shocked at how much he had changed. On the other hand, some of his closest colleagues saw nothing awry, putting it down to too many chocolate biscuits, or brushing aside his tiredness on the grounds that everyone was tired. Such a discrepancy would not be unusual in that hypothyroidism develops slowly, and one may not see the minute degrees of change from day to day, whereas substantial change might be apparent to the occasional observer.[678]

In Campbell's opinion, "Unquestionably, it can now be said, his health was a contributory factor to the uncharacteristic indecisiveness, lethargy, even paralysis of will, with which he met his nemesis in February."[679] Heath's tiredness and irritability could be attributed to hypothyroidism or to the low-grade depression which often accompanies the condition. The symptoms occurred at a critical time, both with respect to the country's economic and industrial difficulties, and Heath's ability to make the correct decision over whether to call an election. Campbell asserts that Heath's political judgment "was plainly affected throughout this period: the psychological effect of his mysterious illness can only have been to reinforce his sense of being under siege and fighting — perhaps literally — for his life."[680] In contrast to Campbell's view, Owen takes a more cautious approach over the role of hypothyroidism in compromising Heath's mental states when prime minister.[681] The truth probably lies somewhere in the middle, since sub-clinical hypothyroidism (i.e., low levels, before any overt "thyroid" manifestations are apparent) can produce depression, which in turn can impair energy, memory, concentration and decision-making.

For several years Heath struggled with this untreated disorder and would be seen sleeping in Parliament. By 1981, his low thyroid state was so severe that he was in obvious need of treatment and was prescribed the thyroid hormone thyroxine. Unfortunately, he had an overreaction and developed atrial fibrillation and heart failure. For two months he had to withdraw from all engagements until his thyroid state was stabilized. What benefit might have accrued if Heath's thyroid problems had been more quickly recognized and treated while he was in power? His story reminds us of the pernicious effect that abnormal thyroid function can have on leaders, and of the importance of prompt detection and treatment. Other recent examples of hypothyroidism or hyperthyroidism in heads of state include George Bush Sr. and Boris Yeltsin.

Heath was a robust child, neither prey to nerves nor to disproportionate feelings of dread or foreboding. He was always rather uneasy around women, which may account for the fact that he never married, and he could easily be embarrassed by public displays of affection towards him by women.[682] He blushed readily, was moody, could be hurt by criticism and was perceived as rather friendless, a characterization which he disputed.[683] If accurate, these tendencies would be compatible with high social anxiety in certain situations, specifically heterosexual intimacy and friendships. While other biographers have mulled over the question of possible homosexual inclinations, or even asexuality, the possibility of social phobia, confined to relationships with women, has not been previously raised. Whether or not he was affected by this disorder, it obviously made no difference to Heath's successful career in politics. Thyroid disorder, unfortunately, appears to have hampered his competency at a critical time.

JAMES CALLAGHAN, LORD CALLAGHAN OF CARDIFF (1912–2005) *(1976–1979)*

James Callaghan, affectionately known as "Sonny Jim," served as Labour prime minister between April 1976 and May 1979. Callaghan was constitutionally robust and was one of the longest-lived of all prime ministers, dying at the age of 92. Apart from an episode of tuberculosis in the 1940s, his health was good, and he prided himself in his general physical fitness.[684] From the psychiatric view, there is some reason to believe that he experienced a single three-week-long episode of depression while in office at a time of conflict between government and trade unions.[685] During these three weeks, Callaghan appeared unable to offer any response to the crisis, remaining "becalmed," refusing appeals to address the country on the economic situation, and turning to others to ask what he should do. A contemporary noted his "deep depression, almost helplessness."[686] As far as is known, this was a single episode in a man not otherwise prone to depression. Without further information to support the occurrence of a major depression, perhaps the most suitable term to describe Callaghan's condition would be adjustment disorder with depressed mood.

MARGARET THATCHER, BARONESS THATCHER OF KESTEVEN (1925–) *(1979–1990)*

Margaret Thatcher has the distinction of being Britain's first woman prime minister and one of the longest-serving of all 20th century premiers. She lead the Conservative government between 1979 and 1990, and prosecuted a successful war (from the British standpoint) against Argentina over the Falkland Islands in 1982. Thatcher is also the first prime minister to have been honored with a statue in Parliament while still alive.

Thatcher was a forceful personality who, like Lloyd George, "always displayed a determination to achieve what she wanted, irrespective of the obstacles in her way."[687] She had the capacity to put in long hours and survive with little sleep. Like Gladstone, she possessed "immense powers of concentration and a quite exceptional memory." Thatcher enjoyed excellent health throughout her life, until in old age she developed dementia, perhaps related to a series of minor strokes. According to her daughter, Mrs. Thatcher first showed changes around 2000 when she reached the age of 75. The decline has been gradual, but it has left Thatcher a "shadow of her former self."[688] Memory decline is noticeable — she sometimes forgets where she lives and that her husband has died. None of these changes took place while Thatcher was in office and so did not affect her leadership abilities.

SIR JOHN MAJOR (1943–) *(1990–1997)*

John Major followed Margaret Thatcher as prime minister in 1990 and remained in office until 1997. He was the youngest prime minister in the 20th century at the time of his appointment.

Major has been in good health in the main, and there is nothing to suggest the occurrence of any mental illness or personality traits which might predispose to depression, anxiety or an impaired ability to cope with the pressures of leadership.[689]

ANTHONY (TONY) BLAIR (1953–) *(1997–2007)*

Tony Blair was born on June 9, 1953, the second of three children. He was educated at Fettes College and Oxford University, and became a barrister prior to entering politics.

Blair entered Parliament in 1983 and rose quickly to leadership of the Labour party in 1994. He served as prime minister between 1997 and 2007, winning three elections, before voluntarily resigning in 2007.

While there is no obvious evidence for mental illness, Owen has indicated that during 2004 Blair was under considerable stress and may have been depressed. Blair divulged the presence of an irregular heart beat, although in a way which suggested some attempt to minimize its true extent. The cause of his condition remains unclear and has been put down by Blair as resulting from lack of sleep and excessive caffeine, but other explanations are possible.[690]

Conclusion

From this overall review it is striking, but perhaps not surprising, that so many prime ministers have shown the effects of stress on their health while in office. In many cases these could be seen as time-limited stress reactions which are readily understandable when taken in context; even the strongest have their limits. But for many premiers, what seems to have occurred could better be understood as exacerbations of disorders which had long been present — mostly depression, anxiety or alcohol/substance use problems.

Thirty-seven (72 percent) of 51 prime ministers appear to have experienced mental disorders or significant symptoms at some time in their lives (Table 1). Even allowing for differences in methods, the findings might be compared to lifetime rates of psychiatric disorder in the general population, as reported in one major study. The rate of 72 percent is far in excess of the 49 percent observed among males in the general population, in whom disease-specific rates were 15 percent, 19 percent and 35 percent for mood disorders, anxiety and alcohol/substance abuse or dependence, respectively.[1] The rates in prime ministers were higher for mood and anxiety, but lower for drug and alcohol problems.

The occurrence of psychiatric problems among prime ministers was independent of era, influence of the monarch, composition of the electorate or selection pool of leaders (i.e., aristocracy, middle class or blue collar). These findings give substance to Ludwig's partly tongue-in-cheek comment that in order to become prime minister of Great Britain, it is almost a requirement to have been depressed.[2] Perhaps as might be expected from its high rate (13 percent) in the general population, depression was the most common disorder, with 22 (43 percent of the entire cohort) being described in the biographies as going through periods of depression, which were often referred to as profound. Out of these 22, eleven had depression without qualification, six seemed to have depression that was associated with chronic grief, three with a seasonal (winter) emphasis and two with bipolar disorder.

If psychiatric disorders only arose after election to office, it would be a simple matter to ascribe them to stress, but such is not the case; some other factors must be at work. Eighteenth century prime ministers were largely chosen by the king, and it would be tempting to wonder if the psychopathology of George III, whether porphyria or bipolar disorder, played a role in his selection of ministers. But since mental disorder appears at a steady rate throughout the entire period of three centuries, this is unlikely to be relevant.

There has been a preponderance of mood and anxiety disorders, and a lack of conditions such as psychopathic personality, paranoia and even bipolar disorder, which are more commonly seen in dictators and autocrats.[3] Ludwig has put forward the idea that democratic systems, particularly those with weak monarchies, are more likely to nurture leaders prone to anxiety or depression and less likely to foster the emergence of personality disorders, paranoia and mania. The kind of person who succeeds in an established democracy is one who is skilled at negotiation and compromise, who knows that elected office is time-limited, that executive power is defined by the constitution, and that overall power comprises a balance between judicial and legislative bodies. President Roosevelt realized the limitations of presidential power when he described his attempts at changing systems within the government—in this case the Navy—as "punching a feather bed."[4] In an established democracy the person at the top, the place where the buck stops, is confronted with the limitations of power.

Depression: Why Is It Common?

Storr argued that Churchill was emotionally deprived and prey to depression, and that the aggression burning under his skin was always looking for an outlet. The epitome of evil, Hitler, gave him the perfect opportunity to direct this energy. As Storr says, "If all depressives could be engaged in fighting wicked enemies, they would never suffer from depression. But in day-to-day existence, antagonists are not wicked enough, and depressives suffer from pangs of conscience about their own hostility."[5] Leaders prone to depression become vulnerable when their grip on power is loosened. Constant activity is a means of staving off depression, and this might be at a frenzied level in those with bipolar features. This is consistent with Theodore Roosevelt's maxim that "black care rarely sits behind a rider whose pace is fast enough."[6] (Roosevelt himself was known to live at a frenetic, even chronically hypomanic, pace).

Childhood deprivation, early parental loss and proneness to depression have often been found in the life stories of prime ministers. What drives some depression-prone people into politics and fires them with ambition to reach the top? The presence of bipolar features is certainly one explanation: constitutional energy, drive, grandiosity and an assertive, dominating manner. A certain level of narcissism is another explanation; Disraeli's sensitivity to rejection has been mentioned as one example of this, along with his and others' assertions that they felt compelled to leave a mark in the world or their lives would amount to nothing. Fear of failure may also be a driving force in some who are prone to depression.

Just as loss of power can trigger depression, so can failure to attain it. Asquith exemplified this when he said, "Of all human troubles, the most hateful is to feel you have the capacity of power and yet you have failed to exercise it. This was for years my case and no one who has not been through it can know the chilly, paralyzing, deadening depression of hope deferred and energy wasted and vitality run to seed."[7] Chamberlain voiced similar feelings when, at 50, he felt he had achieved little and was on the scrap heap.

The story of Philip Burguieres, CEO of a large oilfield service company, reminds us of the link between depression and power in a way which could be relevant to the findings on prime ministers.[8] Burguieres abruptly resigned during a suicidal depression and sought treatment for his illness. Subsequently he has become a spokesman for reducing the stigma of depression in the workplace and to raise awareness of depression among CEOs. He estimates that fully 25 percent of top-level executives experience a severe suicidal depression at some point in their careers, a rate far above suicidal depression in the general population. Contributing to Burguieres' depression was family stress, narrow preoccupation with work, guilt over taking leisure time and the relentless pressure of the job, all of which are determining factors behind mental breakdown in political leaders.[9] These stressors, combined with a presumed genetic risk, tipped him over the edge. Such has been the scenario of some prime ministers in the past and will probably be so in the future.

The Bipolar Spectrum and Prime Ministers for Peace and War

While full-fledged bipolar disorder was believed to have been present in only two, Pitt the Elder and Gladstone, a total of six prime ministers could be classified as falling along the "bipolar spectrum" (Grey, Disraeli, Lloyd George, and Churchill, along with Pitt and Gladstone). That is to say their volatile personalities made them subject to ups and downs beyond most people, and they were prone to depression. When functioning well, they had abundant energy, self-confidence, and dominance, as well as a capacity to make quick decisions and act with authority when necessary. In the cases of Pitt, Lloyd George and Churchill, they were seen as good war leaders, whether of the Seven Years War, World War I or World War II. All three possessed a messianic belief that only they could save their imperiled country. At such times the qualities of the bipolar may be of greater service than the more cautious, self-doubting traits of a Lord North, Lord Liverpool or Arthur Bonar Law. Interestingly, Bonar Law must at some level have recognized this because he was asked by King George V to head a government in the midst of war but declined in favor of Lloyd George, whom he correctly thought was a more suitable leader for the times. Over the next two years his restrained, more deliberate approach was a foil to the Welshman, but when Lloyd George's hubris lead to his downfall after the war was over, Bonar Law became prime minister. Palmerston is another example of a man with a flavor of bipolar qualities succeeding a gloomy, introspective prime minister (Aberdeen) during war.

The Anxious Prime Ministers

Anxiety was seen in 14 (28 percent) subjects, rates which for males are somewhat higher than the 19 percent in general population. This can be broken down by type of anxiety as follows: probable social anxiety in eleven (22 percent), probable generalized anxiety in two (4 percent) and other less clearly defined forms of anxiety in three (6 percent). (It is possible for more than one type to be present.) Military experience was known to have occurred in only nine prime ministers, and, in spite of several with combat experience, none evinced convincing signs of post-traumatic stress disorder. Without diminishing the courage of those prime ministers who did serve in battle, Ludwig has shown that courage, bravery and heroism in battle tends to occur more often among tyrants, visionary and authoritarian leaders than among monarchs or democratic leaders.[10]

Social anxiety is one of the most common psychiatric disorders, with a population prevalence of around 10–14 percent, and 11 percent in men, so the rate here of 20 percent is almost double that found in the general population.[11] For many reasons SAD may sail unrecognized across the horizon. One reason is that SAD is easily conflated with shyness and therefore meets with resistance when it is proclaimed as a medical disorder. While many shy people have SAD, there are important differences, mostly centering on the level of distress and impairment, which is much greater in SAD; shyness describes more of a character disposition. Another reason is the generally low awareness of the disorder, which would therefore not attract the same sort of attention in biographies or lead to the use of terminology suggesting this to be a disorder. For example, consider a person who blushes easily, becomes embarrassed when the center of attention, avoids intimacy, avoids direct eye contact, or is uncomfortable in social gatherings — all of these would make SAD a strong possibility. Another more situational form of social anxiety is performance anxiety, such as fear of public speaking. Twelve (24 percent) prime ministers experienced public speaking anxiety, some of a severe and long-lasting nature, others only occasionally, and four of them either received medical attention or engaged in self-treatment with alcohol, cocaine or opiate narcotics (Table 2). In all other respects, the individual might be quite comfortable in social interaction. If it was necessary to drink alcohol before entering the House of Commons to give a speech, then social anxiety disorder should be considered the cause. Source material does not always give clear ideas about the level of distress of interference, so rather than appending the label of social anxiety disorder, it is better in some cases to be more circumspect and refer to it as "social anxiety." In other cases, the information was more revealing.

The high rate of public speaking anxiety is somewhat unexpected considering that each person willingly chose a profession where public speaking was known to be part of the job. Most overcame the fear, or least learned to live with it. Macmillan is a good example of someone who (a) learned to live with it despite persistently severe anticipatory anxiety, and (b) trained himself by assiduous observation of the masters in how to become an accomplished speaker himself. Others who had to drink or take drugs in order to summon confidence to speak include Rockingham, Addington, Gladstone and Rosebery.

What was the impact of social anxiety? None of the postulated cases were considered to have been good war leaders if and when the test came. This raises the question of "Is it the chicken or egg"? Does the electorate put in office socially anxious leaders in time of peace and avoid doing so in war? Or does the outbreak of war put unmanageable demands on one who has social anxiety? The biographies of at least eleven prime ministers suggest they were mismatched for office and often expressed relief upon departing. These comprised Bute, Rockingham, North, Portland, Addington, Goderich, Aberdeen, Russell, Rosebery, Asquith and Chamberlain (Table 3). Of these, seven showed high social anxiety. Of the remainder, Baldwin had difficulty coping, and Macmillan's anxiety was confined to speech making. While Peel was exceptionally thin-skinned, it did not prevent him from being seen as a success. Melbourne's anxiety was confined to public speaking and improved with time. To the extent that Heath had social anxiety, it was more evident outside political life.

At first sight it is hard to see any advantage for social anxiety in a head of state. It may be commonly believed that shy, hypersensitive people with exaggerated fear of scrutiny, a dislike of being the center of attention, or fear of being humiliated are unlikely to seek out high political office. Yet, if we were to tabulate the rates of shyness, aloofness (i.e., distancing or inapproachability), hypersensitivity and traits of isolation (e.g., having few friends) from the biographies reviewed, there is the unexpected finding that 24 prime ministers demonstrate one or more of these qualities (Table 4). Shyness was noted in 16, hypersensitivity in 13, aloofness in 9 and isolation in 6.

Three possibilities could explain the observed rates of shyness and social fear. One, taking the more positive first, it is conceivable that having a well developed sense of empathy and concern for the feelings of others, which often accompanies social anxiety disorder, could lead a person to identify with social reform or public welfare, and this in turn results in choosing politics as a career. Allusion has been made to Attlee's modesty and shyness, which served him well. Heath, who most likely had elements of social phobia, was known as one driven by idealism. Two, there might be a strong desire to overcompensate for the perceived deficiencies of shyness, sensitivity and introversion. And three, other attributes may be coupled with social anxiety and sensitivity to criticism, as with Peel and Baldwin, and these qualities may fuel political ambition. Peel, for example, was seen as a strange mixture of ambition for power while being nauseated by it, as well as being ultra-sensitive yet bold. Baldwin, a veritable psychiatric textbook, was a man of unshakable conviction and strong stamina who could tear his enemies to pieces; his sense of grandeur eventually led him to believe that he was God's choice to heal the nation. Even the timid Russell had a ruthless streak to him. This third explanation receives support from a study of narcissistic personality (NP) disorder, a condition which is manifest principally by grandiosity, feelings of entitlement, absence of empathy and need for admiration. When NP is put under the microscope, two subtypes have emerged, one of which is characterized as "grandiose-exhibitionistic" and the other as "vulnerable-sensitive."[12] The vulnerable-sensitive type of NP includes proneness to anxiety, emotionality, moodiness, defensiveness and social reticence. Common to both types of NP are tendencies to cruelty, bossiness, intolerance, opportunism, arrogance and a demanding manner, qualities of leadership which have been described in many biographies.

Generalized anxiety was not common, but the 4 percent rate is in line with the 3.6 percent rate observed in U.S. males by Kessler et al.[13] Lord Liverpool's anxiety was more of the generalized variety — diffuse worry and apprehensive anticipation of the worst — although he had some heightened social fear. In his case, while it was excruciating, it may have enhanced his leadership skills when prime minister in that "anxious energy" assured his command of the facts and prepared him well for Parliamentary debate.

No instances of panic disorder or obsessive-compulsive disorder were observed, and, as mentioned, there was nothing to suggest clear-cut post-traumatic stress disorder, which is of some interest given that several prime ministers had been in combat. Therefore, when anxiety was found, it was primarily social anxiety disorder with public speaking fear.

Drugs, Alcohol and Oblivion

There is every reason to worry about the potential menace from misuse of alcohol among leaders. Among world leaders, we can think of President Nixon's intermittently unbridled intake during his booze-laden weekends, which made him inaccessible to his aides, who considered him incapable of conducting any business when in such a state.[14] Alarmingly, at such times an irritable Nixon would threaten to bomb Hanoi and Haiphong. On another occasion, while drunk, he threatened to "nuke" Vietnam. On yet another occasion, when Edward Heath wanted an urgent conversation about the Middle East, Nixon's aides suggested that the call be put off until the next day, the undisclosed reason being that "he was loaded." The manner in which those in power use alcohol demands thoughtful assessment, and raises the issue of when is a head of state "on duty" and when are they "off duty"? Drug and alcohol use syndromes were present in five prime ministers: Pitt the Younger, Derby, Rosebery, Asquith and Eden. While not meeting the complete DSM-IV criteria for a drug or alcohol-related disorder, another five subjects misused or inappropriately used alcohol, including Addington, Churchill, Disraeli, Rockingham and Wilson. Of these 10 individuals (20 percent) (Table 5), nine misused drugs or alcohol while in office. On occasion, colleagues were concerned about the impact of their leader making major decisions while under the influence. Compared to the male population rate of 35 percent, the rate here is much lower.

Disturbances of Sleep

Sleep disturbance was reported in 12 (24 percent) subjects (Table 6), among whom five perhaps experienced this as a separate problem that could not be explained entirely by depression, anxiety or pain, which are well known causes of insomnia. Four experienced excessive sleep: North, Melbourne, Disraeli and Heath. Apart from Heath, who was hypothyroid, the pathology of the others remains conjectural, but sleep apnea merits consideration for North and Melbourne. In Disraeli's case, bipolar depression is known to be associated with hypersomnia (too much sleep), and this could explain things.

Attention to good sleep habits is important for heads of state, just as it is for all of us. Lack of sleep can lead to fatigue, problems concentrating, impaired decision-making, poor immune function and possible increased liability to cancer and infection.[15] Under conditions of high stress this becomes of particular importance. Excessive sleep may bespeak other underlying problems: it can be the end result of poor stress-coping by overeating, which leads to obesity and then sleep apnea. President Taft was a good example of this vicious cycle, and he found it difficult to stay awake in meetings and appeared to lack much interest. Yet after his term was over and his stress levels lowered, he ate less, lost weight and regained his old vitality as chief justice, a position to which he had always aspired.

In managing persistent sleep disturbance, history shows that perils lurk there, as with Eden, Rosebery and Derby. While today it is unlikely that doctors would prescribe drugs that are so addictive, the risk of alcohol abuse is always there, and newer classes of drugs to promote wakefulness might seem inherently appealing for tired, sleep-deprived heads of state. Proper sleep is vital in those who carry heavy responsibility and who work under marked stress. Freeman has pointed out the difficulty of processing vast amounts of information and reaching the best decisions under the influence of fatigue and sleep deprivation.[16] Connected to regular and restful sleep is the need to respect and preserve the inherent circadian rhythms, now much more of a challenge with transcontinental travel, long working days and short stopovers; but it is conceded that some individuals (e.g., Margaret Thatcher and Lord Louis Mountbatten) are at a biological advantage in needing very little sleep. However, there is a limit for everyone before fatigue sets in, and irritability or impatience makes for a poor milieu in which to conduct important matters of state.

Other Disorders

Other conditions which were less commonly noted include Asperger's disorder (Wellington), tic or Tourette's disorders (Melbourne, Baldwin), paraphilia (Gladstone), somatoform problems (Lloyd George), adjustment disorder or marital or bereavement-related difficulties (Campbell-Bannerman, Callaghan), and medical (Heath). The effect of these disorders ranged from negligible to considerable.

Dementia

Dementia affected five (10 percent) prime ministers, three of whom were still in office when changes began to emerge. In one case (Wilson), it is not believed to have significantly impaired his competence, but there are reasons to believe that the onset of dementia lead to his retirement at quite a young age. In the case of Ramsay MacDonald, dementia was much more serious, and in today's world it is doubtful whether things would have been allowed to deteriorate to such an extent without some intervention or delegation of authority. On current evidence, it is impossible to be certain if MacDonald's dementia was primary (e.g., Alzheimer's disorder) or whether it was caused by depression (i.e., "depressive pseudo-dementia"). Either way, it would have lead to marked impairment of essential cognitive and intellectual function, although treatment and prognosis of the two conditions are very different. During Churchill's second term as prime minister he began to show mental decline from a combination of factors, including stroke, cerebrovascular deficiency, cumulative effects of alcohol and perhaps his depressions; it can be presumed that dementia was beginning, with the worst laying in wait for his final years. Many thought that Churchill should have retired much earlier on the grounds of declining health. Of the other two prime ministers, the evidence for dementia in Lord Grenville is weak, and in both his and Thatcher's cases, dementia was not a concern while they were in office.

The risks involved when a political leader has dementia can be illustrated by two examples taken from British and U.S. history. Lord Tweedmouth was First Lord of the Admiralty in 1909 during a tense period of international relations. Under the influence of dementia, he gave away important classified information to the Kaiser. Another damaging example comes from President Woodrow Wilson who, in 1920 and under his own authority, suddenly dismissed his secretary of state. He had also fired Colonel House the previous year, even though House had been his main source of intelligence on European affairs, and such firing was regarded as a mistake.[17]

Aging, Experience and Wisdom

Consideration of dementia and leadership brings up the broader question of aging, experience and wisdom. Although few would argue against the need for paying close attention to the health of older leaders, it would clearly be a mistake to view elder statesmen as a liability simply because of their age. For that reason, some might disagree with L'Etang's assertion that leaders should not remain in office beyond the age of 65. Seniors still enjoy a measure of respect and deference in society.

Thinking is generally regarded as a process which uses step-by-step logic, or cause-and-effect reasoning, to reach conclusions. But there is another type of thinking which is more indirect and intuitive. This type of thinking, known as lateral thinking, makes use of ideas which cannot easily be arrived at with normal logic, and which may not seem immediately obvious. The writer Somerset Maugham said that imaginative (or "lateral") thinking grows by experience and, contrary to popular belief, becomes more powerful with age. One good example of lateral thinking comes from an anecdote about the Duke of Wellington. When he was 81, the royal family consulted the duke about a problem which had proved insoluble to the experts. The Crystal Palace, a fine new all-glass architectural showpiece built to house the 1851 Great Exhibition, came under attack from flocks of sparrows which soiled the glass with their droppings and left an unspeakable mess. None of the authorities could come up with a (logically derived) solution and were close to despair. The queen turned to the duke, a man whom she regarded as a sage, and the duke gave the simplest but most effective of suggestions: "Sparrow-hawks, Ma'am. Sparrow-hawks."[18] This kind of lateral thinking evolves with age as a gradual response to the losses of certain other mental abilities. We should take advantage of the wisdom of leaders, old or young.

Wise leaders are in short supply, while foolish ones seem to be ten a penny. As he died, the Swedish chancellor Count Oxenstierna observed to his son: "Know, my son, with how little wisdom the world is governed."[19]

Just as there is a neurobiology of mental illness, in which neurotransmitters (chemicals in the brain) such as serotonin, noradrenaline and dopamine play a role in the disorders which have been described here, so is there a biology of wisdom.[20] While it would be an obvious error to imply that wisdom and mental illness cannot coexist, a wise leader who is prone to mental disorder (and who is aware of it) is more likely to manage his or her episodes of illness with better judgment. Qualities of wisdom include emotional regulation, impulse control, good decision-making, pro-social attitudes, altruism, a moral compass, and an ability to deal with uncertainty and to see things from different perspectives ("value relativism"). Cultivation of these attributes ("self-improvement") may be expected to strengthen a person who is subject to attacks of depression or anxiety; while their presence in leaders who do not show psychopathology would also benefit the entire community.

One example of wisdom among prime ministers can be seen in Gladstone's persistent and ultimately successful efforts to create a permanent civil service based on merit.[21] While others such as Trevelyan and Northcote take some credit, Gladstone advocated far-reaching changes in the structure of Britain's civil service between 1850 and 1870, eventually passing legislation in his first administration which introduced radical changes to replace a system based on patronage and nepotism. Tuchman has upheld this as a notable example of enterprising, wise and self-critical investigation of government practice, which may have helped protect Britain from the social upheavals that enveloped Europe in the mid–19th century.[22] She contrasted this well-reasoned approach toward stable governance with the panic-driven repressive measures which could easily have been taken — and, in fact, were adopted in some other countries at the time. The Trevelyan-Northcote report of 1854 was commissioned by Gladstone and represents "the counsel of reason...an unusually thoughtful and quite distinctive linking of the ends and means of modern liberal thought with specific public-policy recommendations...one of the more thoughtful responses that have been offered to the specific practical problems of governance."[23] Morley has singled out Gladstone's "unique combination of democratic instinct, spirit of good government, instinct of popular equality and of enlightened bureaucracy," and the triumph of reason over habit.[24]

What is interesting in the above example is that while Gladstone appears to have suffered from bipolar disorder, he embodied many of the features of wisdom: self-discipline over strong passion (impulsivity), a pro-social and altruistic orientation, a moral compass, reflective abilities and self-understanding (e.g., as shown by his diary). His achievements over an exceptionally long political life are hard to match.

Resignation from Office for Reasons Related to Psychiatric Problems

Psychiatric problems were important in the resignation of nine (18 percent) prime ministers, or one out of every six: North, Pitt the Elder, Goderich, Derby, Campbell-Bannerman, MacDonald, Baldwin, Eden and Wilson. There does not seem to have been any decline in this pattern over time.

In addition, of those who had any history of psychiatric problems, active symptoms were present to varying degrees among nearly all (34) of the identified prime ministers when serving in office (Table 1). While it is impossible to gauge the extent to which these were relevant to performance, biographers indicate that in many cases mental health problems did not serve the prime minister well. For example, Salisbury resigned "broken hearted" after the loss of his wife; Russell was a "weak leader" whose personality traits damaged him more after he took office; grief took all the wind out of Bonar Law's sails and he never recovered; Callaghan was frozen into inactivity and inaccessibility for three weeks during a crisis; Rockingham was fortified by large amounts of Madeira before speaking in the Commons; and grief turned Aberdeen and Balfour into quite unapproachable men.

Responsibilities of the Physician and Patient

Others have written about the importance of competent medical care for political leaders. Studies have shown that doctors overlook the extent to which illness affects decision-making capacity, and an even higher threshold has sometimes been used for determining impaired decision-making when doctors care for heads of state.[25]

Doctors can also help or hinder with their treatments, and several examples of poor medical practice by prime ministers' doctors have been presented here. A more historically recent and flagrant therapeutic mishap took place in the United States with President John F. Kennedy, who was treated for most medical problems by his "official" physician, but who received stimulant drugs and accessory hormone treatments for his mental wellbeing from an "unofficial" doctor, with no meaningful coordination of care. The damaging effects of Kennedy's use of amphetamines on policy and international summitry have been described by Owen.[26] Another example of incompetent presidential care, or at least incompetent diagnosis, was provided by Dr. Sawyer, President Harding's personal homeopathic doctor in the 1920s. Dr. Sawyer misdiagnosed a heart attack, which proved fatal, instead calling it mushroom poisoning when there was no evidence to support such a diagnosis.

There is a long history of secrecy over the diagnosis and prognosis of illness in presidents and prime ministers, going back well into the 19th century when President Cleveland's jaw cancer was concealed, then later with regard to Kennedy's Addison's disease, and continuing to the present day, as in the case of Tony Blair, who was reported to be less than forthright, even contradictory, over the duration and nature of his heart problems (although it cannot be said that this compromised his effectiveness in leadership).[27] Among prime ministers, there have been several missed diagnoses, erroneous diagnoses, unwarranted deception in keeping the truth from the public and just plain mistakes, as can unfortunately happen to anyone. For this reason it was thought useful to compile a list of those prime ministers who, from biographical information, may have fallen prey to what is known as iatrogenic, or "doctor-induced," problems of a psychiatric type. As shown in Table 7, there are nine instances where this occurred. Some were more egregious and damaging than others, but they are all reminders of the danger when a head of state is served badly by his or her personal doctor. The most serious instances were associated with the prescription of alcohol, amphetamines and barbiturates, and many would agree, too, that Rosebery became an even more unsuitable premier from the pernicious effect of opiates, cocaine and sulphonel. The same can be said of Eden and the drugs he was prescribed.

Grief has been observed to virtually destroy a statesman's ability to carry out duties.[28] It seems to have had a serious effect on some prime ministers (Table 8), perhaps more apparent in their personal lives, but also in the professional lives of a few, including Rosebery, Salisbury, Campbell-Bannerman and Bonar Law. Over the longer haul it may have also adversely affected Aberdeen and MacDonald while they were in office. Therefore, the potentially destructive and long-lasting impact of grief, which is often borne privately, should be kept in mind by those responsible for providing health care to leaders of government.

As to the prime minister "patient," the fact of the matter is that political leaders are often demanding and want to be in control — quite the opposite of "being a patient." It has been observed by Mishori that U.S. presidents are often "difficult patients ... not compliant.... They don't think the rules apply."[29] In such cases the doctor may have to stand up firmly to his or her patient and perhaps ensure compliance by engaging spousal cooperation. Although Mishori was referring only to United States presidents, the same is likely to be true of other statesman leaders, including prime ministers. Adherence to treatment recommendations is an important responsibility; the same is true for seeking help in the first place — there has been too much denial of sickness, and this is especially true for mental illness.

Of much importance is the need to avoid self-treating, or subverting the system by turning to a doctor who is willing to compromise proper medical standards in acquiescing to the insistent demands of a powerful patient. The quality of medical care given to celebrities appears in the news from time to time. A recent case has been the investigation into the death of the popular entertainer Michael Jackson.[30] Another trap into which a doctor may fall is the hubristic misreading of his/her own skill, since they are looking after such an important patient. This in turn can lead the doctor into realms beyond his everyday competence, which then increases the risk of making a bad error. Additionally, a doctor may be overwhelmed with the enormous responsibility thrust onto his shoulders and make a serious mistake, as happened in Anthony Eden's first surgery.

Lessons and Recommendations

We may look at the findings from a variety of perspectives, but before doing so, it would be remiss not to consider possible sources of error in the reported rates of mental health problems. On one hand, there is the possibility of overestimation. For that to have occurred, either biographers somehow misrepresented alterations in behavior or well-being, or information was misinterpreted by this author as reflecting pathology beyond what was warranted. To guard against this, effort was made to assess whether symptoms resulted in functional impairment or treatment, or were seen by contemporaries (or the biographer) as clearly abnormal. Assessment of confidence levels in diagnostic assessment was also included to help arrive at a more nuanced judgment than simply offering an "either-or" conclusion. On the other hand, there is an equally valid concern that rates were underestimated due to (a) failure of this author to consult primary material, (b) omission by biographers of relevant material on psychopathology or hesitancy to suggest mental disorder ("weakness") because of protective feelings towards their subjects. While absolute certainty cannot be assured, the 72 percent rate is consistent with Ludwig's assertion about the high rates of depression in prime ministers and is not out of line with the nearly 50 percent rate of mental illness in U.S. presidents, a result which was based on more limited sources of information. There is good reason to suspect that all major retrospective epidemiological surveys of mental illness may underestimate the true prevalence, which is reportedly double when a prospective approach is used.

To return to what we can learn from these findings: From the perspective of mental illness in society and the unending battles waged to reduce its stigma, it is in some ways reassuring to know that over 70 percent of a country's elected leaders may have experienced mental illness or significant psychiatric symptoms. If it is still seen as a black mark to have psychiatric difficulties, then how could we possibly let slip unnoticed such high rates in prime ministers? Honesty compels us to accept the reality of psychiatric illness — is it that bad of a thing? If so, many have reached the top despite histories of psychiatric disorder, and can survive or even prosper under conditions of great stress. Consequently, others who are similarly afflicted can hope to fulfill their own goals, no matter how lofty the ambition; there is no need to settle for second best.

From the perspective of competent leadership and national welfare, what are the implications of having a leader who has experienced mental illness? Obviously some disorders are more significant than others — a prime minister who has a phobic disorder is less likely to shipwreck the country than one who has dementia or alcohol problems. Yet at times of incipient war, as during the build-up in Europe in the 1930s, perhaps a premier with significant social anxiety or fatigue is not the most suitable person — the country could be better served by one with more combative temperament or intuitive capacity, such as a Churchill, Palmerston or Pitt. However, we should not dismiss seemingly minor conditions like a dysfunctional marriage situation, as in more than one case family concerns intruded into a prime minister's working day and created problems (e.g., Aberdeen, Campbell-Bannerman). Each case must be taken on an individual basis.

There is some uncertainty as to the best way to conduct independent assessments of leaders, and it may be that different democratic systems call for different procedures. In the U.K., Owen has made a number of suggestions as to the need for openness and a full medical evaluation, either by a neurologist or general internist, but with the possibility that a psychiatric assessment would be called for.[31] In the U.S., two different proposals have been made (perhaps out of many).[32] One of these would take the form of an annual examination by an independent advisory group. As Gilbert has pointed out, there are good reasons to think this would often produce a medically uninformed opinion, since the examiners would have no day-to-day knowledge of the president, especially for mood, behavior and mental illness; it would, moreover, be unworkable and would likely undermine the credibility of the office, produce strongly partisan reactions and essentially cripple the president. In respect of the health of leaders, Marx has noted the importance of the doctor having a sustained period of observation of his (or her) patient.[33]

The Working Group on Presidential Disability offers more viable suggestions in which a physician to the president (the "White House Physician") serves as the chief coordinator in assembling the panel of outside experts, and would be the source of any medical releases concerning impairment or 25th Amendment issues; one big advantage here would be the doctor's knowledge of the president's health and behavior on a day-to-day basis. The Working Group's second major proposal would be to set up "advance directives," with full participation and approval of the president, to specify in detail the parameters of impairment or illness which would give cause for considering transfer of power, whether voluntary or involuntary.

While these proposals have been made with the U.S. presidency in mind, some modification would perhaps be desirable for prime ministers of the United Kingdom, where the situation is somewhat different in that the prime minister can be removed by party decision if that person no longer holds the confidence of his or her colleagues, as has happened in the past (e.g., Thatcher). While other solutions may have greater merit, and one could debate the advantages and disadvantages of various approaches, almost everybody would agree that the present situation leaves the public vulnerable to a head of state whose impairment is concealed, yet who continues to take responsibility for major decisions. Such a state of affairs invites great potential for harm. As Owen has proposed, democracies also should be encouraged to produce legislation which requires public and impartial medical assessment for all candidates who stand for elected office as head of government or of state, as well as private annual follow-up assessments, the results of which would be turned over to a designated senior political person and then handled according to the findings — either kept in confidence or passed along to Cabinet or Parliament.

Honesty may be the best policy. The former Norwegian prime minister

Kjell Bondevik provides one excellent example of what can happen when a leader in office forthrightly discloses that he is depressed. In 1988, Bondevik voluntarily told the country of his plight, that he needed several weeks rest and treatment, and that temporary transfer of power had been arranged. Bondevik indicated that he was unable to cope with unrelentingly heavy work stress, and that these pressures, along with unresolved cumulative bereavements from the deaths of three friends from brain cancer, left him mentally paralyzed — he could not even muster up sufficient energy to get out of bed. Parliament and the electorate greeted this news in a mood of sympathy and, with the exception of one small opposition party, acknowledged his fitness to return to office. Bondevik recovered, resumed office and was later re-elected for a second term. The prime minister has been quoted as saying:

> We know that many outstanding political leaders have had mental health problems, but it was not usual to talk about it, and it was definitely not usual to talk about it while they're in power.... Treatment and discussion of mental illness should become as commonplace as dealing with a broken leg.... Depression should not be seen as a weakness but rather as a human condition that can affect anyone.[34]

Where a prime minister has been confronted with emotional shock or the sudden death of a family member, or who struggles with drugs, alcohol, depression or anxiety, they should be granted space, privacy and the best medical care to see them through their tribulations. In deciding whether, when and how health problems are to be disclosed, there is always the need to strike a balance between privacy and the public interest. This may be of greatest concern for psychosis, degenerative conditions such as dementia, or chronic/relapsing problems like substance abuse or other disorders which affect judgment and where the potential for harm may be greater. Here, proper vigilance, checks and balances are called for, and proposals such as those put forward by Lord Owen deserve consideration. Would the public be better served if they are told the results of health evaluations? Some, like Owen, believe the answer is yes.[35] When the illness is of a psychological nature, there is special need to avoid old prejudices against mental illness in shaping the perception of a leader. While many may say that's impossible, if 72 percent of prime ministers have had some form of mental disorder, then we should move away from asking the simple question of "Did he or didn't he have mental illness?" to "What kind is it and are we better off, are we unaffected, or at a disadvantage because of it?" and "What sort of oversight is required?" As sometimes noted, having endured depression brings out strengths, while in other politicians with thinner skins may be sidelined through "rest cures" or, as a result of alcholism or dementia, even prove incompetent. Could we dare say that since so few prime ministers have come to office with a completely clean bill of psychological health, we should be wary of a candidate who has never experienced a mental illness? That would seem like a return to sanity: to recognize the world for what it is; to realize that our leaders are not demigods but flawed yet talented human beings grappling with tough problems that affect all of us, and that they are individuals who may at times need all the support they can obtain to cope with personal crises or psychological illness as they strive to regain good health and build up resilience.

Appendix: Tables of Psychiatric Issues, by Prime Minister

Table 1. Evidence for Psychiatric Problems by Prime Minister

Prime Minister	Syndrome Present	Type of Problem	Treatment Received	Took Time Off Work	Impaired as Prime Minister	Confidence in Presence of Any Syndrome (Disorder)[1]
Aberdeen	Yes	Depression—grief	No	No	Yes	3–2
Addington	Yes	Social anxiety	No	No	No	4–2
Asquith	Yes	Alcohol abuse; grief	No	No	Yes	4–2
Attlee	No	—	—	—	—	—
Baldwin	Yes	Generalized anxiety; social anxiety; depression; tic disorder	Yes	Yes	Yes	7–3
Balfour	Yes	Depression – grief	No	No	No	1–1
Blair	No	—	—	—	—	—
Bonar Law	Yes	Depression – grief	No	Yes	Yes	4–2
Bute	Yes	Depression; anxiety	Yes	Yes	Yes	5–3
Callaghan	Yes	Adjustment	No	No	No	3–2
Campbell–Bannerman	Yes	Adjustment, grief; marital	No	No	Yes	3–2
Canning	No	—	—	—	—	—
Chamberlain	Yes	Depression	Yes	No	No	3–2
Churchill	Yes	Depression; dementia	Yes	No	Yes	6–3
Derby	Yes	Depression (?seasonal); opioid misuse	No	Yes	Yes	4–2
Devonshire	No	—	—	—	—	—
Disraeli	Yes	Depression (?seasonal)	Yes	Yes	No	5–3
Douglas–Home	No	—	—	—	—	—
Eden	Yes	Anxiety; amphetamine and barbiturate misuse	Yes	Yes	Yes	6–3
Gladstone	Yes	Bipolar; paraphilia	Yes	Yes	Yes	7–3
Goderich	Yes	Anxiety	No	No	Yes	5–3
Grafton	No	—	—	—	—	—
Grenville (George)	No	—	—	—	—	—
Grenville (William)	Yes	Dementia; insomnia	No	No	No	1–1
Grey	Yes	Depression; social anxiety	No	No	Yes	5–3

Name		Condition				Rating
Heath	Yes	Hypothyroidism; social anxiety	Yes	Yes	Yes	4–2
Liverpool	Yes	Generalized anxiety	No	No	No	5–3
Lloyd George	Yes	Depression; somatoform	Yes	Yes	Yes	6–3
MacDonald	Yes	Depression; dementia	Yes	Yes	Yes	7–3
Macmillan	Yes	Depression (?seasonal); social anxiety	Yes	Yes	No	6–3
Major	No	—	—	—	—	—
Melbourne	Yes	Depression; sleep apnea; tic disorder	No	No	Yes	3–3
Newcastle	Yes	Anxiety	Yes	No	No	5–3
North	Yes	Depression; sleep apnea	No	No	Yes	6–3
Palmerston	No	—	—	—	—	—
Peel	Yes	Social anxiety	No	No	No	2–1
Pelham	No	—	—	—	—	—
Perceval	No	—	—	—	—	—
Pitt (Elder)	Yes	Bipolar	Yes	Yes	Yes	6–3
Pitt (Younger)	Yes	Alcohol abuse; Social anxiety	Yes	No	Yes	6–3
Portland	Yes	Social anxiety	No	No	No	1–1
Rockingham	Yes	Social anxiety	Yes	No	No	4–2
Rosebery	Yes	Depression (grief); insomnia; drug use disorder	Yes	No	Yes	5–3
Russell	Yes	Depression (grief); social anxiety	No	No	Yes	5–3
Salisbury	Yes	Depression	Yes	Yes	No	2–1
Shelburne	No	—	—	—	—	—
Thatcher	Yes	Dementia	Yes	No	No	5–3
Walpole	No	—	—	—	—	—
Wellington	Yes	Asperger's disorder; depression	No	No	No	3–2
Wilmington	No	—	—	—	—	—
Wilson	Yes	Dementia	No	No	No	5–3

[1] Seven criteria were used for establishing a syndrome (disorder), as described in text. Evidence of 1–2 criteria corresponds to low confidence (1), 3–4 to moderate confidence (2), and 5–7 to high confidence (3). The paired numbers refer to (i) number of criteria met (range 1 to 7) and (ii) overall confidence level (rating of 1 to 3) based on the number of criteria. These judgments refer to the existence of any syndrome rather than to confidence in each individual condition.

Table 2. Performance and Public Speaking Anxiety as Reported in Accounts

Addington*	Lloyd George
Baldwin	Macmillan
Chamberlain	Melbourne
Gladstone*	Portland
Grey	Rockingham*
Liverpool	Rosebery*

*Took alcohol, opiates, or other drugs to cope with anticipatory anxiety.

Table 3. Prime Ministers Reported to Be Misfits for Office

Aberdeen*	North*†
Addington*†	Portland†
Asquith*	Rockingham†
Bute†	Rosebery†
Chamberlain*	Russell†
Goderich†	

*Not well suited as a war leader; † poor match on the basis of personality or neurosis.

Table 4. Presence of Shy (S), Aloof (A), Isolated (I), or Hypersensitive (H) Personality Traits

Prime Minister	Trait
Aberdeen	S
Addington	S
Attlee	S
Baldwin	I, S
Balfour	A
Bute	A, H, S
Chamberlain	A, H, I, S
Disraeli	H
Eden	H
Goderich	H
Grafton	H, S
Grenville (Lord)	A
Grey	H
MacDonald	A, H, I, S
Macmillan	S
Newcastle	H
Peel	A, H, S
Perceval	H, S
Pitt (Younger)	S
Portland	H, S
Rockingham	S
Rosebery	A, H, I
Russell	A, H, I, S
Salisbury	S
Wilson	A, I

Table 5. Prime Ministers with Alcohol or Drug–Related Problems

Alcohol	Drugs
Addington	Derby
Asquith	Eden
Churchill	Rosebery
Disraeli	
Eden	
Pitt (Younger)	
Rockingham	
Wilson	

With the exception of Disraeli, the problems occurred during time as prime minister. Inclusion in this list does not necessarily mean the presence of a DSM–IV diagnosis, but reflects the fact that excessive or inappropriate consumption took place and/or that others were concerned.

Table 6. Prime Ministers Who Were Troubled by Sleep Disturbance

Insomnia	Hypersomnia
Eden	Disraeli
Gladstone	Heath
Goderich	Melbourne
Grenville (Lord)	North
Grey	
MacDonald	
Pitt (Elder)	
Rosebery	

Table 7. Possible Iatrogenically Produced Psychiatric Problems

Prime Minister	Problem
Derby	Opiate drugs prescribed for pain impaired his mental state
Eden	Adverse behavioral effects of prescribed amphetamines and barbiturates
Heath	Excessive dose of thyroid medication was prescribed
Macmillan	Veganin caused some depression
Pitt (Elder)	Dr. Addington prescribed opiates, which worsened his depression
Pitt (Younger)	Dr. Addington advised liberal use of alcohol to a teenaged Pitt, which may well have set him on a path to alcoholism
Rockingham	Self-prescribed drugs may have worsened his problems
Rosebery	Side effects from opium, cocaine and sulphonel for insomnia
Wilson	Dr. Evans advised use of alcohol for "metabolism," which may have hastened progress towards alcohol misuse.

Table 8. Prime Ministers Who Either Were Reportedly Sensitive to Effects of Bereavement or Had Significant Grief-Related Problems in Office

Aberdeen	Goderich
Asquith	Liverpool
Baldwin	Lloyd George
Balfour	MacDonald
Bonar Law	Rosebery
Campbell–Bannerman	Russell
Chamberlain	Salisbury

Notes

Preface

1. Jonathan R. T. Davidson, Kathryn M. Connor, and Marvin Swartz, "Mental Illness in U.S. Presidents Between 1776 and 1974: A Review of Biographical Sources," *Journal of Nervous and Mental Disease*, 194 (2006): 47–51.
2. American Psychiatric Association. *Diagnostic and Statistical Manual of Mental Disorders*, 4th Edition. Washington, DC: American Psychiatric Association, 2000.

Introduction

1. William Sargant. *The Unquiet Mind*. Boston, MA: Little, Brown, 1967, p. 16.
2. Hugh L'Étang. *The Pathology of Leadership*. London: William Heinemann Medical Books, 1969, pp. 206–207.
3. J. M. Jones and J. I. Jones, "Presidential Stroke: United States Presidents and Cerebrovascular Disease," *CNS Spectrums*, 11 (2006): 674–678.
4. Norman Sartorius, "Leadership," *International Psychiatry*, 6 (2009): 1.
5. Hugh L'Étang. *The Pathology of Leadership*. London: William Heinemann Medical Books, 1969, p. 7.
6. A. L. Kennedy. *Salisbury 1830–1903: Portrait of a Statesman*. London: John Murray, 1953, p. 356.
7. W. B. Yeats, "The Second Coming" in *Selected Poetry*, ed. A. Norman Jeffares (London: Macmillian & Co. Ltd., 1962), pp. 99–100.
8. L'Étang, pp. 70–72, 77–78.
9. American Psychiatric Association. *The Principles of Medical Ethics: Principles with Annotations Especially Applicable to Psychiatry*. Arlington, VA: American Psychiatric Press, 2008.
10. Mark Moran, "Lingering Questions Prompt 'Goldwater Rule' Evaluation," *Psychiatric News*, October 17, 2008, p. 8.
11. D. Owen, J.R.T. Davidson, "Hubris Syndrome: An Acquired Personality Disorder? A Study of U.S. Presidents and U.K. Prime Ministers Over the Last 100 Years," *Brain* 132 (2009): 1396–1406.
12. American Psychiatric Association. *Diagnostic and Statistical Manual of Mental Disorders*, 4th Edition. Washington, DC: American Psychiatric Association, 2000; World Health Organization. *The ICD-10 Classification of Mental and Behavioural Disorders*. Washington, DC: American Psychiatric Press, 1994.
13. Michael Brown, "Were We All Alcoholics in Parliament Back Then?" *The Independent*, August 30, 2006, http://www.independent.co.uk/opinion/commentators/michael-brown-were-we-all-alcoholics-in-parliament-back-then-413888.html.
14. Michael Vestey, "Sobering Thoughts," *Spectator*, January 28, 2006, http://findarticles.com/p/articles/mi_qa3724/is_200601/ai_n17186010/print (accessed May 12, 2008).
15. B. Z. Paulshock, "Dr. Cheyne," *Journal of the American Medical Association* 284 (2000): 1305.
16. Joshua Wolf Schenk. *Lincoln's Melancholy: How Depression Challenged a President and Fuelled His Greatness*. Boston: Houghton Mifflin, 2005; Anthony Storr. *Churchill's Black Dog and Other Phenomena of the Human Mind*. London: Fontana/Collins, 1989.
17. K.R. Jamison, R.H. Gerner, C. Rammen, C. Padesky, "Clouds and Silver Linings: Positive Experiences Associated with Primary Affective Disorder," *American Journal of Psychiatry*, 137 (1980): 198–202.
18. Jonathan R. T. Davidson, Kathryn M. Connor, "The Impairment of Presidents Pierce and Coolidge After Traumatic Bereavement," *Comprehensive Psychiatry* 49 (2008): 413–419.
19. E. Slater, "The Problems of Pathogra-

phy," *Acta Psychiatrica Scandinavica*, Supplement 219 (1970): 209–215.

THE PRIME MINISTERS

Sir Robert Walpole

1. Paul Smith, ed. *Bagehot: The English Constitution*. New York: Cambridge University Press, 2001, p. 44.
2. Steven Taylor, "Robert Walpole, First Earl of Orford (1676–1745)," in *Oxford Dictionary of National Biography* (Oxford University Press, September, 2004), January, 2008, http://www.oxforddnb.com/view/article/28601 (accessed January 6, 2009).
3. Dermot Englefield, Janet Seaton, and Isobel White. *Facts About the British Prime Ministers*. New York: H.W. Wilson, 1995, p. 5.
4. B. A. Paulshock, "Dr. Cheyne," *Journal of the American Medical Association*, 284 (2000): 1305.

Earl of Wilmington

5. A. A. Hanham, "Compton, Spencer, Earl of Wilmington (c.1674–1743)," in *Oxford Dictionary of National Biography* (Oxford University Press, September 2004), January, 2008, http://www.oxforddnb.com/view/article/6036 (accessed January 6, 2009).
6. Englefield, et al., p. 10.

Henry Pelham

7. Englefield, et al., p. 13.
8. P. J. Kulisheck, "Pelham, Henry (1674–1754)," in *Oxford Dictionary of National Biography* (Oxford University Press, September 2004), January, 2008, http://www.oxforddnb.com/view/article/21789 (accessed January 6, 2009).

Thomas Pelham-Holles

9. Reed Browning, "Holles, Thomas Pelham, Duke of Newcastle upon Tyne and First Duke of Newcastle under Lyme (1693–1768)," in *Oxford Dictionary of National Biography* (Oxford University Press, September 2004), January, 2008, http://www.oxforddnb.com/view/article/21801 (accessed January 6, 2009).
10. Ray A. Kelch. *Newcastle: A Duke Without Money*. Berkeley and Los Angeles: University of California Press, 1974, p. 14.
11. Englefield, et al., p. 20.
12. Reed Browning. *The Duke of Newcastle*. New Haven: Yale University Press, 1975, p. 85.
13. Browning, "Holles, Thomas Pelham, Duke of Newcastle upon Tyne and First Duke of Newcastle under Lyme (1693–1768)."
14. Kelch, pp. 7–17.
15. Kulisheck.
16. Browning.

William Cavendish

17. Karl Wolfgang Schweizer, "Cavendish, William, Fourth Duke of Devonshire (bap. 1720, d. 1764)," in *Oxford Dictionary of National Biography* (Oxford University Press, September, 2004), January, 2008, http://www.oxforddnb.com/view/article/4949 (accessed January 6, 2009).
18. Englefield, et al., p. 26.

John Stuart

19. Peter D. Brown, "Bute in Retirement," in *Lord Bute: Essays in Re-Interpretation*, ed. Karl W. Schweizer (Leicester: Leicester University Press, 1988), p, 243.
20. Karl Wolfgang Schweizer, "Stuart, John, Third Earl of Bute (1713–1792)," in *Oxford Dictionary of National Biography*, Oxford University Press, September 2004, October 2007, http://www.oxforddnb.com/view/article/26716 (accessed January 6, 2009).
21. Christopher Hibbert. *George III*. New York: Basic Books, 1998, p. 22.
22. Richard B. Sher, "The Favourite of the Favourite," in *Lord Bute: Essays in Re-Interpretation*, ed. Karl W. Schweizer (Leicester University Press, 1988), 207.
23. Sian Busby, "On Scottish Prime Ministers" Telegraph.co.uk, June 28, 2007, http://my.telegraph.co.uk/sian_busby/blog/2007/06/28/on_scottish_prime_ministers (accessed August 19, 2009).
24. Brown, p. 246.
25. Sher, p. 190.
26. R. R. Sedgwick, ed.. *Letters from George III to Lord Bute*. London: Macmillan, 1939, pp. 44–46.
27. David P. Miller, "My Favourite Studdys: Lord Bute as Naturalist," in *Lord Bute: Essays in Re-Interpretation*, ed. Karl W. Schweizer (Leicester: Leicester University Press, 1988), p. 235.
28. Frank O'Gorman, "The Myth of Lord Bute's Secret Influence," in *Lord Bute: Essays in Re-Interpretation*, ed. Karl. W. Schweizer (Leicester: Leicester University Press, 1988), p. 69.
29. Marjie Bloy, "John Stuart, Third Earl of Bute (1713–1792)," *The Victorian Web*, February 27, 2002, http://www.victorianweb.org/history/pms/bute.html (accessed July 16, 2008).
30. Englefield, et al., p. 31.

George Grenville

31. J. V. Beckett and P. D. G. Thomas, "Grenville, George (1712–1770)," in *Oxford Dictionary of National Biography* (Oxford University Press, September 2004), October, 2007, http://www.oxforddnb.com/view/article/11489 (accessed January 6, 2009).

Charles Wentworth

32. Horace Walpole, *Memoirs of the Reign of King George III, Vol. 2*. London: Lawrence and Bullen, 1894, pp. 139–140.
33. W. H. G. Armytage, "Charles Watson-Wentworth, Second Marquess of Rockingham, F. R. S. (1730–1782): Some Aspects of His Scientific Interests," *Notes and Records of the Royal Society of London*, 12 (1965): 61–76.
34. R. J. S. Hoffman. *The Marquis: A Study of Lord Rockingham, 1730–1782*. New York: Fordham University Press, 1973, p. 178.
35. I. R. Christie, "Review: The Rise of Party in England. The Rockingham Whigs, 1760–1782. By Frank O'Gorman. London: Allen and Unwin, 1975," *The English Historical Review*, 91 (1976): 390–393.
36. S. M. Farrell, "Wentworth, Charles Watson, Second Marquess of Rockingham (1730–1782)," in *Oxford Dictionary of National Biography* (Oxford University Press, September 2004), October, 2007, http://www.oxforddnb.com/view/article/28878 (accessed January 6, 2009).
37. Ibid.
38. Hoffman, pp. 27–28.
39. Armytage, p. 75; C. Ritcherson, "Review: Hoffman RJS. The Marquis: A Study of Lord Rockingham, 1730–1782, New York: Fordham University Press, 1973," *The American Historical Review*, 80 (1975): 640–641; Armytage, 64.
40. Christie, p. 391.
41. Ritcherson, p. 641.
42. Farrell.

William Pitt the Elder

43. Vera M. White, "William Pitt 'The Elder' (1708–1778)," Encyclopaedia Britannica, Inc., 2002, http://www.gwleibniz.com/britannica_pages/pitt_elder/pitt_elder.html (accessed May 17, 2008).
44. Stanley Ayling. *The Elder Pitt*. New York: David McKay, 1976, p. 118.
45. Ibid., p. 249.
46. Ibid., p. 250.
47. Paul Smith, ed. *Bagehot: The English Constitution*. New York: Cambridge University Press, 2001, p. 84.
48. Jeremy Black. *Pitt the Elder*. New York: Cambridge University Press, 1992, p. 272.

49. Ayling, p. 132.
50. Ibid., p. 135.
51. White.
52. Ayling, p. 364.
53. Ibid., p. 368.
54. Ibid., p. 368.
55. Marie Peters, "William Pitt, First Earl of Chatham," in *Biographical Dictionary of British Prime Ministers*. Robert Eccleshall and Graham Walker (eds.). New York: Routledge, 1998, p. 62.
56. Ayling, p. 417.
57. Black, p. 274.
58. Ibid., p. 275.
59. David Owen and Jonathan R. T. Davidson, "Hubris Syndrome: An Acquired Personality Disorder? A Study of U.S. Presidents and U.K. Prime Ministers Over the Last 100 Years," *Brain*, 132 (2009): 1396–1406.
60. White.
61. Barbara Tuchman. *The March of Folly*. New York: Ballantine Books, 1984, p. 160.
62. Black, pp. 225, 304.

Augustus Henry Fitzroy

63. Marjorie Bloy, "Augustus Henry Fitzroy, Third Duke of Grafton," in *Biographical Dictionary of British Prime Ministers*. Robert Eccleshall and Graham Walker (eds.). New York: Routledge, 1998, p. 61.
64. Peter Durrant, "Fitzroy, Augustus Henry, Third Duke of Grafton (1735–1811)," in *Oxford Dictionary of National Biography* (Oxford University Press, September, 2004), October 2007, http://www.oxforddnb.com/view/article/9628 (accessed January 6, 2009).
65. Ibid.
66. Englefield, et al., p. 56.

Lord North

67. Tuchman, pp. 127–231.
68. Peter Thomas, "Frederick North, Styled Lord North, 1752–1790, Second Earl of Guilford," in *Biographical Dictionary of British Prime Ministers*. Robert Eccleshall and Graham Walker (eds.). New York: Routledge, 1998, p. 64.
69. Matthew Snow, "A Biography of Lord North (1732–1792)," *From Revolution to Reconstruction*, May 5, 2003, www.let.rug.nl/usa/B/north/north.htm (accessed May 25, 2008).
70. Peter Whiteley. *Lord North: The Prime Minister Who Lost America*. Rio Grande, OH: Hambledon Press, 1996, p. 81.
71. Ibid., p. 83.
72. Butterfield H., "Lord North and Mr. Robinson, 1779," *Cambridge Historical Journal*, 5 (1937): 255–279.
73. Ibid., p. 276.
74. Ibid., p. 267.

75. Ibid., p. 268.
76. Ibid.
77. Ibid., p. 275.
78. Ibid., p. 275.
79. Ibid., p. 276.
80. Whiteley, pp. 83–85.
81. Ibid., p. 115.
82. Ibid., p. 116.
83. Ibid., p. 168.
84. American Psychiatric Association. *Diagnostic and Statistical Manual of Mental Disorders, 4th Edition.* Washington, DC: American Psychiatric Association, 2000, pp. 615–617.
85. Charles Smith. *The Early Career of Lord North the Prime Minister.* Cranbury, NJ: Associated University Press, 1979, pp. 236–238.
86. Ibid., p. 237.

William Petty

87. Dermot Englefield, Janet Seaton, and Isobel White, *Facts About the British Prime Ministers* (New York: H.H. Wilson, 1995), 66.

William Cavendish Cavendish-Bentinck

88. David Wilkinson, "William Henry Cavendish-Bentinck, 3rd Duke of Portland," in *Biographical Dictionary of British Prime Ministers*, eds. Robert Eccleshall and Graham Walker (New York: Routledge, 1998), pp. 77–78.
89. David Wilkinson, "Bentinck, William Henry Cavendish Cavendish, Third Duke of Portland (1738–1809)," in *Oxford Dictionary of National Biography* (Oxford University Press, September 2004), October 2007, http://www.oxforddnb.com/view/article/2162 (accessed January 6, 2009).
90. Wilkinson, *Oxford Dictionary of National Biography.*

William Pitt the Younger

91. Pembroke College Cambridge Society, *Annual Gazette*, 8 (June, 1934): 18; William Hague. *William Pitt the Younger: A Biography.* New York: Alfred A. Knopf, 2005, p. 25.
92. Marjorie Bloy, "William Pitt the Younger," http://www.victorianweb.org/history/pms/pitt.html (accessed May 25, 2008).
93. http://www.number-10.gov.uk/output/Page 161.asp (accessed May 15, 2008).
94. Ibid.
95. William Hague. *William Pitt the Younger: A Biography.* New York: Alfred A. Knopf, 2005, p. 189.
96. Ibid., p. 211.
97. Ibid., p. 261; J. H. Rose. *William Pitt and National Revival.* London: G. Bell and Sons, 1911, p. 279.
98. L.V. Harcourt. *The Diaries and Correspondence of the Right Hon. George Rose, Vol. 1.* London: Richard Bentley, 1860, p. 130.
99. Hague, p. 290.
100. G. Pellew. *The Life and Correspondence of the Right Hon. Henry Addington, Vols. 1–3.* London: John Murray, 1849, p. 91.
101. J. Ehrman. *The Younger Pitt, Vol. 2.* London: Constable, 1969, p. 463; Hague, p. 314.
102. Lord Rosebery. *Letters Relating to the Love Episode of William Pitt.* Published privately, 1900, pp. 31–32; Hague, p. 315.
103. Hague, p. 361.
104. Pitt to Lady Chatham. Chatham Papers, Public Record Office 30/8/12, fol. 484; Hague, p. 361.
105. Duchess of Cleveland. *Life and Letters of Lady Hester Stanhope.* London: John Murray, 1914, p. 62; Hague, p. 450.
106. T. Raikes. *A Portion of the Journal Kept by Thomas Raikes, Vol. 4.* London: Longman, 1856–1857, p. 217.
107. W. S. Taylor and J. H. Pringle, eds. *Correspondence of William Pitt, Earl of Chatham, Vols. I–IV, Earl of Chatham to Lady Chatham, April, 3, 1772.* London: John Murray, 1838–1840, pp. 207–208; Hague, p. 20.
108. G. Tomline. *Memoirs of the Life of the Right Honorable William Pitt, Vol. 1.* London: John Murray, 1825, p. 5.; Hague, p. 30.
109. Hague, p. 30.
110. Ibid., p. 31.
111. Wilberforce, "Sketch of Mr. Pitt," quoted in Lord Rosebery, *Pitt and Wilberforce* (published privately: Edinburgh, 1897), p. 16; Hague, p. 112.
112. Furneaux, R. *William Wilberforce.* London: Hamish Hamilton, 1974, p. 13; Hague, p. 112.
113. Hague, p. 116.

Henry Addington

114. Philip Ziegler. *Addington: A Life of Henry Addington, First Viscount Sidmouth.* New York: John Day, 1965, p. 16.
115. www.number-10.gov.uk/output/Page 162.asp (accessed May 29, 2008).
116. Ziegler, 186.
117. Ibid., p. 46.
118. Ibid., p. 4.
119. Ibid., p. 186.
120. Ibid., p. 218.
121. Ibid., p. 219.
122. Ibid.
123. Hague, pp. 188–189.
124. Ziegler, p. 46; www.number-10.gov.uk/output/Page 162. asp (accessed May 29, 2008).

William Wyndham Grenville

125. P. J. Jupp, "Grenville, William Wyndham, Baron Grenville (1759-1834)," in *Oxford Dictionary of National Biography* (Oxford University Press, September 2004), October 2007, *http://www.oxforddnb.com/view/article/11501* (accessed January 6, 2009).
126. Englefield, et al., p. 96.

Spencer Perceval

127. Peter Jupp, "Spencer Perceval," in *Biographical Dictionary of British Prime Ministers*. Robert Eccleshall and Graham Walker (eds.). New York: Routledge, 1998, p. 102.
128. Englefield, et al., p. 102.
129. Iremonger, Lucille. *Lord Aberdeen: A Biography of the Fourth Earl of Aberdeen KG, KT, Prime Minister 1852-1855*. London: Collins, 1978, p. 49.
130. Englefield, et al., p. 103.
131. Iremonger, 45.
132. Ibid., p. 47.
133. Ibid., p. 51.

Robert Banks Jenkinson

134. *http://www.number-10.gov.uk/output/Page 157.asp* (accessed May 24, 2008).
135. Eric Evans, "Robert Banks Jenkinson, Second Earl of Liverpool," in *Biographical Dictionary of British Prime Ministers*. Robert Eccleshall and Graham Walker (eds.). New York: Routledge, 1998, pp. 106-116.
136. Ibid., pp. 106-107.
137. Iremonger, pp. 51-57.
138. B. Hilton, "The Political Arts of Lord Liverpool," *Transactions of the Royal Historical Society*, 38 (1988): 147-170.
139. Iremonger, pp. 51-57.
140. Ibid., p. 54.
141. Sir Archibald Alison [Bart.]. *History of Europe: From the Fall of Napoleon in MDCCCXV to the Accession of Louis Napoleon in MDCCCLII, Vol. 2, Chapter XXI*. New York: Harper & Brothers Publishers, Google Books, MDCCCLV, p. 282.
142. D. Beales, "Book Review: Lord Liverpool by Norman Gash," *Journal of Modern History*, 59 (1987): 831-833.
143. Norman Gash. *Lord Liverpool*. Cambridge, MA: Harvard University Press, 1984, pp. 101-102.
144. John Plowright. *Regency England: The Age of Lord Liverpool*. New York: Routledge, 1996, p. 4.
145. Gash, p. 246.
146. Ibid., p. 189.

George Canning

147. Wendy Hinde. *George Canning*. New York: Basil Blackwell, 1989, p. 80.
148. Iremonger, p. 63.
149. Ibid., p. 69.

Frederick Robinson

150. Michael Fry, "Frederick John Robinson, First Viscount Goderich, First Earl of Ripon," in *Biographical Dictionary of British Prime Ministers*. Robert Eccleshall and Graham Walker (eds.). New York: Routledge, 1998, p. 120.
151. Iremonger, p. 76.
152. Ibid., p. 78.
153. Ibid., p. 79.
154. Ibid., p. 81.
155. W. D. Jones. *Prosperity Robinson: The Life of Viscount Goderich, 1782-1859*. London: Macmillan, 1967.
156. Iremonger, p. 80.
157. Ibid., p. 80.
158. Fry, p. 122.
159. *http://www.number-10.gov.uk/output/Page 155.asp* (accessed June 6, 2008).

Arthur Wellesley

160. Richard English, "Arthur Wellesley, First Duke of Wellington," in *Biographical Dictionary of British Prime Ministers*. Robert Eccleshall and Graham Walker (eds.). New York: Routledge, 1998, p. 127.
161. American Psychiatric Association. *Diagnostic and Statistical Manual of Mental Disorders, 4th Edition*. Washington, DC: American Psychiatric Association, 2000, pp. 80-84.
162. Iremonger, p. 85.
163. Marjorie Bloy, "Arthur Wellesley, First Duke of Wellington (1769-1852)," *A Web of English History*, January 28, 2008, *http://www.historyhome.co.uk/pms/wellingt.htm* (accessed July 12, 2008).
164. Iremonger, p. 87.
165. English, p. 124.
166. *http://www.number-10.gov.uk/output/Page153.asp* (accessed July 6, 2008).
167. Richard Holmes. *Wellington: The Iron Duke*. London: HarperCollins, 2003, p. 96.
168. Ibid., p. 96.
169. Iremonger, p. 95.
170. Ibid., p. 92.
171. Bloy, p. 35.
172. Holmes, p. 288.
173. Iremonger, p. 93.
174. Ibid., p. 94.
175. C. McElearney and M. Fitzgerald, "Did the Duke of Wellington Have Asperger's Syndrome?" *Irish Psychiatrist*, 7 (2006): 7-10.

176. A. Roberts. *Napoleon and Wellington*. London: Orion Publishing, 2001. Cited in McElearney and Fitzgerald.
177. Philip H. Stanhope, 5th Earl. *Notes of Conversations with the Duke of Wellington, 1831–1851*. London: John Murray, 1888, p. 28.
178. Elizabeth Longford. *Wellington: Pillar of State*. St. Albans, England: Panther Books, 1975, p. 370; McElearney and Fitzgerald, p. 9.
179. A. Klin, W. Jones, R. Schultz, F. Volkmar, D. Cohen, "Visual Fixation Patterns During Viewing of Naturalistic Social Situations as Predictors of Social Competence in Individuals with Autism," *Archives of General* Psychiatry, 59 (2002): 809–816.
180. Stanhope, p. 236.

Charles Grey

181. G.M. Trevelyan. *Lord Grey of the Reform Bill*. Westport, CT: Greenwood Press, 1970, p. 350.
182. Ibid., p. 352.
183. E. A. Smith. *Lord Grey, 1764–1845*. Stroud, Gloucestershire: Alan Sutton Publishing, 1990, p. 68.
184. Ibid., p. 83.
185. Ibid., p. 135.
186. Ibid., p. 206.
187. Ibid., p. 25.
188. Trevelyan, p. 184.
189. J. W. Derry. *Charles, Earl Grey: Aristocratic Reformer*. Cambridge, MA: Blackwell, 1992), 92.
190. Trevelyan, p. 164.
191. Ibid.
192. Smith, p. 135.
193. Ibid., p. 84.
194. Trevelyan, p. 257.
195. Ibid., p. 362.
196. Smith, p. 8.
197. Iremonger, pp. 310–311.

William Lamb

198. James Leavesley. *Mere Mortals: Diseases of the Famous*. Sydney, NSW: ABC Books, 2004, p. 114.
199. "March 15th," *Ward's Book of Days*, http://www.wardsbookofdays.com/15march.htm (accessed July 31, 2008).
200. Cecil, Lord David. *Melbourne*. New York: Harmony Books, 1966, p. 48.
201. Philip Ziegler. *Melbourne: A Biography*. New York: Atheneum, 1982, p. 61.
202. Ibid., p. 62.
203. Ibid.
204. Leavesley, pp. 113–114.
205. Ziegler, p. 123.
206. Cecil, pp. 182–183.
207. Ibid., p. 184.
208. Ziegler, p. 241.
209. Ibid., p. 242.
210. Cecil, p. 347.
211. Ziegler, p. 341.
212. Leavesley, p. 114.
213. Cecil, p. 418.
214. Ibid., 358.
215. Ibid., 418.
216. Ibid.
217. Ibid., p. 424.
218. Ibid., p. 425.
219. Ibid., p. 428.
220. Ibid., p. 429.
221. Ibid., p. 431.
222. Ibid., p. 432.
223. Ibid., p. 176.
224. Ibid., p. 324.
225. Ibid., p. 176.
226. American Psychiatric Association. *Diagnostic and Statistical Manual of Mental Disorders, 4th Edition*. Washington, DC: American Psychiatric Association, 2000, p. 116.
227. Cecil, pp. 324, 377.
228. Ziegler, p. 17.
229. Ibid., p. 119.
230. Ibid., p. 242.
231. Ibid., pp. 156–157.
232. Cecil, p. 324.
233. Leavesley, p. 114.
234. Ziegler, p. 242.
235. S. Nishino, "Narcolepsy: Pathophysiology and Pharmacology," *Journal of Clinical Psychiatry*, 68 [Suppl. 13] (2007): 9–15.
236. American Psychiatric Association, pp. 613–614.
237. Jonathan R.T. Davidson and Wei Zhang, "Treatment of Post-Stroke Depression with Antidepressants," *Journal of Alternative and Complementary Medicine*, 14 (2008): 795–796.
238. Eric Evans, "William Lamb, Second Viscount Melbourne," in *Biographical Dictionary of British Prime Ministers*. Robert Eccleshall and Graham Walker (eds.). New York: Routledge, 1998, p. 141.
239. Ziegler, p. 363.

Sir Robert Peel

240. Dermot Englefield, Janet Seaton, and Isobel White. *Facts About the British Prime Ministers*. New York: H.W. Wilson, 1995, p. 153.
241. F. Post, "Creativity and Psychopathology: A Study of 291 World-Famous Men," *British Journal of Psychiatry*, 165 (1994): 22–34.
242. Lucille Iremonger. *The Fiery Chariot: A Study of British Prime Ministers and the Search for Love*. London: Secker & Warburg, 1970, p. 99.
243. Ibid., p. 104.

244. Algernon Cecil. *Queen Victoria and Her Prime Ministers*. London: Eyre & Spottiswoode, 1953, p. 109.
245. Ibid., p. 103.
246. Cecil, p. 118.
247. Christopher Hibbert, "Queen Victoria and Her Prime Ministers," *BBC British History: Victorians*, November 14, 2008, http://www.bbc.co.uk/history/british/victorians/victoria_ministers_02.shtml (accessed November 14, 2008).
248. Boyd Hilton, "Robert Peel," in *Biographical Dictionary of British Prime Ministers*. Eds. Robert Eccleshall and Graham Walker. New York: Routledge, 1998, p. 142.
249. Cecil, p. 109.

Lord John Russell

250. Lucille Iremonger. *The Fiery Chariot: A Study of British Prime Ministers and the Search for Love*. London: Secker & Warburg, 1970, p. 116.
251. Ibid., pp. 110–111.
252. Ibid., p. 111.
253. Jonathan Parry, "Lord John Russell, First Earl Russell," in *Biographical Dictionary of British Prime Ministers*. Robert Eccleshall and Graham Walker (eds.). New York: Routledge, 1998, 155.
254. Iremonger, p. 111.
255. Parry, pp. 151–161.
256. Iremonger, p. 113.
257. Ibid., p. 114.
258. Ibid., p. 116.

Edward Stanley

259. Valerie Cromwell, "Edward George Geoffrey Smith Stanley, Fourteenth Earl of Derby," in *Biographical Dictionary of British Prime Ministers*. Robert Eccleshall and Graham Walker (eds.). New York: Routledge, 1998, p. 162.
260. Lucille Iremonger. *The Fiery Chariot: A Study of British Prime Ministers and the Search for Love*. London: Secker & Warburg, 1970, p. 313.
261. Rene Dubos. *Mirage of Health: Utopias, Progress and Biological Change*. Piscataway, NJ: Rutgers University Press, 1987, p. 187.
262. Stanley Weintraub. *Disraeli: A Biography*. New York: Truman Talley Books/Dutton, 1993, pp. 318, 337.
263. Marjie Bloy, "Edward George Geoffrey Smith Stanley, 14th Earl of Derby (1799–1869)," *The Victorian Web*, March 12, 2002, http://victorianweb.org/history/pms/derby1.html (accessed August 6, 2008).
264. Dermot Englefield, Janet Seaton, and Isobel White. *Facts About the British Prime Ministers*. New York: H.W. Wilson, 1995, p. 167.
265. Angus Hawkins, "Stanley, Edward George Geoffrey Smith, Fourteenth Earl of Derby (1799–1869)," in *Oxford Dictionary of National Biography* (Oxford University Press, September, 2004), January, 2008, http://www.oxforddnb.com/view/article/26265, September 30, 2008.
266. Angus Hawkins. *The Forgotten Prime Minister: The 14th Earl of Derby, Vol. 1, Ascent: 1799–1851*. New York: Oxford University Press, 2007, pp. 13 and 422.
267. Cromwell, p. 162.
268. R. Machado-Vieira et al., "A Double-Blind, Randomized, Placebo-Controlled Study on the Efficacy and Safety of the Purinergic Agents Allopurinol and Dipyridamole Adjunctive to Lithium in Acute Bipolar Mania," *Journal of Clinical Psychiatry*, 69 (2008): 1237–1245.
269. George Saintsbury. *The Earl of Derby*. New York: Harper & Brothers, 1892, p. 219.
270. David Owen and Jonathan R. T. Davidson, "Hubris: An Acquired Personality Disorder? A Study of U.S. Presidents and U.K. Prime Ministers over the Last 100 Years," *Brain*, 132 (2009): 1396–1406; Kathryn M. Connor and Jonathan R. T. Davidson, "Development of a New Resilience Scale: The Connor-Davidson Resilience Scale (CD-RISC)," *Depression and Anxiety*, 18 (2003): 76–82.

George Gordon

271. Lucille Iremonger. *Lord Aberdeen: A Biography of the Fourth Earl of Aberdeen KG, KT, Prime Minister 1852–1855*. London: Collins, 1978.
272. Muriel Chamberlain, "George Gordon (Later Hamilton-Gordon), Fourth Earl of Aberdeen," in *Biographical Dictionary of British Prime Ministers*. Robert Eccleshall and Graham Walker (eds.). New York: Routledge, 1998, p. 167.
273. Roy Jenkins. *Gladstone: A Biography*. New York: Random House, 1997, pp. 40–41.
274. Iremonger, p. 238.
275. Ibid., p. 309.
276. Ibid., p. 124.
277. Ibid., p. 130.
278. Muriel E. Chamberlain, "Gordon, George Hamilton, Fourth Earl of Aberdeen (1784–1860)," in *Oxford Dictionary of National Biography* (Oxford University Press, September, 2004), January, 2008, http://www.oxforddnb.com/view/article/11044, 10 (accessed January 25, 2009).
279. Muriel E. Chamberlain, "Gordon, George Hamilton, Fourth Earl of Aberdeen (1784–1860)," in *Oxford Dictionary of National Biography* (Oxford University Press, September, 2004), p. 18.

Henry John Temple

280. Lucille Iremonger. *The Fiery Chariot: A Study of British Prime Ministers and the Search*

for Love. London: Secker & Warburg, 1970, p, 314.
281. F. Post, "Creativity and Psychopathology: A Study of 291 World-Famous Men," *British Journal of Psychiatry*, 165 (1994): 22–34; Dermot Englefield, Janet Seaton, and Isobel White. *Facts About the British Prime Ministers*. New York: H.W. Wilson, 1995, p. 184.
282. Iremonger, p. 318; Paul Smith, ed. *Bagehot: The English Constitution*. New York: Cambridge University Press, 2001, pp. 122–123.

Benjamin Disraeli

283. "Benjamin Disraeli," *The National Archives, www.spartacus.schoolnet.co.uk/PRdisraeli.htm* (accessed May 22, 2008).
284. William Kuhn. *The Politics of Pleasure*. London: Free Press, Simon & Shuster, 2006, p. 68.
285. Kuhn, pp. 1–2.
286. Ibid., p. 163.
287. Ibid., p. 73; Donald F. Klein et al. *Diagnosis and Drug Treatment of Psychiatric Disorders: Adults and Children*. Baltimore: Williams & Wilkins, 1980, pp. 263–266.
288. Charles Richmond and Jerrold Post, "Disraeli's Crucial Illness," *The Self-Fashioning of Disraeli 1818–1851*. Charles Richmond and Paul Smith (eds.). London: Cambridge University Press, 1988, p. 75.
289. Richmond and Post, p. 75.
290. Ibid., p. 190.
291. Ibid., p. 70.
292. Kuhn, p. 3.
293. Paul Smith. *Disraeli: A Brief Life*. Google Books, 1999, p. 108.
294. Kuhn, p. 47.
295. Ibid., p. 313.
296. Ibid., p. 147.
297. Ibid., p. 73.
298. Richmond and Post, p. 188.
299. Lucille Iremonger. *The Fiery Chariot: A Study of British Prime Ministers and the Search for Love*. London: Secker and Warburg, 1970, pp. 314–315.
300. Kuhn, p. 3; Iremonger, p. 314.
301. Kuhn, p. 81.
302. Weintraub, p. 79.
303. Ibid., p. 298.
304. Richmond and Post, p. 77.
305. Weintraub, p. 83–84.

William Ewart Gladstone

306. F. Post, "Creativity and Psychopathology: A Study of 291 World-Famous Men," *British Journal of Psychiatry*, 165 (1994): 22–34.
307. Travis L. Crosby. *The Two Mr. Gladstones: A Study in Psychology and History*. New Haven: Yale University Press, 1997.
308. Colin Matthew. *Gladstone: 1809–1874*. New York: Clarendon Press, 1986, pp. 231–232.
309. Lucille Iremonger. *The Fiery Chariot: A Study of British Prime Ministers and the Search for Love*. London: Secker & Warburg, 1970, p. 317.
310. Charles Richmond and Jerrold Post, "Disraeli's Crucial Illness," in *The Self-Fashioning of Disraeli 1818–1851*. Charles Richmond and Paul Smith (eds.). London: Cambridge University Press, 1988, p. 76.
311. Philip Magnus. *Gladstone: A Biography*. New York: E.P. Dutton, 1954, p. 74.
312. John. R. Vincent (ed.). *Disraeli, Derby and the Conservative Party: Journals and Memoirs of Edward Henry, Lord Stanley 1849–1869*. New York: Harper & Row, 1978, pp. 233, 334, 380.
313. Crosby, p. 27.
314. Ibid., p. 28.
315. Ibid., p. 60.
316. Magnus, p. 51.
317. Ibid., p. 71.
318. Ibid., p. 96.
319. Crosby, p. 62.
320. Ibid., p. 78.
321. Magnus, p. 131.
322. Ibid., p. 174.
323. Roy Jenkins. *Gladstone: A Biography*. New York: Random House, 1997, p. 265.
324. Crosby, p. 127.
325. Magnus, p. 217.
326. Ibid.
327. Ibid.
328. Ibid.
329. Ibid.
330. Magnus, p. 220.
331. Ibid., pp. 221–222.
332. Ibid., p. 226.
333. Jenkins, p. 367.
334. Ibid., p. 229.
335. Jenkins, p. 368.
336. Ibid., p. 466.
337. Matthew, pp. 284–285.
338. Ibid., p. 285.
339. Ibid., p. 287.
340. Magnus, p. 323.
341. Ibid., p. 404.
342. Ibid., p. 10.
343. Jenkins, p. 372.
344. Ibid., p. 402.
345. Magnus, p. 175.
346. Jenkins, p. 457.
347. Crosby, p. 11.
348. Jenkins, p. 373.
349. Vincent, p. 252.
350. Jenkins, p. 464.
351. Crosby, p. 176.
352. Vincent, p. 216.
353. Crosby, p. 85.

354. Vincent, p. 312.
355. Ibid., p. 267.
356. Jenkins, p. 502.
357. Richard Davenport-Hines. *The Pursuit of Oblivion: A Global History of Narcotics.* New York: W.W. Norton, 2004, pp. 82–83.
358. Jenkins, pp. 44 and 104.
359. Crosby, p. 64.
360. Ibid., p. 65; Jenkins, p. 106.
361. Matthew, p. 363.
362. Crosby, p. 161.
363. Magnus, p. 305.
364. Matthew, p. 69.
365. Jenkins, p. 308.
366. E. Slater and A. Meyer, "Contributions to a Pathography of the Musicians: 2. Organic and Psychotic Disorders," *Confinia Psychiatrica,* 3 (1960): 129–140.
367. American Psychiatric Association. *Diagnostic and Statistical Manual of Mental Disorders,* 4th Edition. Washington, DC: American Psychiatric Association, 2000, pp. 566–576.
368. E. Slater, "The Creative Personality," *The Cambridge Review,* 27 (February, 1981): 114–120.
369. Matthew, p. 241.

Robert Gascoyne-Cecil

370. A. L. Kennedy. *Salisbury 1830–1903: Portrait of a Statesman.* London: John Murray, 1953, p. 6.
371. Kennedy, p. 11.
372. Ibid., pp. 27–28.
373. Ibid., p. 28.
374. K. Rose. *The Later Cecils.* New York: Harper & Row, 1975, pp. 23–24.
375. Ibid., p. 23.
376. Dermot Englefield, Janet Seaton, and Isobel White. *Facts About the British Prime Ministers.* New York: H.H. Wilson, 1995, p. 210.
377. Rose, p. 24.
378. Lucille Iremonger. *The Fiery Chariot: A Study of British Prime Ministers and the Search for Love.* London: Secker & Warburg, 1970, p. 144.
379. Arnold White in *Harper's Weekly,* "England's Foreign Office," *New York Times,* August 21, 1898, http://query.nytimes.com/gst/abstract.html?res=F60E14FA3B5416738DDDA80A94D0405B8885F0D3 (accessed October 12, 2008); "Lord Salisbury's Illness," *New York Times,* March 20, 1898, http://query.nytimes.com/gst/abstract.html?res=F30A15F63D5C11738DDDA90A94DB405B8885F0D3 (accessed October 12, 2008).
380. Kennedy, p. 9.
381. Ibid., p. 50; Ibid., p. 353.
382. Englefield, p. 210.
383. Kennedy, p. 356.

Archibald Philip Primrose

384. Leo McKinstry, "Enjoy It While You Can, Prime Minister, There Could Be Trouble Ahead," *Daily Express,* August 3, 2007.
385. Lucille Iremonger. *The Fiery Chariot: A Study of British Prime Ministers and the Search for Love.* London: Secker & Warburg, 1970, pp. 146–148.
386. Robert Rhodes James. *Rosebery.* New York: Macmillan, 1963, p. 10.
387. Iremonger, p. 152.
388. Graham Walker, "Archibald Philip Primrose, 5th Lord Rosebery, 1847–1929," in *Biographical Dictionary of British Prime Ministers.* Robert Eccleshall and Graham Walker (eds.). New York: Routledge, 1998, p. 223.
389. James, p. 76.
390. Leo McKinstry, *Daily Telegraph,* December 27, 2005, http://www.telegraph.co.uk/opinion/main.jhtml?xlm=/opinion/2005/12/27/do2701.xml, October 9, 2008.
391. James, p. 251.
392. Ibid., p. 369.
393. Algernon Cecil. *Queen Victoria and Her Prime Ministers.* London: Eyre & Spottiswoode, 1953, p. 271.
394. Marjie Bloy, "Archibald Philip Primrose, 5th Earl of Rosebery (1847–1929)," *The Victorian Web,* January 16, 2005, http://www.victorianweb.org/history/pms/rosebery.html (accessed July 16, 2008).
395. Leo McKinstry. *Rosebery, a Statesman in Turmoil.* London: John Murray, 2005, p. 93.
396. James, p. 227.
397. Ibid., pp. 228 and 229.
398. McKinstry, *Rosebery, a Statesman in Turmoil,* p. 215.
399. James, p. 373.
400. McKinstry, *Daily Telegraph,* 2005.
401. Richard Davenport-Hines. *The Pursuit of Oblivion.* New York: W.W. Norton, 2004, p. 173.
402. James, p. 463.
403. Ibid., p. 467.
404. Ibid., p. 476.
405. Ibid., p. 485.
406. Ibid., p. 474.

Arthur Balfour

407. "Arthur James Balfour," Answers.com, http://www.answers.com/topic/arthur-balfour?print=true (accessed October 13, 2008).
408. Jim Stagle, "Arthur Balfour," OregonLive.com, http://blog.oregonlive.com/religion/2007/07/arthur_balfour.html (October 12, 2008).
409. Dermot Englefield, Janet Seaton, and Isobel White. *Facts About the British Prime Ministers.* New York: H.W. Wilson, 1995, p. 217.
410. Geoffrey Searle, "Arthur James Balfour, First Earl of Balfour," in *Biographical Diction-*

ary of British Prime Ministers. Robert Eccleshall and Graham Walker (eds.). New York: Routledge, 1998, pp. 236–237.
411. Englefield, p. 221.
412. A. Wolf, "The Earl of Balfour," *Journal of Philosophical Studies*, 20 (1930): 503–515.
413. Harold Begbie. *A Gentleman with a Duster: The Mirrors of Downing Street, Some Political Reflections*. New York: Putnam's, 1921, p. 65.
414. Lucille Iremonger. *The Fiery Chariot: A Study of British Prime Ministers and the Search for Love*. London: Secker & Warburg, 1970, p. 171.
415. Iremonger, p. 166.
416. Ibid., p. 167.

Sir Henry Campbell-Bannerman

417. Iain Hutchinson, "Henry Campbell-Bannerman," in *Biographical Dictionary of British Prime* Ministers. Robert Eccleshall and Graham Walker (eds.). New York: Routledge, 1998, p. 240.
418. Lord David Owen. *In Sickness and in Power: Illness in Heads of Government During the Last 100 Years*. London: Methuen, 2008, p. 10.
419. Ibid., p. 9.
420. J. A. Spender. *The Life of the Right Hon. Sir Henry Campbell-Bannerman GCB, Vol. 2*. London: Hodder & Stoughton, 1923, p. 288.
421. Lucille Iremonger. *The Fiery Chariot: A Study of British Prime Ministers and the Search for Love*. London: Secker & Warburg, 1970, p. 319.
422. Roy Hattersley, *Campbell-Bannerman*. London: Haus Publishing, 2006, p. 94.
423. Iremonger, p. 320; Dermot Englefield, Janet Seaton, and Isobel White. *Facts About the British Prime Ministers*. New York: H.W. Wilson, 1995, p. 224.
424. Iremonger, p. 320.
425. Spender, p. 289.
426. Iremonger, p. 320.
427. Hattersley, p. 94.
428. Spender, p. 297.
429. Ibid., p. 394.
430. Ibid., p. 297.
431. American Psychiatric Association. *Diagnostic and Statistical Manual of Mental Disorders, 4th Edition*. Washington, DC: American Psychiatric Association, 2000, pp. 680, 737, 740.

Herbert Henry Asquith

432. The Rt. Hon. Lord Riddell. *Lord Riddell's War Diary, 1914–1918*. London: Ivor Nicholson and Watson, 1933, p. 97.
433. Michael Brock, "Biography of 1st Earl of Oxford and Asquith Herbert Henry Asquith" *Liberal History Democrat Group, http://www.liberalhistory.org.uk/item_single.php?item_id=3&item=biography&PHPSESSI* (accessed August 8, 2008).
434. Kenneth Brown, "Herbert Henry Asquith, Earl of Oxford and Asquith," in *Biographical Dictionary of British Prime Ministers*. Robert Eccleshall and Graham Walker (eds.). New York: Routledge, 1998, p. 244.
435. Colin Clifford. *The Asquiths*. London: John Murray, 2002, p. 471.
436. Ibid., p. 98.
437. Ibid., p. 186.
438. Lucille Iremonger. *The Fiery Chariot: A Study of British Prime Ministers and the Search for Love*. London: Secker & Warburg, 1970, p. 232.
439. Clifford, pp. 192–193.
440. Michael Brock and Eleanor Brock, eds. *H. H. Asquith: Letters to Venetia Stanley*. New York: Oxford University Press, 1985, pp. 10–11.
441. Claire Hu, "Is There a Drinks Cabinet in the House?" *Harpers Wine and Spirit Magazine*, July 23, 2007.
442. Clifford, p. 186.
443. D. Owen, "Hubris Syndrome," *Clinical Medicine*, 8 (2008): 428–432.
444. Eddie Ford, "Booze and Moral Panics," *Weekly Worker*, December 15, 2005, p. 605.
445. Hu, 2007.
446. Brock and Brock, p. 11.
447. Ford, 2005.
448. Iremonger, p. 232.
449. Hugh L'Étang. *The Pathology of Leadership*. London: William Heinemann Medical Books, 1969, p. 61.
450. Ibid., p. 61.
451. Clifford, p. 380.
452. Brock and Brock, p. 606.
453. Riddell, p. 293.
454. Ibid., p. 293.
455. Iremonger, p. 235.

David Lloyd George

456. Thomas Jones. *Lloyd George*. Cambridge, MA: Harvard University Press, 1951, p. 178.
457. Kenneth O. Morgan, "George, David Lloyd, First Earl Lloyd-George of Dwyfor 1863–1945)," in *Oxford Dictionary of National Biography* (Oxford University Press, September, 2004), October, 2008, *http://www.oxforddnb.com/view/article/34570*, 47 (accessed December 19, 2008).
458. Lucille Iremonger. *The Fiery Chariot: A Study of British Prime Ministers and the Search for Love*. London: Secker & Warburg, 1970, p. 207.
459. Kenneth O. Morgan. *David Lloyd George: Welsh Radical as World Statesman*. Cardiff: University of Wales Press, 1963, p. 7.

460. Lord Beaverbrook. *The Decline and Fall of Lloyd George*. London: Collins, 1963, p. 10; D. Owen and J.R.T. Davidson, "Hubris Syndrome: An Acquired Personality Disorder? A Study of U.S. Presidents and U.K. Prime Ministers Over the Last 100 Years," *Brain*, 132 (2009): 1396–1406.
461. F. Post, "Creativity and Psychopathology, a Study of 291 World-Famous Men," *British Journal of Psychiatry*, 165 (1994): 22–34.
462. Arnold M. Ludwig. *King of the Mountain: The Nature of Political Leadership*. Louisville, KY: University Press of Kentucky, 2002, p, 236; Iremonger, pp. 194 and 205.
463. Kenneth O. Morgan, "George, David Lloyd, First Earl Lloyd-George of Dwyfor 1863–1945)," in *Oxford Dictionary of National Biography* (Oxford University Press, September, 2004), October, 2004, http://www.oxforddnb.com/view/article/34570 (accessed December 19, 2008).
464. Frank Owen. *Tempestuous Journey*. London: Hutchinson, 1954, p. 236.
465. Ibid., p. 240.
466. Iremonger, p. 208.
467. Lord David Owen. *In Sickness and in Power: Illness in Heads of Government During the Last 100 Years*. London: Methuen, 2008, p. 14.
468. Frank Owen, p. 156.
469. A.J.P. Taylor, ed. *Lloyd George: A Diary by Frances Stevenson*. New York: Harper & Row, 1971, p. 23.
470. Kenneth O. Morgan, "George, David Lloyd, First Earl Lloyd-George of Dwyfor 1863–1945," in *Oxford Dictionary of National Biography* (Oxford University Press, September, 2004), p. 5.
471. Physicians and Surgeons of the Principal London Hospitals. *The Family Physician: A Manual of Domestic Medicine, New and Enlarged Edition*. London: Cassell, 1886, p. 513.
472. Iremonger, p. 194.
473. Hugh L'Étang. *The Pathology of Leadership*. London: William Heinemann Medical Books, 1969, p. 64.
474. Jones, p. 121.
475. Ibid.
476. F. W. Burton-Fanning, "Neurasthenia in Soldiers of the Home Forces," *Lancet*, 1 (1917): 907–911.
477. Beaverbrook, p. 264.
478. Ibid., pp. 138–139.
479. Ibid., pp. 293–294.
480. L'Étang, p. 65.
481. Ibid.
482. Morgan, "George, David Lloyd, First Earl Lloyd-George of Dwyfor 1863–1945," *Oxford Dictionary of National Biography* (Oxford University Press, September, 2004), 45; David Owen, 14; Morgan, "George, David Lloyd, first Earl Lloyd-George of Dwyfor 1863–1945," *Oxford Dictionary of National Biography*, 47; Ludwig, 215.
483. Ludwig, p. 215.
484. Morgan, "George, David Lloyd, First Earl Lloyd-George of Dwyfor 1863–1945," *Oxford Dictionary of National Biography*, p. 47.
485. Iremonger, p. 175.
486. Ibid., p, 197; Morgan, "George, David Lloyd, First Earl Lloyd-George of Dwyfor 1863–1945," *Oxford Dictionary of National Biography*, pp. 45–46.
487. Morgan, "George, David Lloyd, First Earl Lloyd-George of Dwyfor 1863–1945," *Oxford Dictionary of National Biography*, p. 8.
488. Jones, p. 89.
489. Ibid., p. 92.
490. Ibid.
491. Morgan, "George, David Lloyd, first Earl Lloyd-George of Dwyfor 1863–1945," *Oxford Dictionary of National Biography*, p. 24.

Andrew Bonar Law

492. D. Owen and J.R.T. Davidson, "Hubris Syndrome: An Acquired Personality Disorder? A Study of U.S. Presidents and U.K. Prime Ministers Over the Last 100 Years," *Brain*, 132 (2009): 1396–1406.
493. H. Berrington, "Review Article — The Fiery Chariot: British Prime Ministers and the Search for Love," *British Journal of Political Science*, 4 (1974): 345.
494. Andrew Taylor. *Bonar Law*. London: Haus Publishing, 2006, p. 5.
495. J. Vincent, ed. *The Crawford Papers: The Journals of David Lindsay, Twenty-Seventh Earl of Crawford and Tenth Earl of Balcarres, 1871–1940, During the Years 1892 to 1940*. Manchester: Manchester University Press, 1984, p. 263.
496. Robert Blake. *The Unknown Prime Minister: The Life and Times of Andrew Bonar Law, 1858–1923*. London: Eyre & Spottiswoode, 1935, p. 61.
497. Ibid., p. 61.
498. Robert Rhodes James, ed. *Memoirs of a Conservative: J. C. C. Davidson's Memoirs and Papers, 1910–37*. London: Weidenfeld and Nicholson, 1969, p. 72.
499. Vincent, p. 248.
500. Blake, p. 61.
501. Lord Riddell. *War Diary, 1914–1918*. London: Ivor, Nicholson & Watson, 1933, p. 258.
502. Blake, p. 356.
503. Ibid., p. 360.
504. Ibid., p. 423.
505. E. H. H Green, "Law, Andrew Bonar (1858–1923)," *Oxford Dictionary of National Biography* (Oxford University Press, September

2004), January 25, 2008, *http:www.oxforddnb.com/view/article/34426*.

Stanley Baldwin

506. John Gunther. *Inside Europe*. London: Hamish Hamilton, 1937, p. 269.
507. Lucille Iremonger. *The Fiery Chariot: A Study of British Prime Ministers and the Search for Love*. London: Secker & Warburg, 1970, p. 321.
508. Keith Middlemas and John Barnes. *Baldwin: A Biography*. London: Macmillan, 1969, p. 259; Andrew Lycett, 'Oliver Baldwin: A Life of Dissent. Christopher J. Walker. Arcadia Books," *New Statesman*, March 29, 2004, *http://www.newstatesman.com/print/200403290045* (accessed July 27, 2008).
509. Gunther, p. 273.
510. Ibid., p. 275.
511. Iremonger, p. 324; Middlemas, p. 1083.
512. Middlemas, pp. 27, 171–172.
513. Gunther, p. 270.
514. Iremonger, p. 323.
515. Middlemas, p. 500; A. W. Baldwin (3rd Earl Baldwin of Bewdley). *My Father: The True Story*. London: George, Allen & Unwin, 1955, p. 50.
516. G. M. Young. *Stanley Baldwin*. London: Rupert Hart-Davis, 1952, pp. 57–58, 128, 167.
517. P. Williamson, "Baldwin's Reputation: Politics and History, 1937–1967," *The Historical Journal*, 47 (2004): 127–168.
518. Iremonger, p. 321.
519. Arnold M. Ludwig. *King of the Mountain: The Nature of Political Leadership*. Lexington, KY: University Press of Kentucky, 2002, p. 244; Middlemas, 960–965.
520. Iremonger, p. 324.
521. American Psychiatric Association. *Diagnostic and Statistical Manual of Mental Disorders, Fourth Edition*. Washington, DC: American Psychiatric Association, 2000, pp. 111–114.
522. Baldwin, p. 135.
523. Iremonger, p. 323.
524. Andrew Thorpe, "Stanley Baldwin, First Earl Baldwin of Bewdley," in *Biographical Dictionary of British Prime Ministers*. Robert Eccleshall and Graham Walker (eds.). New York: Routledge, 1998, p. 280.
525. Gunther, p. 275.
526. Roy Jenkins. *Baldwin*. London: Collins, 1987, p. 143.
527. Dominique Enright. *The Wicked Wit of Winston Churchill*. London: Michael O'Mara Books, 2001, p. 58.
528. Middlemas, p. 930.
529. Ibid., p. 1035.
530. Gunther, p. 276.
531. Thorpe, p. 279.
532. Hugh L'Étang. *Fit to Lead*. London: William Heinemann Medical Books, 1979, p. 35.
533. Thorpe, p. 279.
534. American Psychiatric Association, p. 410.
535. Ibid., p. 484.
536. Ibid., pp. 450–456.
537. Ibid., pp. 472–476.
538. Ibid., p. 116.
539. M. Francis, "Tears, Tantrums, and Bared Teeth: The Emotional Economy of Three Conservative Prime Ministers," *Journal of British Studies*, 41 (2002): 354–387.

James Ramsay MacDonald

540. Duncan Tanner, "(James) Ramsay MacDonald," in *Biographical Dictionary of British Prime Ministers*. Robert Walker and Graham Eccleshall (eds.). New York: Routledge, 1998, p. 281.
541. Lucille Iremonger. *The Fiery Chariot: A Study of Prime Ministers and the Search for Love*. London: Secker & Warburg, 1970, p. 265.
542. Ibid., p. 275.
543. Ibid., p. 274.
544. David Marquand. *Ramsay MacDonald*. London: Jonathan Cape, 1977, p. 134; Jonathan R. T. Davidson and Kathryn M. Connor, "The Impairment of Presidents Pierce and Coolidge After Traumatic Bereavement," *Comprehensive Psychiatry*, 49 (2008): 413–419.
545. Tanner, p. 283.
546. L. M. Weir. *The Tragedy of Ramsay MacDonald*. London: Secker and Warburg, 1938, p. 552.
547. Bert E. Park. *The Impact of Illness on World Leaders*. Philadelphia: University of Pennsylvania Press, 1996, p. 94.
548. L. Lafore. *The End of Glory: An Interpretation of the Origins of World War II*. New York: J. P. Lippincott, 1970, p. 86.
549. Park, p. 95.
550. Weir, pp. 473–474.
551. Park, p. 103.
552. Ibid., p. 99.
553. Marquand, p. 697.
554. Park, p. 101.
555. Ibid., p. 103.
556. Marquand, p. 700.
557. Sir Arthur Salter. *Personality in Politics*. London: Faber, 1938, p. 64.
558. Park, p. 112.

Neville Chamberlain

559. Dermot Englefield, Janet Seaton, and Isobel White. *Facts About the British Prime Ministers*. New York: H. W. Wilson, 1995, p. 270.

560. Lucille Iremonger. *The Fiery Chariot: A Study of British Prime Ministers and Their Search for Love*. London: Secker & Warburg, 1970, p. 300.
561. Stuart Ball, "(Arthur) Neville Chamberlain," in *Biographical Dictionary of British Prime Ministers*. Robert Eccleshall and Graham Walker (eds.). New York: Routledge, 1998, p. 289.
562. David Dutton. *Neville Chamberlain*. London: Arnold, 2001, p. 10.
563. Andrew J. Crozier, "Chamberlain, (Arthur) Neville (1869–1940)," in *Oxford Dictionary of National Biography* (Oxford University Press, September 2004), October 2008, http://www.oxforddnb.com/view/article/32347 (accessed January 12, 2009).
564. Ibid., 19.
565. Ibid., p. 22.
566. Ibid.
567. Lord David Owen. *In Sickness and in Power: Illness in Heads of Government During the Last 100 Years*. London: Methuen, 2008, p. 26; David Owen and Jonathan R. T. Davidson, "Hubris Syndrome: An Acquired Personality Disorder? A Study of U.S. Presidents and U.K. Prime Ministers Over the Last 100 Years," *Brain*, 132 (2009): 1396–1406.
568. Iremonger, p. 297.
569. Ibid., p. 298.
570. Crozier, p. 10.
571. Iremonger, p. 298.
572. Keith Feiling. *The Life of Neville Chamberlain*. London: Macmillan, 1946, p. 119.
573. Ibid., p. 112.
574. Ibid., p. 119.
575. Iremonger, p. 302.
576. Owen, 2009.
577. Frederick K. Goodwin and Kay R. Jamison. *Manic Depressive Illness*. New York: Oxford University Press, 1990, p. 357.
578. Paul Smith, ed. *Bagehot: The English Constitution*. New York: Cambridge University Press, 2001, p. 19–20.

Sir Winston Churchill

579. David Owen. *In Sickness and in Power: Illness in Heads of Government During the Last 100 Years*. London: Methuen, 2008, p. 41.
580. Arnold M. Ludwig. *King of the Mountain*. Lexington, KY: University Press of Kentucky, 2002, p. 168.
581. Clive Ponting. *Churchill*. London: Sinclair-Stevenson, 1994, p. 21; Ludwig, p. 167.
582. Anthony Storr. *Churchill's Black Dog and Other Phenomena of the Human Mind*. Glasgow: Fontana/Collins, 1969, p. 9.
583. Roy Jenkins. *Churchill: A Biography*. New York: Farrar, Straus & Giroux, 2001, p. 20–21.
584. Storr, p. 5.

585. Winston S. Churchill. *Painting as a Pastime*. New York: McGraw-Hill, 1950, p. 16.
586. Churchill, p. 19.
587. "Winston Churchill and Manic Depression," Bipolar Lives.com, July 20, 2008, http://www.bipolar-lives.com/winston-churchill-and-manic-depression.html.
588. Mary Soames. *Clementine Churchill by Her Daughter*. London: Cassell, 1979, p. 253.
589. Storr, p. 17.
590. Ibid., p. 22.
591. Ibid., p. 6.
592. Donald F. Klein, et al. *Diagnosis and Drug Treatment of Psychiatric Disorders: Adults and Children, Second Edition*. Baltimore: Williams & Wilkins, 1980, pp. 233–243.
593. Sarah Churchill. *A Thread in the Tapestry*. London: Deutsch, 1967; Winston S. Churchill. *Savrola*. Bath: Cedric Chivers, 1973, p. 39–40.
594. John Gunther. *Inside Europe*. London: Hamish Hamilton, 1937, p. 293; Owen, p. 41.
595. "Winston Churchill and Manic Depression," Bipolar Lives.com, July 20, 2008, http://www.bipolar-lives.com/winston-churchill-and-manic-depression.html.
596. Frederick K. Goodwin and Kay R. Jamison. *Manic Depressive Illness*. New York: Oxford University Press, 1990, p. 359.
597. Storr, pp. 14–15.
598. Ronald Fieve. *Moodswing*. New York: Bantam Books, 1969, p. 115.
599. Storr, p. 45.
600. Ludwig, p. 225.
601. Ponting, pp. 287–289.
602. John H. Mather, "Lord Randolph Churchill: Malades et Mort," *The Churchill Centre*, July 20, 2008, http://www.winstonchurchill.org/learn/myths/myths/his-father-died-of-syphilis (accessed September 6, 2009).
603. Lord David Owen, "Diseased, Demented, Depressed: Serious Illness in Heads of State," *Quarterly Journal of Medicine*, 96 (2003): 325–336; I. Robertson, "Soundings: Interpreting Problems," *British Medical Journal*, 309 (1994): 1519.
604. Norman Rose. *Churchill: An Unruly Life*. New York: Simon & Schuster, 1998, p. 194.
605. Ponting, pp. 287–288.
606. Robertson, p. 1994.
607. Ponting, pp. 619–620.
608. David Reynolds, "Selected Extracts From 'After Dark' Programme (Channel 4 TV)," The International Campaign for Real History, July 20, 2008, http://www.fpp.co.uk/docs/Irving/broadcasts/AfterDark280588.html.
609. American Psychiatric Association. *Diagnostic and Statistical Manual of Mental Disorders, Fourth Edition*. Washington, DC: American Psychiatric Association, 2000, pp. 192–199, 213–214.

610. Ludwig, p. 262; John H. Mather, "Lord Randolph Churchill: Malades et Mort," *The Churchill Centre,* July 20, 2008, http://www.winstonchurchill.org/learn/myths/myths/his-father-died-of-syphilis (accessed September 6, 2009).
611. Norman Rose. *Churchill: The Unruly Giant.* New York: Free Press, 1994, pp. 410–411.

Clement Attlee

612. R. C. Whiting, "Attlee, Clement Richard, First Earl Attlee (1883–1967)," in *Oxford Dictionary of National Biography* (Oxford University Press, September 2004), January 2008, http://www.oxforddnb.com/view/article/30498 (accessed December 28, 2008).

Sir Anthony Eden

613. Hugh L'Étang. *The Pathology of Leadership.* London: William Heinemann Medical Books, 1969, pp. 21–24.
614. David Owen. *In Sickness and in Power: Illness in Heads of Government During the Last 100 Years.* London: Methuen, 2008, p. 140.
615. D. R. Thorpe, "Eden (Robert) Anthony, First Earl of Avon (1897–1977)," in *Oxford Dictionary of National Biography* (Oxford University Press, September 2004), May 2008, http://www.oxforddnb.com/view/article/31060 (accessed December 28, 2008); David Dutton. *Anthony Eden: A Life and Reputation.* New York: Arnold, 1997, p. 461; Ibid., p. 239; Ibid., p. 463; L'Étang, p. 163; Dutton, p. 466.
616. L'Étang, pp. 161–162.
617. A. Morison, "The Soldier's Heart and the Strained Heart," *British Medical Journal,* 1 (1916): 184.
618. Owen, p. 110.
619. J. W. Braasch, "Anthony Eden's (Lord Avon) Biliary Tract Saga," *Annals of Surgery,* 238 (2003): 772–775.
620. Dermot Englefield, Janet Seaton, and Isobel White. *Facts About the British Prime Ministers.* New York: H.W. Wilson, 1995, p. 295.
621. Owen, p. 113
622. Robert Rhodes James. *Anthony Eden.* London: Weidenfeld & Nicolson, 1986, p. 432.
623. Owen, p. 120.
624. Francis Beckett, "Secrets and Lies," *New Statesman,* January, 16, 2006, http://www.newstatesman.com/print/200601160005 (accessed August 18, 2009).
625. Bert E. Park. *Ailing, Aging, Addicted: Studies of Compromised Leadership.* Lexington, KY: University Press of Kentucky, 1993, pp. 146–147.
626. Owen, p. 122.

627. Winston S. Churchill. *The Gathering Storm.* London: Houghton Mifflin, 1948, p. 257.

Harold Macmillan

628. H. C. G. Matthew, "Macmillan, (Maurice) Harold, First Earl of Stockton (1894–1986)," *Oxford Dictionary of National Biography* (Oxford University Press, September 2004), January 2008, http://www.oxforddnb.com/view/article/40185 (accessed December 28, 2008).
629. Alastair Horne. *Harold Macmillan, Volume 1, 1894–1956.* New York: Penguin Books, 1988, p. 98.
630. Dermot Englefield, Janet Seaton, and Isobel White. *Facts About the British Prime Ministers.* New York: H. W. Wilson, 1995, p. 301.
631. David Owen. *In Sickness and in Power: Illness in Heads of Government During the Last 100 Years.* London: Methuen, 2008, p. 70.
632. Horne, *Volume 1,* pp. 1 and 13.
633. Alastair Horne. *Harold Macmillan, Volume 2, 1957–1986.* New York: Penguin Books, 1989, p. 613.
634. Horne, *Volume 1,* p. 303.
635. Horne, *Volume 2,* p. 267.
636. Ibid., p. 529.
637. Ibid., pp. 529–530.
638. Ibid., p. 631.
639. Horne, *Volume 1,* p. 13.
640. Horne, *Volume 2,* p. 153.
641. Horne, *Volume 1,* p. 75.
642. Ibid., p. 390.
643. Horne, *Volume 2,* pp. 189 and 195.
644. R. E. Taylor, "Death of Neurasthenia and Its Psychological Reincarnation," *British Journal of Psychiatry,* 179 (2001): 550–557.
645. Horne, *Volume 1,* p. 215.
646. F. W. Burton-Fanning, "Neurasthenia in Soldiers of the Home Forces," *Lancet* (1917): 907–911.
647. Wei Zhang, et al., "Symptoms of Neurasthenia Following Earthquake Trauma: Re-Examination of a Discarded Syndrome," *Psychiatry Research,* 153 (2007): 171–177.
648. Horne, *Volume 1,* pp. 45–46.
649. S. Galea, et al., "Psychological Sequelae of September 11 Terrorist Attacks in New York City," *New England Journal of Medicine,* 346 (2002): 482–487.
650. Horne, *Volume 1,* p. 49.
651. Ibid., p. 36.
652. Ibid., p. 48.
653. Ibid., p. 240.
654. Ibid., p. 98.

Sir Alec Douglas-Home

655. Dermot Englefield, Janet Seaton, and Isobel White. *Facts About the British Prime*

Ministers. New York: H.W. Wilson, 1995, p. 310.

Harold Wilson

656. Roy Jenkins, "Wilson, (James) Harold, Baron Wilson of Rievaulx (1916-1995)," in *Oxford Dictionary of National Biography* (Oxford University Press, September 2004), January 2009, *http://www.oxforddnb.com/view/article/58000* (assessed January 15, 2009).
657. David Owen. *In Sickness and in Power: Illness in Heads of Government During the Last 100 Years*. London: Methuen, 2008, pp. 83-85; Philip Ziegler. *Wilson*. London: Weidenfeld & Nicholson, 1993; Ben Pimlott. *Harold Wilson*. London: HarperCollins, 1993; Arnold M. Ludwig. *King of the Mountain: The Nature of Political Leadership*. Lexington, KY: University Press of Kentucky, 2002, pp. 228-229 and 263.
658. Ziegler, pp. 486-487.
659. Ibid., pp. 468-469.
660. Ibid., p. 468.
661. Ibid., p. 467.
662. Pimlott, pp. 674-675.
663. Peter Paterson, "Harold Was a Toper Too," *The Spectator*, January 9, 1999, *http://findarticles.com/p/articles/mi_qa3724/is_199901/ai_n8834583/print?tag=artBody* (accessed December 31, 2008).
664. Ziegler, p. 166.
665. Ibid., p. 470.
666. Ibid., p. 471.
667. Ibid., p. 487.
668. P. Garrard, "Cognitive Archaeology: Uses, Methods and Results," *Journal of Neurolinguistics* (2008), DOI: 10.1016/j.jneuroling.2008.07.006.
669. Ludwig, p. 263.
670. Owen, p. 85.
671. Michael Kenny, "(James) Harold Wilson, Lord Wilson of Rievaulx," in *Biographical Dictionary of British Prime Ministers*. Robert Eccleshall and Graham Walker (eds.). New York: Routledge, 1998, p. 337.
672. Barbara Tuchman. *The March of Folly*. New York: Ballantine Books, 1984, p. 17.

Sir Edward Heath

673. George Hutchinson. *Edward Heath: A Personal and Political Biography*. London: Longman, 1970, p. 198.
674. Andrew Gamble, "Edward Richard George Heath," in *Biographical Dictionary of British Prime Ministers*. Robert Eccleshall and Graham Walker (eds.). New York: Routledge, 1998, p. 343.
675. John Campbell. *Edward Heath: A Biography*. London: Jonathan Cape, 1993, p. 574.

676. Dermot Englefield, Janet Seaton, and Isobel White. Facts About the British Prime Ministers. New York: H.W. Wilson, 1995, p. 327.
677. Thomas Stuttaford, "The Telltale Loss of Power," *Times Online*, April 27, 2007, *http://www.martinfrost.ws/htmlfiles/april2007/politics_thyroid.html* (accessed January 6, 2009).
678. Lord David Owen. *In Sickness and in Power: Illness in Heads of Government During the Last 100 Years*. London: Methuen, 2008, p. 86.
679. Campbell, pp. 576-577.
680. Ibid., p. 659.
681. Owen, p. 86.
682. Margaret Laing. *Edward Heath, Prime Minister*. New York: Third Press, 1973, p. 151.
683. Laing, p. 205; Ibid., p. 172; Ibid., p. 205.

James Callaghan

684. Dermot Englefield, Janet Seaton, and Isobel White. *Facts About the British Prime Ministers*. New York: H.W. Wilson, 1995, p. 336.
685. Kenneth O. Morgan. *Callaghan: A Life*. New York: Oxford University Press, 1997, pp. 664-665.
686. Ibid., p. 665.

Margaret Thatcher

687. Dermot Englefield, Janet Seaton, and Isobel White. *Facts About the British Prime Ministers*. New York: H. W. Wilson, 1995, p. 346.
688. James Kirkup, "Margaret Thatcher's Mental Decline Revealed by Her Daughter," Telegraph.co.uk, August 25, 2008, *http://www.telegraph.co.uk/news/newstopics/politics/conservative/2614020/Margaret-Thatchers-mental-decline-revealed-by-her-daughter.html* (accessed January 15, 2009).

Sir John Major

689. Dermot Englefield, Janet Seaton, and Isobel White. *Facts About the British Prime Ministers*. New York: H.W. Wilson, 1995, p. 354.

Anthony (Tony) Blair

690. Lord David Owen. *In Sickness and in Power: Illness in Heads of Government During the Last 100 Years*. London: Methuen, 2008, pp. 300-302 and 317.

Conclusion

1. R. C. Kessler, et al., "Lifetime and 12-Month Prevalence of DSM-III-R Psychiatric

Disorders in the United States: Results from the National Comorbidity Survey," *Archives of General Psychiatry*, 51 (1994): 8–19.

2. Arnold Ludwig. *King of the Mountain: The Nature of Political Leadership*. Lexington, KY: University Press of Kentucky, 2002, p. 236.

3. Ibid., pp. 221–271.

4. Ibid., p. 40.

5. Anthony Storr. *Churchill's Black Dog and Other Phenomena of the Human Mind*. London: Fontana Collins, 1989, pp. 34–35.

6. Marvin Olasky, "Theodore Roosevelt: Manly Compassion in Troubled Times," *Compassion and Culture*, Capital Research Center, November 2008, http://www.capitalresearch.org/pubs/pdf/v1225674429.pdf (accessed August 20, 2009).

7. Ludwig, p. 237.

8. Stefanie Marsh, "Losing It," *Times Online*, August 2, 2007, http://www.timesonline.co.uk/tol/life_and_style/health/features/article2180877.ece?print (accessed February 17, 2009); Irving Muszynski and Clare Miller, "Burguieres Recovers from Depression by Helping Other CEOs," *Mental Health Works* (American Psychiatric Association and the American Psychiatric Foundation, Fourth Quarter 2008), pp. 5–6.

9. H. Freeman, "The Human Brain and Political Behaviour," *British Journal of Psychiatry* 159 (1991): 19–32.

10. Ludwig, p. 211.

11. R. C. Kessler, et al., "Lifetime Prevalence and Age-of-Onset Distributions of DSM-IV Disorders in the National Comorbidity Survey Replication," *Archives of General Psychiatry*, 62 (2005): 593–602.

12. P. Wink, "Two Faces of Narcissism," *Journal of Personality and Social Psychology*, 61 (1991): 590–597.

13. Kessler, et al., 1994.

14. Freeman, 1991, p. 24.

15. P. A. Bryant, J. Trinder, N. Curtis, "Sick and Tired: Does Sleep Have a Vital Role in the Immune System?" *Nature Reviews: Immunology*, 4 (2004): 457–467.

16. Freeman, 1991.

17. Ibid.

18. Leo Abse. *Tony Blair: The Man Behind the Smile*. London: Robson Books, 2001, p. 160.

19. Barbara Tuchman. *The March of Folly*. New York: Ballantine Books, 1984, p. 8.

20. T. W. Meeks and D. V. Jeste, "Neurobiology of Wisdom," *Archives of General Psychiatry*, 66 (2009): 355–365.

21. D. Marion, "The British Civil Service: A Political Excavation and Review," *Administration & Society*, 24 (1993): 470–486.

22. Tuchman, p. 385.

23. Marion, p. 483.

24. J. Morley. *The Life of William Ewart Gladstone*. New York: Macmillan, 1903, pp. 512 and 650.

25. Lord David Owen. *In Sickness and in Power: Illness in Heads of Government During the Last 100 Years*. London: Methuen, 2008, p. 329; V. Raymont, et al., "Prevalence of Mental Incapacity in Medical Inpatients and Associated Risk Factors: Cross-Sectional Study," *Lancet*, 364 (2004): 1421–1427.

26. Owen, 2008, pp. 141–190.

27. Owen, pp. 318–320.

28. Jonathan R. T. Davidson and Kathryn M. Connor, "The Impairment of Presidents Pierce and Coolidge After Traumatic Bereavement," *Comprehensive Psychiatry*, 49 (2008): 413–419.

29. Ranit Mishori, "When the Patient Is the President," *Parade*, August 15, 2009, p. 10.

30. Jana Winter, "Source: Michael Jackson's Doctor to Be Charged with Manslaughter," FoxNews.com, August 19, 2009, http://www.foxnews.com/printer_friendly_story/0,3566,54054 0,00.html (accessed September 5, 2009).

31. Owen, 2008, pp. 338–347.

32. R. E. Gilbert, "Psychological Illness in Presidents: A Medical Advisory Commission and Disability Determinations," *Political Psychology*, 27 (2006): 55–75.

33. R. Marx. *The Health of Presidents*. New York: Putnam's, 1960, p. 11.

34. Joanna Burlison, "USF Honors Former Norwegian Prime Minister Kjell Bondevik," *Foghorn Online*, October 10, 2009, http://foghorn.usfca.edu/2009/10/usf-honors-former-norwegian-prime-minister-kjell-bondevik/ (accessed October 10, 2009).

35. Owen, 2008, pp. 338–347.

Bibliography

Abse, Leo. *Tony Blair: The Man Behind the Smile*. London: Robson Books, 2001.

"Addington, Henry." Number-10.gov.uk. http://www.number-10.gov.uk/output/Page 162.asp (accessed May 29, 2008).

Alison, Sir Archibald [Bart.]. *History of Europe: From the Fall of Napoleon in MDCCCXV to the Accession of Louis Napoleon in MDCCCLII, Volume II, Chapter XXI*. New York: Harper & Brothers, Google Books, MDCCCLV.

American Psychiatric Association. *Diagnostic and Statistical Manual of Mental Disorders, Fourth Edition, Text Revision*. Washington, DC: American Psychiatric Association, 2000.

———. *The Principles of Medical Ethics: Principles with Annotations Especially Applicable to Psychiatry*. Arlington, VA: American Psychiatric Press, 2008.

Armytage, W. H. G. "Charles Watson-Wentworth, Second Marquess of Rockingham, F. R. S. (1730–1782): Some Aspects of His Scientific Interests." *Notes and Records of the Royal Society of London*, 12 (1965): 61–76.

"Arthur James Balfour." Answers.com. http://www.answers.com/topic/arthurbalfour?print=true (accessed October 13, 2008).

Ayling, Stanley. *The Elder Pitt*. New York: David McKay, 1976.

Baldwin, A. W. (3rd Earl Baldwin of Bewdley). *My Father: The True Story*. London: George, Allen & Unwin, 1955.

Ball, Stuart. "(Arthur) Neville Chamberlain." In *Biographical Dictionary of British Prime Ministers*, by Robert Eccleshall and Graham Walker (eds.). New York: Routledge, 1998.

Beales, D. "Book Review: Lord Liverpool by Norman Gash." *Journal of Modern History*, 59 (1987): 831–833.

Beaverbrook, Lord Max. *The Decline and Fall of Lloyd George*. London: Collins, 1963.

Beckett, Francis. "Secrets and Lies." *New Statesman*, January 16, 2006. http://www.newstatesman.com/print/200601160005 (accessed August 18, 2009).

Beckett, J. V., and P. D. G. Thomas. "Grenville, George (1712–1770)." In *Oxford Dictionary of National Biography*. Oxford University Press, September 2004; online edition October 2007, http://www.oxforddnb.com/view/article/11489 (accessed January 6, 2009).

Begbie, Harold. *A Gentleman with a Duster: The Mirrors of Downing Street, Some Political Reflections*. New York: Putnam's, 1921.

"Benjamin Disraeli." *The National Archives*. http://www.spartacus.schoolnet.co.uk/PRdisraeli.htm (accessed May 22, 2008).

Berrington, H. "Review Article—The Fiery Chariot: British Prime Ministers and the Search for Love." *British Journal of Political Science*, 4 (1974): 345.

Black, Jeremy. *Pitt the Elder*. New York: Cambridge University Press, 1992.

Blake, Robert. *The Unknown Prime Minister: The Life and Times of Andrew Bonar Law, 1858–1923*. London: Eyre & Spottiswoode, 1935.

Bloy, Marjie. "Archibald Philip Primrose, 5th Earl of Rosebery (1847–1929)." *The Victorian Web*. January 16, 2005. http://www.victorianweb.org/history/pms/rosebery.html (accessed July 16, 2008).

_____. "Arthur Wellesley, First Duke of Wellington (1769–1852)." *A Web of English History*. January 28, 2008. *http://www.historyhome.co.uk/pms/wellingt.htm* (accessed July 12, 2008).

_____. "Augustus Henry Fitzroy, Third Duke of Grafton." In *Biographical Dictionary of British Prime Ministers*, by Robert Eccleshall and Graham Walker (eds.). New York: Routledge, 1998.

_____. "Edward George Geoffrey Smith Stanley, 14th Earl of Derby (1799–1869)." *The Victorian Web*. March 12, 2002. *http://victorianweb.org/history/pms/derby1.html* (accessed August 6, 2008).

_____. "John Stuart, Third Earl of Bute (1713–1792)." *The Victorian Web*. February 27, 2002. *http://www.victorianweb.org/history/pms/bute.html* (accessed July 16, 2008).

_____. "William Pitt the Younger." *The Victorian Web*. *http://www.victorianweb.org/history/pms/pitt.html* (accessed May 25, 2008).

Braasch, J. W. "Anthony Eden's (Lord Avon) Biliary Tract Saga." *Annals of Surgery*, 238 (2003): 772–775.

Brock, Michael. "Biography of 1st Earl of Oxford and Asquith Herbert Henry Asquith." *Liberal History Democrat Group*. *http://www.liberalhistory.org.uk/item_single.php?item_id=3&item=biography&PHPSESSI* (accessed August 8, 2008).

Brock, Michael, and Eleanor Brock, eds. *H.H. Asquith: Letters to Venetia Stanley*. New York: Oxford University Press, 1985.

Brown, Kenneth. "Herbert Henry Asquith, Earl of Oxford and Asquith." In *Biographical Dictionary of British Prime Ministers*, by Robert Eccleshall and Graham Walker (eds.). New York: Routledge, 1998.

Brown, Michael. "Were We All Alcoholics in Parliament Back Then?" *The Independent*, August 30, 2006. *http://www.independent.co.uk/opinion/commentators/michael-brown-were-we-all-alcoholics-in-parliament-back-then-413888.html*.

Brown, Peter D. "Bute in Retirement." In *Lord Bute: Essays in Re-Interpretation*, by Karl W. Schweizer (ed.). Leicester: Leicester University Press, 1988.

Browning, Reed. *The Duke of Newcastle*. New Haven: Yale University Press, 1975.

_____. "Holles, Thomas Pelham—Duke of Newcastle Upon Tyne and First Duke of Newcastle Under Lyme (1693–1768)." *Oxford Dictionary of National Biography*. Oxford University Press, September 2004; online edition, January 2008, *http://www.oxforddnb.com/view/article/21801* (accessed January 6, 2009).

Bryant, P. A., J. Trinder, and N. Curtis. "Sick and Tired: Does Sleep Have a Vital Role in the Immune System?" *Nature Reviews: Immunology*, 4 (2004): 457–467.

Burlison, Joanna. "USF Honors Former Norwegian Prime Minister Kjell Bondevik." *Foghorn Online*, October 10, 2009. *http://foghorn.usfca.edu/2009/10/usf-honors-former-norwegian-prime-minister-kjell-bonevik/* (accessed October 10, 2009).

Burton-Fanning, F. W. "Neurasthenia in Soldiers of the Home Forces." *Lancet* (1917): 907–911.

Busby, Sian. "On Scottish Prime Ministers." *Telegraph.co.uk*, June 28, 2007. *http://my.telegraph.co.uk/sian_busby/blog/2007/06/08/on_scottish_prime_ministers* (accessed August 19, 2009).

Butterfield, H. "Lord North and Mr. Robinson, 1779." *Cambridge Historical Journal*, 5 (1937): 255–279.

Campbell, John. *Edward Heath: A Biography*. London: Jonathan Cape, 1993.

Cecil, Algernon. *Queen Victoria and Her Prime Ministers*. London: Eyre & Spottiswoode, 1953.

Cecil, Lord David. *Melbourne*. New York: Harmony Books, 1966.

Chamberlain, Muriel. "George Gordon (Later Hamilton-Gordon), Fourth Earl of Aberdeen." In *Biographical Dictionary of British Prime Ministers*, by Robert Eccleshall and Graham Walker (eds.). New York: Routledge, 1998.

_____. "Gordon, George Hamilton, Fourth Earl of Aberdeen (1784–1860)." *Oxford Dictionary of National Biography*. Oxford University Press; online edition, January 2008, *http://www.oxforddnb.com/view/article/11044* (accessed January 25, 2009).

Christie, I.R. "Review—The Rise of Party in England: The Rockingham Whigs, 1760–1782, by Frank O'Gorman; London: Allen and Unwin, 1975." *The English Historical Review*, 91 (1976): 390–393.

Churchill, Sarah. *A Thread in the Tapestry*. London: Deutsch, 1967.

Churchill, Winston S. *The Gathering Storm*. London: Houghton Mifflin, 1948.

_____. *Painting as a Pastime*. New York: McGraw-Hill, 1950.
_____. *Savrola*. Bath: Cedric Chivers, 1973.
Clifford, Colin. *The Asquiths*. London: John Murray, 2002.
Coles, A.J. "Fit to Decide?" *Brain*, 132 (2009): 1407–1409.
Connor, Kathryn M., and Jonathan R. T. Davidson. "Development of a New Resilience Scale: The Connor-Davidson Resilience Scale (CD-RISC)." *Depression and Anxiety*, 18 (2003): 76–82.
Cromwell, Valerie. "Edward George Geoffrey Smith Stanley, Fourteenth Earl of Derby." In *Biographical Dictionary of British Prime Ministers*, by Robert Eccleshall and Graham Walker (eds.). New York: Routledge, 1998.
Crosby, Travis L. *The Two Mr. Gladstones: A Study in Psychology and History*. New Haven: Yale University Press, 1997.
Crozier, Andrew J. "Chamberlain, (Arthur) Neville (1869–1940)." *Oxford Dictionary of National Biography*, Oxford University Press, September 2004; online edition, October 2008, *http://www.oxforddnb.com/view/article/32347* (accessed January 12, 2009).
Davenport-Hines, Richard. *The Pursuit of Oblivion: A Global History of Narcotics*. New York: W.W. Norton, 2004.
Davidson, Jonathan R. T., and Kathryn M. Connor. "The Impairment of Presidents Pierce and Coolidge After Traumatic Bereavement." *Comprehensive Psychiatry*, 49 (2008): 413–419.
Davidson, Jonathan R. T., Kathryn M. Connor, and Marvin Swartz. "Mental Illness in U.S. Presidents Between 1776 and 1974: A Review of Biographical Sources." *Journal of Nervous and Mental Disease*, 194 (2006): 47–51.
Davidson, Jonathan R. T., and Wei Zhang. "Treatment of Post-Stroke Depression with Antidepressants." *Journal of Alternative and Complementary Medicine*, 14 (2008): 795–796.
Derry, J. W. *Charles, Earl Grey: Aristocratic Reformer*. Cambridge, MA: Blackwell, 1992.
Dubos, Rene. *Mirage of Health: Utopias, Progress and Biological Change*. Piscataway, NJ: Rutgers University Press, 1971.
Duchess of Cleveland. *Life and Letters of Lady Hester Stanhope*. London: John Murray, 1914.
Durrant, Peter. "Fitzroy, Augustus Henry, Third Duke of Grafton (1735–1811)." *Oxford Dictionary of National Biography*, Oxford University Press, September 2004; online edition, October 2007, *http://www.oxforddnb.com/view/article/9628* (accessed January 6, 2009).
Dutton, David. *Anthony Eden: A Life and Reputation*. New York: Arnold, 1997.
_____. *Neville Chamberlain*. London: Arnold, 2001.
Ehrman, J. *The Younger Pitt, Volume II*. London: Constable, 1969.
Englefield, Dermot, Janet Seaton, and Isobel White. *Facts About British Prime Ministers*. New York: H.W. Wilson, 1995.
English, Richard. "Arthur Wellesley, First Duke of Wellington." In *Biographical Dictionary of British Prime Ministers*, by Robert Eccleshall and Graham Walker (eds.). New York: Routledge, 1998.
Enright, Dominique. *The Wicked Wit of Winston Churchill*. London: Michael O'Mara Books, 2001.
Evans, Eric. "Robert Banks Jenkinson, Second Earl of Liverpool." In *Biographical Dictionary of British Prime Ministers*, by Robert Eccleshall and Graham Walker (eds.). New York: Routledge, 1998.
_____. "William Lamb, Second Viscount Melbourne." In *Biographical Dictionary of British Prime Ministers*, by Robert Eccleshall and Graham Walker (eds.). New York: Routledge, 1998.
Farrell, S.M. "Wentworth, Charles Watson, Second Marquess of Rockingham (1730–1782)." *Oxford Dictionary of National Biography*, Oxford University Press, September 2004; online edition, October 2007, *http://www.oxforddnb.com/view/article/28878* (accessed January 6, 2009).
Feiling, Keith. *The Life of Neville Chamberlain*. London: Macmillan, 1946.
Fieve, Ronald. *Moodswing*. New York: Bantam Books, 1969.
Ford, Eddie. "Booze and Moral Panics." *Weekly Worker*, 605, December 15, 2005.
Francis, M. "Tears, Tantrums, and Bared Teeth: The Emotional Economy of Three Conservative Prime Ministers." *Journal of British Studies*, 41 (2002): 354–387.
Freeman, H. "The Human Brain and Political Behaviour." *British Journal of Psychiatry*, 159 (1991): 19–32.
Friedman, Robert A. "Role of Physicians and

Mental Health Professionals in Discussions of Public Figures." *Journal of American Medical Association*, 300 (2008): 1348–1350.
Fry, Michael. "Frederick John Robinson, First Viscount Goderich, First Earl of Ripon." In *Biographical Dictionary of British Prime Ministers*, by Robert Eccleshall and Graham Walker (eds.). New York: Routledge, 1998.
Furneaux, R. *William Wilberforce*. London: Hamish Hamilton, 1974.
Galea, S., J. Ahern, H. Resnick, D. Kilpatrick, M. Bucuvalas, J. Gold, D. Vlahov. "Psychological Sequelae of September 11 Terrorist Attacks in New York City." *New England Journal of Medicine*, 346 (2002): 482–487.
Gamble, Andrew. "Edward Richard George Heath." In *Biographical Dictionary of British Prime Ministers*, by Robert Eccleshall and Graham Walker (eds.). New York: Routledge, 1998.
Garrard, P. "Cognitive Archaeology: Uses, Methods and Results." *Journal of Neurolinguistics* (2008), doi: 10.1016/j.jneuroling.2008.07.006.
Gash, Norman. *Lord Liverpool*. Cambridge, MA: Harvard University Press, 1984.
Gilbert, R. E. "Psychological Illness in Presidents: A Medical Advisory Commission and Disability Determinations." *Political Psychology*, 27 (2006): 55–75.
Goodwin, Frederick K., and Kay R. Jamison. *Manic Depressive Illness*. New York: Oxford University Press, 1990.
Green, E. H. H. "Law, Andrew Bonar (1858–1923)." *Oxford Dictionary of National Biography*, Oxford University Press, September 2004; online edition, January 25, 2008, http://www.oxforddnb.com/view/artcle/34426.
Gunther, John. *Inside Europe*. London: Hamish Hamilton, 1937.
Hague, William. *William Pitt the Younger: A Biography*. New York: Alfred A. Knopf, 2005.
Hanham, A. A. "Compton, Spencer, Earl of Wilmington (c.1674–1743)." *Oxford Dictionary of National Biography*, Oxford University Press, September 2004; online edition, January 2008, http://www.oxforddnb.com/view/article/6036 (accessed January 6, 2009).
Harcourt, L. V. *The Diaries and Correspondence of the Right Hon. George Rose, Volume 1*. London: Richard Bentley, 1860.
Hattersley, Roy. *Campbell-Bannerman*. London: Haus Publishing, 2006.

Hawkins, Angus. *The Forgotten Prime Minister: The 14th Earl of Derby, Volume I, Ascent: 1799–1851*. New York: Oxford University Press, 2007.
_____. "Stanley, Edward George Geoffrey Smith, Fourteenth Earl of Derby (1799–1869)." *Oxford Dictionary of National Biography*, Oxford University Press, September 2004; online edition, January 2008, http://www.oxforddnb.com/view/article/26265 (accessed September 30, 2008).
Hibbert, Christopher. *George III*. New York: Basic Books, 1998.
_____. "Queen Victoria and Her Prime Ministers." *BBC British History: Victorians*. November 14, 2008, http://www.bbc.co.uk/history/british/victorians/victoria_ministers_02.shtml (accessed November 14, 2008).
Hilton, B. "The Political Arts of Lord Liverpool." *Transactions of the Royal Historical Society*, 38 (1988): 147–170.
Hilton, Boyd. "Robert Peel." In *Biographical Dictionary of British Prime Ministers*, by Robert Eccleshall and Graham Walker (eds.). New York: Routledge, 1998.
Hinde, Wendy. *George Canning*. New York: Basil Blackwell, 1989.
Hoffman, J.S. *The Marquis: A Study of Lord Rockingham, 1730–1782*. New York: Fordham University Press, 1973.
Holmes, Richard. *Wellington: The Iron Duke*. London: HarperCollins, 2003.
Horne, Alastair. *Harold Macmillan, Volume 1: 1894–1956*. New York: Penguin, 1988.
_____. *Harold Macmillan, Volume II: 1957–1986*. New York: Penguin, 1989.
Hu, Claire. "Is There a Drinks Cabinet in the House?" *Harpers Wine and Spirit Magazine*, July 23, 2007.
Hughes, J.R. "Did All These Famous People Really Have Epilepsy?" *Epilepsy & Behavior*, 6 (2005): 115–139.
Hutchinson, George. *Edward Heath: A Personal and Political Biography*. London: Longman, 1970.
Hutchinson, Iain. "Henry Campbell-Bannerman." In *Biographical Dictionary of British Prime Ministers*, edited by Robert Eccleshall and Graham Walker. New York: Routledge, 1998.
Iremonger, Lucille. *The Fiery Chariot: A Study of British Prime Ministers and the Search for Love*. London: Secker & Warburg, 1970.
_____. *Lord Aberdeen: A Biography of the*

Fourth Earl of Aberdeen, KG., KT., Prime Minister 1852–1855. London: Collins, 1978.
James, Robert Rhodes. *Anthony Eden.* London: Weidenfeld & Nicolson, 1986.
_____, ed. *Memoirs of a Conservative: J.C.C. Davidson's Memoirs and Papers, 1910–37.* London: Weidenfeld and Nicholson, 1969.
_____. *Rosebery.* New York: Macmillan, 1963.
Jamison, K. R., R. H. Gerner, C. Rammen, and C. Padesky. "Clouds and Silver Linings: Positive Experiences Associated with Primary Affective Disorder." *American Journal of Psychiatry*, 137 (1980): 198–202.
Jenkins, Roy. *Baldwin.* London: Collins, 1987.
_____. *Churchill: A Biography.* New York: Farrar, Straus & Giroux, 2001.
_____. *Gladstone: A Biography.* New York: Random House, 1997.
_____. "Wilson, (James) Harold, Baron Wilson of Rievaulx (1916–1995)." *Oxford Dictionary of National Biography*, Oxford University Press, September 2004; online edition, January 2009, http://www.oxforddnb.com/view/article/58000 (accessed January 15, 2009).
"Jenkinson, Robert Banks." Number-10.gov.uk. http://www.number10.gov.uk/output/Page157.asp (accessed May 24, 2008).
Jones, J. M., and J. I. Jones. "Presidential Stroke: United States Presidents and Cerebrovascular Disease." *CNS Spectrums*, 11 (2006): 674–678.
Jones, Thomas. *Lloyd George.* Cambridge, MA: Harvard University Press, 1951.
Jones, W. D. *Prosperity Robinson: The Life of Viscount Goderich, 1782–1859.* London: Macmillan, 1967.
Jupp, P. J. "Grenville, William Wyndham, Baron Grenville (1759–1834)." *Oxford Dictionary of National Biography*, Oxford University Press, September 2004; online edition, October 2007, http://www.oxforddnb.com/view/article/11501 (accessed January 6, 2009).
Jupp, Peter. "Spencer Perceval." In *Biographical Dictionary of British Prime Ministers*, by Robert Eccleshall and Graham Walker (eds.). New York: Routledge, 1998.
Kelch, Ray A. *Newcastle: A Duke Without Money.* Berkeley and Los Angeles: University of California Press, 1974.
Kennedy, A. L. *Salisbury, 1830–1903: Portrait of a Statesman.* London: John Murray, 1953.
Kenny, Michael. "(James) Harold Wilson, Lord Wilson of Rievaulx." In *Biographical Dictionary of British Prime Ministers*, by Robert Eccleshall and Graham Walker (eds.). New York: Routledge, 1998.
Kessler, R. C., P. Berglund, O. Demler, R. Jin, and E. F. Walters. "Lifetime Prevalence and Age-of-Onset Distributions of DSM-IV Disorders in the National Comorbidity Survey Replication." *Archives of General Psychiatry*, 62 (2005): 593–602.
Kessler, R. C., K. A. McGonagle, S. Zhao, C. B. Nelson, M. Hughes, S. Eshleman, H. U. Wittchen, and K. S. Kendler. "Lifetime and 12-Month Prevalence of DSM-III-R Psychiatric Disorders in the United States: Results from the National Comorbidity Survey." *Archives of General Psychiatry*, 51 (1994): 8–19.
Kidd, Joseph. "The Last Illness of Lord Beaconsfield." In *Homoeopathy in the Irish Potato Famine, an Essay by Francis Treuhertz.* London: Samuel Press, 1995.
Kirkup, James. "Margaret Thatcher's Mental Decline Revealed by Her Daughter." *Telegraph.co.uk*, August 25, 2008, http://www.telegraph.co.uk/news/newstopics/politics/conservative/2614020/Margaret-Thatchers-mental-decline-revealed-by-her-daughter.html (accessed January 15, 2009).
Klein, Donald F., Rachel Gittelman, Frederic Quitkin, and Arthur Rifkin. *Diagnosis and Drug Treatment of Psychiatric Disorders: Adults and Children.* Baltimore: Williams & Wilkins, 1980.
Klin, A., W. Jones, R. Schultz, F. Volkmar, and D. Cohen. "Visual Fixation Patterns During Viewing of Naturalistic Social Situations as Predictors of Social Competence in Individuals with Autism." *Archives of General Psychiatry*, 59 (2002): 809–816.
Korda, Michael. *With Wings Like Eagles: A History of the Battle of Britain.* New York: HarperCollins, 2009.
Kuhn, William. *The Politics of Pleasure.* London: Free Press, Simon & Shuster, 2006.
Kulisheck, P. J. "Pelham, Henry (1674–1754)." *Oxford Dictionary of National Biography*, Oxford University Press, September 2004; online edition, January 2008, http://www.oxforddnb.com/view/article/21789 (accessed January 6, 2009).
Lafore, L. *The End of Glory: An Interpretation of the Origins of World War II.* New York: J.P. Lippincott, 1970.

Laing, Margaret. *Edward Heath, Prime Minister.* New York: Third Press, 1973.

Leavesley, James. *Mere Mortals: Diseases of the Famous.* Sydney, NSW: ABC Books, 2004.

L'Etang, Hugh. "Alcohol and Leadership." *British Journal of Alcohol and Addiction,* 15: 167–171.

———. *Fit to Lead.* London: William Heinemann Medical Books, 1979.

———. *The Pathology of Leadership.* London: William Heinemann Medical Books, 1969.

Longford, Elizabeth. *Wellington: Pillar of State.* St. Albans, England: Panther Books, 1975.

"Lord Salisbury's Illness." *New York Times,* March 20, 1898, http://query.nytimes.com/gst/abstract.html?res=F30A15F63D5C11738DDDA90A94DB405B8885F0D3 (accessed October 12, 2008).

Ludwig, Arnold M. *King of the Mountain: The Nature of Political Leadership.* Louisville, KY: University Press of Kentucky, 2002.

Lycett, Andrew. "Oliver Baldwin: A Life of Dissent, by Christopher J. Walker, Arcadia Books." *New Statesman,* March 29, 2004, http://www.newstatesman.com/print/200403290045 (accessed July 27, 2008).

Machado-Vieira, R., J. C. Soares, D. R. Lara, et al. "A Double-Blind, Randomized, Placebo-Controlled Study on the Efficacy and Safety of the Purinergic Agents Allopurinol and Dipyridamole Adjunctive to Lithium in Acute Bipolar Mania." *Journal of Clinical Psychiatry,* 69 (2008): 1237–1245.

Magnus, Philip. *Gladstone: A Biography.* New York: E.P. Dutton, 1954.

Mandela, Nelson. *Long Walk to Freedom.* New York: Little, Brown, 1995.

Marion, D. "The British Civil Service: A Political Excavation and Review." *Administration & Society,* 24 (1993): 470–486.

Marquand, David. *Ramsay MacDonald.* London: Jonathan Cape, 1977.

Marr, Andrew. *A History of Modern Britain.* London: Macmillan, 2007.

Marsh, Stefanie. "Losing It." *Times Online,* August 2, 2007, http://www.timesonline.co.uk/tol/life_and_style/health/features/article2180877.ece?print (accessed February 17, 2009).

Marx, Rudolf. *The Health of the Presidents.* New York: Putnam's, 1960.

Mather, John H. "Lord Randolph Churchill: Malades et Mort." *The Churchill Centre,* July 20, 2008, http://www.winstonchurchill.org/learn/myths/myths/his-father-died-of-syphilis (accessed September 6, 2009).

Matthew, Colin. *Gladstone: 1809–1874.* New York: Clarendon Press, 1986.

Matthew, H. C. G. "Macmillan, (Maurice) Harold, First Earl of Stockton (1894–1986)." *Oxford Dictionary of National Biography,* Oxford University Press, September 2004; online edition, January 2008, http://www.oxforddnb.com/view/article/40185 (accessed December 28, 2008).

McElearney, C., and M. Fitzgerald. "Did the Duke of Wellington Have Asperger's Syndrome?" *Irish Psychiatrist,* 7 (2006): 7–10.

McKinstry, Leo. *Daily Telegraph,* December 27, 2005, http://www.telegraph.co.uk/opinion/main.jhtml?xlm=/opinion/2005/12/27/do2701.xml (accessed October 9, 2008).

———. "Enjoy It While You Can, Prime Minister, There Could Be Trouble Ahead." *Daily Express,* August 3, 2007.

———. *Rosebery: A Statesman in Turmoil.* London: John Murray, 2005.

Meeks, T.W., and D.V. Jeste. "Neurobiology of Wisdom." *Archives of General Psychiatry,* 66 (2009): 355–365.

"Melbourne, Lord, March 15." *Ward's Book of Days,* http://www.wardsbookofdays.com/15march.htm (accessed July 31, 2008).

Middlemas, Keith, and John Barnes. *Baldwin: A Biography.* London: Macmillan, 1969.

Miller, David P. "My Favourite Studdys: Lord Bute as Naturalist." In *Lord Bute: Essays in Re-Interpretation,* by Karl W. Schweizer (ed.). Leicester: Leicester University Press, 1988.

Mishori, Ranit. "When the Patient Is the President." *Parade,* August 15, 2009.

Moffitt, T.E., A. Caspi, A. Taylor, J. Kokaua, B.J. Milne, G. Polanczyk, and R. Poulton. "How Common Are Common Mental Disorders? Evidence that Lifetime Prevalence Rates are Doubled by Prospective *Versus* Retrospective Ascertainment." *Psychological Medicine,* doi:10.1017/S0033291709991036 (2009): 1–11.

Moran, Mark. "Lingering Questions Prompt 'Goldwater Rule' Evaluation." *Psychiatric News,* October 17, 2008.

Morgan, Kenneth O. *Callaghan: A Life.* New York: Oxford University Press, 1997.

———. *David Lloyd George: Welsh Radical as World Statesman.* Cardiff: University of Wales Press, 1963.

_____. "George, David Lloyd, First Earl Lloyd-George of Dwyfor (1863–1945)." *Oxford Dictionary of National Biography*, Oxford University Press, September 2004; online edition, October 2008, *http://www.oxforddnnb.com/view/article/34570* (accessed December 19, 2008).

Morison, A. "The Soldier's Heart and the Strained Heart." *British Medical Journal*, 1 (1916): 184.

Morley, J. *The Life of William Ewart Gladstone*. New York: Macmillan, 1903.

Muszynski, Irving, and Clare Miller. "Burguieres Recovers from Depression by Helping Other CEOs." *Mental Health Works, American Psychiatric Association and the American Psychiatric Foundation*, Fourth Quarter 2008.

Nishino, S. "Narcolepsy: Pathophysiology and Pharmacology." *Journal of Clinical Psychiatry*, 68 [Suppl. 13] (2007): 9–15.

O'Gorman, Frank. "The Myth of Lord Bute's Secret Influence." In *Lord Bute: Essays in Re-Interpretation*, by Karl W. Schweizer (ed.). Leicester: Leicester University Press, 1988.

Olasky, Marvin. "Theodore Roosevelt: Manly Compassion in Troubled Times." *Compassion and Culture*, Capital Research Center, November 2008, *http://www.capitalresearch.org/pubs/pdf/v1225674429.pdf* (accessed August 20, 2009).

Owen, D. "Hubris Syndrome." *Clinical Medicine*, 8 (2008): 428–432.

Owen, D., and J.R.T. Davidson. "Hubris Syndrome: An Acquired Personality Disorder? A Study of U.S. Presidents and U.K. Prime Ministers Over the Last 100 Years." *Brain*, 132 (2009): 1396–1406.

Owen, Frank. *Tempestuous Journey*. London: Hutchinson, 1954.

Owen, Lord David. "Diseased, Demented, Depressed: Serious Illness in Heads of State." *Quarterly Journal of Medicine*, 96 (2003): 325–336.

_____. *In Sickness and in Power: Illness in Heads of Government During the Last 100 Years*. London: Methuen, 2008.

Park, Bert E. *Ailing, Aging, Addicted: Studies of Compromised Leadership*. Lexington, KY: University Press of Kentucky, 1993.

Park, Bert E. *The Impact of Illness on World Leaders*. Philadelphia: University of Pennsylvania Press, 1996.

Parry, Jonathan. "Lord John Russell, First Earl Russell." In *Biographical Dictionary of British Prime Ministers*, by Robert Eccleshall and Graham Walker (eds.). New York: Routledge, 1998.

Paterson, Peter. "Harold Was Toper Too." *The Spectator*, January 9, 1999, *http://findarticles.com/p/articles/mi_qa3724/is_199901/ai_n8834583/print?tag=artBody* (accessed December 31, 2008).

Paulshock, B. Z. "Dr. Cheyne." *Journal of the American Medical Association*, 284 (2000): 1305.

Pellew, G. *The Life and Correspondence of the Right Hon. Henry Addington, Volumes I–III*. London: John Murray, 1849.

Pembroke College Cambridge Society. *Annual Gazette*, 8 (June 1934): 18.

Peters, Marie. "William Pitt, First Earl of Chatham." In *Biographical Dictionary of British Prime Ministers*, by Robert Eccleshall and Graham Walker (eds.). New York: Routledge, 1998.

Physicians and Surgeons of the Principal London Hospitals. *The Family Physician: A Manual of Domestic Medicine — New and Enlarged Edition*. London: Cassell, 1886.

Pimlott, Ben. *Harold Wilson*. London: HarperCollins, 1993.

"Pitt to Lady Chatham." Chatham Papers, Public Record Office 30/8/12, fol. 484.

"Pitt, William, the Younger." Number-10.gov.uk. *http://www.number10.gov.uk/output/Page161.asp* (accessed May 15, 2008).

Plowright, John. *Regency England: The Age of Lord Liverpool*. New York: Routledge, 1996.

Ponting, Clive. *Churchill*. London: Sinclair-Stevenson, 1994.

Post, F. "Creativity and Psychopathology: A Study of 291 World-Famous Men." *British Journal of Psychiatry*, 165 (1994): 22–34.

Post, J.M., and R.S. Robins. "The Captive King and His Captive Court: The Psychopolitical Dynamics of the Disabled Leader and His Inner Circle." *Political Psychology*, 11 (1990): 331–351.

Raikes, T. *A Portion of the Journal Kept by Thomas Raikes, Volume IV*. London: Longman, 1856–1857.

Raymont, V., W. Bingley, A. Buchanan, A. S. David, P. Hayward, S. Wessely, and M. Hotopf. "Prevalence of Mental Incapacity in Medical Inpatients and Associated Risk Factors: Cross-Sectional Study." *Lancet*, 364 (2004): 1421–1427.

Reynolds, David. "Selected Extracts from 'After Dark' Programme (Channel 4 TV)." *The International Campaign for Real History.* July 20, 2008, *http://www.fpp.co.uk/docs/Irving/broadcasts/AfterDark280588.html*.

Richmond, Charles, and Jerrold Post. "Disraeli's Crucial Illness." In *The Self-Fashioning of Disraeli, 1818–1851*, by C. Richmond and P. Smith (eds.). London: Cambridge University Press, 1988.

"Riddell, Lord George." *Lord Riddell's War Diary, 1914–1918*. London: Ivor, Nicholson & Watson, 1933.

Ritcherson, C. "Review — 'The Marquis: A Study of Lord Rockingham, 1730–1782,' by R.J.S. Hoffman, New York: Fordham University Press, 1973." *The American Historical Review*, 80 (1975): 640–641.

Roberts, A. *Napoleon and Wellington*. London: Orion Publishing Group, 2001. Cited in McElearney, C., and M. Fitzgerald. "Did the Duke of Wellington Have Asperger's Syndrome?" *Irish Psychiatrist*, 7 (2006): 7–10.

Robertson, I. "Soundings: Interpreting Problems." *British Medical Journal*, 309 (1994): 1519.

"Robinson, Frederick John." *Number-10.gov.uk. http://www.number-10.gov.uk/output/Page 155.asp* (accessed June 6, 2008).

Rose, J. H. *William Pitt and National Revival.* London: G. Bell and Sons, 1911.

Rose, K. *The Later Cecils*. New York: Harper & Row, 1975.

Rose, Norman. *Churchill: The Unruly Giant.* New York: Free Press, 1994.

_____. *Churchill: An Unruly Life.* New York: Simon & Schuster, 1998.

"Rosebery, Lord." *Letters Relating to the Love Episode of William Pitt.* Published privately, 1900.

Saintsbury, George. *The Earl of Derby.* New York: Harper & Brothers, 1892.

Salter, Sir Arthur. *Personality in Politics.* London: Faber, 1938.

Sargant, William. *The Unquiet Mind.* Boston, MA: Little, Brown, 1967.

Sartorius, Norman. "Leadership." *International Psychiatry*, 6 (2009): 1.

Schenk, Joshua Wolf. *Lincoln's Melancholy: How Depression Challenged a President and Fuelled His Greatness.* Boston: Houghton Mifflin, 2005.

Schweitzer, Karl Wolfgang. "Cavendish, William, Fourth Duke of Devonshire (bap. 1720, d. 1764)." *Oxford Dictionary of National Biography*, Oxford University Press, September 2004; online edition, January 2008, *http://www.oxforddnb.com/view/article/4949* (accessed January 6, 2009).

_____. "Stuart, John, Third Earl of Bute (1713–1792)." *Oxford Dictionary of National Biography*, Oxford University Press, September 2004; online edition, October 2007, *http://www.oxforddnb.com/view/article/26716* (accessed January 6, 2009).

Searle, Geoffrey. "Arthur James Balfour, First Earl of Balfour." In *Biographical Dictionary of British Prime Ministers*, by Robert Eccleshall and Graham Walker (eds.). New York: Routledge, 1998.

Sedgwick, R.R., ed. *Letters from George III to Lord Bute.* London: Macmillan, 1939.

Sher, Richard B. "The Favourite of the Favourite." In *Lord Bute: Essays in Re-Interpretation*, by Karl W. Schweizer (ed.). Leicester: Leicester University Press, 1988.

"Sir George Downing." *Encyclopaedia Britannica Online, http://www.britannica.com/EB checked/topic/170489/Sir-George-Downing*.

Slater, E. "The Creative Personality." *The Cambridge Review*, 27 (February 1981): 114–120.

_____. "The Problems of Pathography." *Acta Psychiatrica Scandinavica*, Supplement 219 (1970): 209–215.

Slater, E., and A. Meyer. "Contributions to a Pathography of the Musicians: 2. Organic and Psychotic Disorders." *Confinia Psychiatrica*, 3 (1960): 129–140.

Smith, Charles. *The Early Career of Lord North the Prime Minister.* Cranbury, NJ: Associated University Press, 1979.

Smith, E. A. *Lord Grey, 1764–1845*. Stroud, Gloucestershire: Alan Sutton Publishing, 1990.

Smith, Paul, ed. *Bagehot: The English Constitution.* New York: Cambridge University Press, 2001.

Smith, Paul. *Disraeli: A Brief Life.* Google Books, 1999.

Snashall, D. "Commentary: The Ailing Leader — A Suitable Case for Occupational Medicine?" *Occupational Medicine*, 53 (2003): 502–504.

Snow, Matthew. "A Biography of Lord North (1732–1792)." *From Revolution to Reconstruction*, May 5, 2003, *http://www.let.rug.nl/usa/B/north/north.htm* (accessed May 25, 2008).

Soames, Mary. *Clementine Churchill by her Daughter.* London: Cassell, 1979.
Spender, J. A. *The Life of the Right Hon. Sir Henry Campbell-Bannerman GCB, Volume II.* London. Hodder & Stoughton, 1923.
Stagle, Jim. "Arthur Balfour." *OregonLive.com*, http://blog.oregonlive.com/religion/2007/07/arthur_balfour.html (accessed October 12, 2008).
Stanhope, Philip H. *5th Earl, Notes of Conversations with the Duke of Wellington, 1831–1851.* London: John Murray, 1888.
Storr, Anthony. *Churchill's Black Dog and Other Phenomena of the Human Mind.* London: Fontana/Collins, 1989.
Stuttaford, Thomas. "The Telltale Loss of Power." *Times Online*, April 27, 2007, http://www.martinfrost.ws/htmlfiles/april2007/politics_thyroid.html (accessed January 6, 2009).
Tanner, Duncan. "(James) Ramsay MacDonald." In *Biographical Dictionary of British Prime Ministers*, by Robert Walker and Graham Eccleshall (eds.). New York: Routledge, 1998.
Taylor, A. J. P., ed. *Lloyd George: A Diary by Frances Stevenson.* New York: Harper & Row, 1971.
Taylor, Andrew. *Bonar Law.* London: Haus Publishing, 2006.
Taylor, R. E. "Death of Neurasthenia and Its Psychological Reincarnation." *British Journal of Psychiatry*, 179 (2001): 550–557.
Taylor, Steven. "Robert Walpole, First Earl of Oxford (1676–1745)." *Oxford Dictionary of National Biography*, Oxford University Press, September 2004; online edition, January 2008, http://www.oxforddnb.com/view/article/28601 (accessed January 6, 2009).
Taylor, W. S., and J. H. Pringle, eds. *Correspondence of William Pitt, Earl of Chatham, Volumes I-IV: Earl of Chatham to Lady Chatham, 3 April, 1772.* London: John Murray, 1838–1840.
Thomas, Peter. "Frederick North, Styled Lord North, 1752–1790, Second Earl of Guilford." In *Biographical Dictionary of British Prime Ministers*, by Robert Eccleshall and Graham Walker (eds.). New York: Routledge, 1998.
Thorpe, Andrew. "Stanley Baldwin, First Earl Baldwin of Bewdley." In *Biographical Dictionary of British Prime Ministers*, by Robert Eccleshall and Graham Walker (eds.). New York: Routledge, 1998.
Thorpe, D. R. "Eden, (Robert) Anthony, First Earl of Avon (1897–1977)." *Oxford Dictionary of National Biography*, Oxford University Press, September 2004; online edition, May 2008, http://www.oxforddnb.com/view/article/31060 (accessed December 28, 2008).
Tomline, G. *Memoirs of the Life of the Right Honorable William Pitt, Volume I.* London: John Murray, 1825.
Trevelyan, G. M. *Lord Grey of the Reform Bill.* Westport, CT: Greenwood Press, 1970.
Tuchman, Barbara. *The March of Folly.* New York: Ballantine Books, 1984.
Vestey, Michael. "Sobering Thoughts." *Spectator*, January 28, 2006, http://findarticles.com/p/articles/mi_qa3724/is_200601/ai_n17186010/print (accessed May 12, 2008).
Vincent, J., ed. *The Crawford Papers: The Journals of David Lindsay, Twenty-Seventh Earl of Crawford and Tenth Earl of Balcarres, 1871–1940, During the Years 1892 to 1940.* Manchester: Manchester University Press, 1984.
Vincent, John. R., ed. *Disraeli, Derby and the Conservative Party: Journals and Memoirs of Edward Henry, Lord Stanley, 1849–1869.* New York: Harper & Row, 1978.
Walker, Graham. "Archibald Philip Primrose, Fifth Lord Rosebery, 1847–1929." In *Biographical Dictionary of British Prime Ministers*, by Robert Eccleshall and Graham Walker (eds.). New York: Routledge, 1998.
Walpole, Horace. *Memoirs of the Reign of King George III, Volume 2.* London: Lawrence and Bullen, 1894.
Weintraub, Stanley. *Disraeli: A Biography.* New York: Truman Talley Books/Dutton, 1993.
Weir, L.M. *The Tragedy of Ramsay MacDonald.* London: Secker and Warburg, 1938.
"Wellesley, Arthur." *Number-10.gov.uk.* http://www.number10.gov.uk/output/Page153.asp (accessed July 6, 2008).
White, Arnold. "England's Foreign Office." *New York Times*, August 21, 1898, http://query.nytimes.com/gst/abstract.html?res=F60E14FA3B5416738DDDA80A94D0405B8885F0D3 (accessed October 12, 2008).
White, Vera M. "William Pitt 'The Elder' (1708–1778)." *Encyclopaedia Britannica*, 2002, http://www.gwleibniz.com/britannica_pages/pitt_elder/pitt_elder.html (accessed May 17, 2008).
Whiteley, Peter. *Lord North: The Prime Minister Who Lost America.* Rio Grande, OH: Hambledon Press, 1996.

Whiting, R. C. "Attlee, Clement Richard, First Earl Attlee (1883–1967)." *Oxford Dictionary of National Biography*, Oxford University Press, September 2004; online edition, January 2008, *http://www.oxforddnb.com/view/article/30498* (accessed December 28, 2008).

Wilberforce, W. "Sketch of Mr. Pitt," quoted in Lord Rosebery, *Pitt and Wilberforce*. Edinburgh: Published privately, 1897.

Wilkinson, David. "Bentinck, William Henry Cavendish-Bentinck, Third Duke of Portland (1738–1809)." *Oxford Dictionary of National Biography*, Oxford University Press, September 2004; online edition, October 2007, *http://www.oxforddnb.com/view/article/2162* (accessed January 6, 2009).

———. "William Henry Cavendish-Bentinck, Third Duke of Portland." In *Biographical Dictionary of British Prime Ministers*, by Robert Eccleshall and Graham Walker (eds.). New York: Routledge, 1998.

Williamson, P. "Baldwin's Reputation: Politics and History, 1937–1967." *The Historical Journal*, 47 (2004): 127–168.

Wink, P. "Two Faces of Narcissism." *Journal of Personality and Social Psychology*, 61 (1991): 590–597.

"Winston Churchill and Manic Depression." July 20, 2008, *http://www.bipolar-lives.com/winston-churchill-and-manic-depression.html*.

Winter, Jana. "Source: Michael Jackson's Doctor to Be Charged with Manslaughter." *FoxNews.com*, August 19, 2009, *http://www.foxnews.com/printer_friendly_story/0,3566,540540,00.html* (accessed September 5, 2009).

Wolf, A. "The Earl of Balfour." *Journal of Philosophical Studies*, 20 (1930): 503–515.

World Health Organization. *The ICD-10 Classification of Mental and Behavioral Disorders*. Washington, DC: American Psychiatric Press, 1994.

Young, G. M. *Stanley Baldwin*. London: Rupert Hart-Davis, 1952.

Zhang, Wei, Li-Ching Lee, Kathryn M. Connor, Chia-Ming Chang, Te-Jen Lai, and Jonathan R. T. Davidson. "Symptoms of Neurasthenia Following Earthquake Trauma: Re-Examination of a Discarded Syndrome." *Psychiatry Research*, 153 (2007): 171–177.

Ziegler, Philip. *Addington: A Life of Henry Addington, First Viscount Sidmouth*. New York: John Day, 1965.

———. *Melbourne: A Biography*. New York: Atheneum, 1982.

———. *Wilson*. London: Weidenfeld & Nicholson, 1993.

Index

Aberdeen, Fourth Earl of 73–75, 166, 167, 173, 175, 176; dysthymia 74; *see also* grief
Addington, Dr. Anthony 36
Addington, Henry 40–42, 167; alcohol intake 41; public speaking fear 40, 167; and son's suicide 42; *see also* public speaking fear
adjustment disorder 161, 170; *see also* Callaghan, James; Campbell-Bannerman, Sir Henry
Albert, Prince 61–62
alcohol 11, 13, 22, 36–40, 71, 77–78, 109–111, 112, 139–140, 145, 155–157, 169, 185; parliamentary culture of 11; *see also* Addington, Henry; Asquith, Herbert; Churchill, Sir Winston; Derby, Lord; Disraeli, Benjamin; Eden, Sir Anthony; Nixon, President Richard; Rockingham, Marquess of; Rosebery, Fifth Earl of; Wilson, Harold
anxiety (unspecified type) 49, 127, 155–156; *see also* Baldwin, Stanley; Bute, Third Earl of; Goderich, Viscount; North, Lord; Wilson, Harold
Asperger's disorder 13, 49, 53–54, 170; *see also* developmental disorders; Wellington, Duke of
Asquith, Herbert 13, 107–112, 167; alcohol problems 11, 109–111, 169; on effect of failure to achieve power 165; family history 107–108; grief 111–112; *see also* alcohol; grief
assessment guidelines *see* disabled leaders
Attlee, Clement 141–142, 168
avoidant personality disorder 45

Baldwin, Stanley 7, 9, 10, 92, 121–127, 167, 168, 170, 173; Churchill on 124–125; depression 124–126; generalized anxiety 123; likeness to Lincoln 124; nervous breakdowns 125; social anxiety 122–123; Tourette's disorder 123–124; *see also* depression; generalized anxiety disorder; social anxiety; tics; Tourette's disorder

Balfour, Arthur 103–105; contributions to theology 103; grief 104–105, 173; spiritualism and 103–104; *see also* grief
bereavement *see* grief
bipolar disorder 12, 26–27, 57, 77, 81, 87–89, 116–117, 137–140, 165, 166; *see also* Churchill, Sir Winston; *see also* Disraeli, Benjamin; Gladstone, William; Grey, Second Earl; Lloyd George, David; Palmerston, Viscount; Pitt the Elder
Blair, Anthony (Tony) 162, 174
Bonar Law, Andrew 13, 118–121; depression 119–121, 166; grief 119–121, 173, 175; melancholy temperament 118; *see also* depression; grief
Bondevik, Kjell 178
bravery in battle 166
Bush, President George H.W. 160; *see also* thyroid disease
Bute, Third Earl of 18–20, 167; *see also* depression; social anxiety
Byron, Lord 74

Callaghan, James 160–161, 170, 173; depression 161; *see also* adjustment disorder
Campbell-Bannerman, Sir Henry 105–107, 170, 173, 175, 176; *see also* adjustment disorder; grief
Canning, George 46, 47
Chamberlain, Neville 7, 131–135, 167; depression 133–134; on effect of failure to achieve power 165; grief 133; hubris of 133; public speaking fear 132–133; as war leader 131–132; *see also* depression; grief; hubris; public speaking fear
Churchill, Sir Winston 7, 8, 12, 41, 78, 93, 110, 135–142, 164, 166, 176; alcohol intake 11, 109, 139–140, 169; Beaverbrook on 113; bipolar features 137, 140; dementia 140, 171; depression 136, 138–139; and painting as

213

214 Index

therapy 136–137; sense of mission 136; strokes 140; *see also* bipolar disorder; dementia; depression; stroke
classification of disease *see* psychiatric diagnosis
clergyman's throat 114–115; *see also* Lloyd George, David
Coolidge, President Calvin 12, 39; *see also* grief; social anxiety

dementia 10–11, 13, 42, 129–131, 140, 155, 157–158, 161, 170–171; *see also* Churchill, Sir Winston; Grenville, William; MacDonald, Ramsay; Thatcher, Margaret; Tweedmouth, Lord; Wilson, Harold; Wilson, President Woodrow
depression 12, 13, 19–20, 46, 57–49, 61–63, 93–96, 113–114, 119–121, 133–134, 136, 138–139, 150–151; *see also* Bonar Law, Andrew; Bute, Third Earl of; Chamberlain, Neville; Churchill, Sir Winston; Grey, Second Earl; Liverpool, Second Earl of; Lloyd George, David; Macmillan, Harold; Melbourne, Second Viscount; Salisbury, Third Marquess of
Derby, Lord 69–73, 170, 173; alcohol intake 11, 71, 169; depression 70–72; on Gladstone 88–89; opium problem 71; seasonal depression 72; *see also* alcohol; depression; drug use and misuse; seasonal depression
developmental disorders 13; *see also* Asperger's disorder
Devonshire, Fourth Duke of 17–18
disabled leaders 177
disclosure of psychiatric illness 178
Disraeli, Benjamin 12, 66, 76–79, 84, 136; bipolar disorder 77–78; depression benefits 78; digitalis 79; drinking 77–78; family history 78; hypersomnia 169; rejection sensitivity 165; on Salisbury 95; seasonal factors 78–79; *see also* alcohol; bipolar disorder; hypersomnia
Douglas-Home, Sir Alec 154–155
Downing, Sir George 2
drug use and misuse 12, 13, 71–72, 101–102, 145–146, 185; *see also* Derby, Lord; Eden, Sir Anthony; Gladstone, William; Rosebery, Fifth Earl of

Eden, Sir Anthony 11, 142–147, 173, 174; acute anxiety episode 143–144; alcohol misuse 13, 145, 169; barbiturate misuse 145–146; Churchill on 147; gall bladder problems 143–144; insomnia 144, 170; stimulant misuse 145–146; and Suez crisis 144–146; temperament 142–143; *see also* alcohol; drug use and misuse; insomnia
ethical guidelines for assessing public figures 8

Farquhar, Sir Walter (physician to Pitt the Younger) 37–38

generalized anxiety disorder 13, 45–46, 123, 168–169; *see also* Baldwin, Stanley; Liverpool, Second Earl of
George III, King 15, 16, 18, 20, 21, 25, 26, 28–32, 34, 35, 40, 44, 95, 164
George IV, King 47–49
George V, King 166
Gladstone, William 12, 43, 66, 68, 78, 79–93, 98, 99, 117, 170; bipolar features 81, 87–89; and civil service 172–173; depressive episodes 82–87; family history 80–83; insomnia 85–86; risky sexual behavior 80, 83, 90–92; and spiritualism 93; use of drugs before speeches 11, 89; *see also* insomnia; public speaking fear; sexual deviations; wisdom
Goderich, Viscount 47–49, 167, 173; *see also* anxiety; grief
Goldwater, Senator Barry 8
Grafton, Third Duke of 27
Grant, President Ulysses 39; *see also* social anxiety
Grenville, George 20–21
Grenville, William 42, 171; *see also* dementia; insomnia; stroke
Grey, Second Earl 56–59; bipolar qualities 56–57; chronic depression 57–59; insomnia 58; public speaking fear 58; *see also* bipolar disorder; insomnia; public speaking fear
grief 12–13, 49, 69, 74, 95, 104–105, 106–107, 111–112, 114, 119–121, 133, 186; *see also* Aberdeen, Fourth Earl of; Asquith, Herbert; Balfour, Arthur; Bonar Law, Andrew; Campbell-Bannerman, Sir Henry; Chamberlain, Neville; Coolidge, President Calvin; Goderich, Viscount; Lloyd George, David; Pierce, President Franklin; Russell, Lord; Salisbury, Third Marquess of; Wellington, Duke of

Handel, George Frederick 91
Heath, Sir Edward 158–160, 167, 168, 169, 170; hypersomnia 169; hypothyroidism 159–160; social anxiety 160; *see also* hypersomnia; hypothyroidism; social anxiety
Hitler, Adolf 7, 130, 134, 135, 164
hubris 26, 101–102, 113; 133; *see also* Chamberlain, Neville; Lloyd George, David; Pitt the Elder; Rosebery, Fifth Earl of
hubris syndrome 26
hypersomnia 76–77, 169, 185; *see also* Disraeli, Benjamin; Heath, Sir Edward; Melbourne, Second Viscount; North, Lord

iatrogenic disorders 185
insomnia 10, 24, 42, 58, 85–86, 99–100, 144, 170, 185; *see also* Eden, Sir Anthony; Gladstone, William; Grenville, William; Grey, Second Earl; Pitt the Elder; Rosebery, Fifth Earl of
Jefferson, President Thomas 39; *see also* social anxiety

Kidd, Dr. Joseph 5
King George III *see* George III, King
King George IV *see* George IV, King
King George V *see* George V, King

Lincoln, President Abraham 93
Liverpool, Second Earl 44–47, 135; depression 46; generalized anxiety 45–46, 168; social anxiety 45; *see also* depression; generalized anxiety; social anxiety
Lloyd George, David 6, 13, 41, 104, 112–117, 166, 170; on Asquith 111; Beaverbrook on 113; bipolar qualities 116–117; clergyman's throat 114–115; depression 113–114; grief 114; hubris 113; neuritis 114–115; *see also* bipolar disorder; clergyman's throat; depression; grief; hubris; neuritis

MacDonald, Ramsay 7, 10, 92, 127–131, 173; Churchill on 130; dementia 129–131, 171, 173; depression 128–131; grief 128–129, 175; ineptness at Stresa conference 130–131; *see also* dementia; depression; grief
Macmillan, Harold 9, 147–154, 167; bipolar symptoms considered 150; depression 150–151; family history of 149; frequent sickness at school 148; neurasthenia 152–153; panic attack in World War I 148; possible posttraumatic stress disorder 153–154; prostate surgery and resignation 150; public speaking fear 148, 152; recurrent pain from war injuries 148, 151; seasonal depression 150; *see also* depression; public speaking fear; seasonal depression
Major, Sir John 161–162
manic depression *see* bipolar disorder
medical care quality 174–175
Melbourne, Second Viscount 59–66, 167, 170; depression 61–63; narcolepsy 64–65; public speaking fear 60–61; sleep apnea 64–65; stroke 65; Tourette's disorder 63–64; *see also* depression; narcolepsy; public speaking fear; sleep apnea; stroke; tic disorder; Tourette's disorder
Moran, Lord Charles 5
Mountbatten, Lord Louis 170
Mussolini, Benito 130

narcissistic personality disorder types 168
narcolepsy 61, 64–65
neuralgia *see* neuritis
neuritis 114–115; *see also* Lloyd George, David
Newcastle, Duke of 16–17
Nixon, President Richard 169; *see also* alcohol
North, Lord 27–33, 101, 166, 173; paralyzing depression 30; self doubt 28–29; sleep apnea 32; *see also* depression; sleep apnea

Oxenstierna, Count *see* wisdom

Palmerston, Viscount 75, 176; bipolar qualities 166
paraphilias *see* sexual deviations
Peel, Sir Robert 63, 66–68, 76, 167, 168; social anxiety 67; *see also* social anxiety
Pelham, Henry 16
Perceval, Spencer 42–44
personality traits and suitability for office 184
Pierce, President Franklin 12; *see also* grief
Pitt (the Elder), William 9, 23–27, 39, 135, 166, 173, 176; bipolar disorder 26–27; family history 23; insomnia 24; *see also* bipolar disorder; hubris; insomnia
Pitt (the Younger), William 34–40; alcohol misuse 11, 36–40, 169; social anxiety 38–40; *see also* alcohol; social anxiety
Portland, Third Duke of 34, 167; *see also* public speaking fear
psychiatric diagnosis 2, 9–10, 13, 19, 182–183; *Diagnostic and Statistical Manual of Mental Disorders, Fourth Edition Text Revision (DSM-IV-TR)* 2, 9, 13, 19; distinction between normal and pathological 13; potential benefits of mental illness 12; *World Health Organization International Classification of Diseases 10th Edition (ICD-10)* 9
public speaking fear 21–22, 34, 40, 58, 60–61, 89, 132–133, 148, 152, 167, 184; *see also* Addington, Henry; Chamberlain, Neville; Gladstone, William; Grey, Second Earl; Macmillan, Harold; Melbourne, Second Viscount; Portland, Third Duke of; Rockingham, Marquess of; Rosebery, Fifth Earl of

Queen Victoria *see* Victoria, Queen

relationship disorder *see* relationship problem
relationship problem 13, 107; *see also* Campbell-Bannerman, Sir Henry
resignation from office 173
Rockingham, Marquess of 21–23, 167, 169, 173; *see also* alcohol; public speaking fear
Roosevelt, President Franklin 164
Roosevelt, President Theodore 164
Rosebery, Fifth Earl of 10, 86, 92, 96–103, 167, 170, 174, 175; alcohol intake 11, 169; depression 100; drug problems 101–102; grief after loss of wife 99–100; grief as child 96; hubris 101–102; insomnia 99–100; stroke 102; *see also* depression; drug misuse; grief; hubris; insomnia; public speaking fear; stroke
Russell, Lord 61, 68–69, 167, 168, 173; *see also* social anxiety

Salisbury, Third Marquess of 93–96; depression 93–96; grief 95, 173, 175; social anxiety 96; *see also* depression; grief; social anxiety
Sargant, William 5
seasonal affective disorder *see* seasonal depression

seasonal depression 13, 72, 78–79, 150; *see also* Derby, Lord; Disraeli, Benjamin; Macmillan, Harold
sexual deviations 13, 52, 90–92, 170; *see also* Gladstone, William; Wellington, Duke of
Shelburne, Second Earl of 33
sleep apnea 32, 64–65, 101, 170; *see also* Melbourne, Second Viscount; North, Lord; Taft, President William
sleep disorders 13
social anxiety 19, 38–40, 45, 67, 96, 122–123, 160, 166–168; *see also* Baldwin, Stanley; Bute, Third Earl of; Coolidge, President Calvin; Grant, President Ulysses; Heath, Sir Edward; Jefferson, President Thomas; Liverpool, Second Earl of; Peel, Sir Robert; Pitt the Younger; Salisbury, Third Marquess of
somatoform disorder 13, 170; *see also* Lloyd George, David
Stockmar, Baron 62
stroke 6, 42, 54–55, 65, 102, 140 ; *see also* Churchill, Sir Winston; Grenville, William; Melbourne, Second Viscount; Rosebery, Fifth Earl of; Wellington, Duke of
suicidal depression in chief executives 165

Taft, President William Howard 101, 170; *see also* sleep apnea
Tennyson, Alfred Lord 93
Thatcher, Margaret 161, 170; dementia 161, 171; *see also* dementia
thyroid disease 13, 160; *see also* Bush, President George H.W.; Heath, Sir Edward; Yeltsin, Boris
tics *see* Tourette's disorder
Tourette's disorder 13, 61, 63–64, 123–124, 170; *see also* Baldwin, Stanley; Melbourne, Second Viscount
Tweedmouth, Lord 171; *see also* dementia

Victoria, Queen 59, 61–64, 66, 67, 79, 84–85, 95

Walpole, Sir Robert 15
war leaders' characteristics 135
Wellington, Duke of 38, 49–55, 90, 170; epileptic seizures 55; lateral thinking 172; *see also* Asperger's disorder; grief; sexual deviations
Wilberforce, William 39
Wilde, Oscar 101
Wilmington, Earl of 15–16
Wilson, Harold 155–158, 173; alcohol intake 11, 112, 155–157; anxiety 155–156; dementia 155, 157–158, 171; early retirement 158; and President Carter 157; *see also* alcohol; anxiety; dementia
Wilson, President Woodrow 171; *see also* dementia
wisdom 172–173

Yeats, William Butler 7
Yeltsin, Boris 160; *see also* thyroid disease

www.ingramcontent.com/pod-product-compliance
Lightning Source LLC
Chambersburg PA
CBHW032053300426
44116CB00007B/712